For Revolt

Also Available from Bloomsbury

The Politics of Aesthetics, Jacques Rancière
Althusser's Lesson, Jacques Rancière
Egalitarian Moments: From Descartes to Rancière, Devin Zane Shaw
Art, Politics and Rancière, Tina Chanter

For Revolt

Rancière, Abstract Space and Emancipation

Jussi Palmusaari

BLOOMSBURY ACADEMIC
LONDON • NEW YORK • OXFORD • NEW DELHI • SYDNEY

BLOOMSBURY ACADEMIC
Bloomsbury Publishing Plc, 50 Bedford Square, London, WC1B 3DP, UK
Bloomsbury Publishing Inc, 1385 Broadway, New York, NY 10018, USA
Bloomsbury Publishing Ireland, 29 Earlsfort Terrace, Dublin 2, D02 AY28, Ireland

BLOOMSBURY, BLOOMSBURY ACADEMIC and the Diana logo
are trademarks of Bloomsbury Publishing Plc

First published in Great Britain 2024
This paperback edition published 2025

Copyright © Jussi Palmusaari, 2024

Jussi Palmusaari has asserted his right under the Copyright, Designs
and Patents Act, 1988, to be identified as Author of this work.

For legal purposes the Acknowledgements on p. vi constitute
an extension of this copyright page.

Cover design: Ben Anslow
Cover image: Red Guards read announcements to be pasted on walls during the
Cultural Revolution. China 1967 (© World History Archive / Alamy Stock Photo)

All rights reserved. No part of this publication may be: i) reproduced or transmitted in any form, electronic or mechanical, including photocopying, recording or by means of any information storage or retrieval system without prior permission in writing from the publishers; or ii) used or reproduced in any way for the training, development or operation of artificial intelligence (AI) technologies, including generative AI technologies. The rights holders expressly reserve this publication from the text and data mining exception as per Article 4(3) of the
Digital Single Market Directive (EU) 2019/790.

Bloomsbury Publishing Inc does not have any control over, or responsibility for, any third-party websites referred to or in this book. All internet addresses given in this book were correct at the time of going to press. The author and publisher regret any inconvenience caused if addresses have changed or sites have ceased to exist, but can accept no responsibility for any such changes.

A catalogue record for this book is available from the British Library.

A catalog record for this book is available from the Library of Congress.

ISBN: HB: 978-1-3502-7402-0
PB: 978-1-3502-7713-7
ePDF: 978-1-3502-7401-3
eBook: 978-1-3502-7400-6

Typeset by Newgen KnowledgeWorks Pvt. Ltd., Chennai, India

For product safety related questions contact productsafety@bloomsbury.com.

To find out more about our authors and books visit www.bloomsbury.com
and sign up for our newsletters.

Contents

Acknowledgements	vi
Note on Text	vii
List of Abbreviations	viii
Introduction: Spatiality, equality, intelligence	1
1 Can rupture be thought?	19
2 Rancière's literary Maoism	63
3 Politics of staging and the primacy of space	97
4 Time and its discontents	121
5 The Jacobin anachronism	149
Conclusion	167
Notes	171
Bibliography	209
Index	229

Acknowledgements

This book originated in a PhD which I completed in the Centre for Research in Modern European Philosophy, Kingston University London. Fragments of introduction and Chapter 4 were published earlier as an afterword for Jacques Rancière, *Marx in the Woods*. An earlier, Finnish version of parts of Chapter 2 was published in Anna Tuomikoski (ed.), *Erimielisyyden näyttämöt*. I thank Rab-Rab Press and Tutkijaliitto for permission to use this material here. I wish to thank the staff and students of the CRMEP for creating such a stimulating and inspiring environment for doing research. I am most grateful to my supervisor Peter Hallward. I want to thank also my second supervisor Howard Caygill as well Éric Alliez, Étienne Balibar, Giovanni Campailla, Stephen Howard and Sanja Perovic for commenting on various drafts; Bruno Bosteels and Catherine Malabou, who examined my PhD, for their insightful feedback; an anonymous reviewer of the manuscript for many valuable suggestions; Liza Thompson at Bloomsbury for her enthusiasm for this project; Sezgin Boynik, Katrine Høghøj, Anna Tuomikoski and Moritz Herrmann for opportunities to discuss and write about Rancière in different contexts; Nicolas Schneider for countless discussions concerning the concepts of time, space and place over recent years; and Oliver Davis and Eddie Hughes for their generosity and help. Heartfelt thanks to my sister Maria and my mother Riitta-Maija for their continuous support. My deepest gratitude goes to Anne for her infinite patience and encouragement and to Kaiho for his ever-intelligent revolt.

Note on Text

Where the reference is to a non-English text, the translation is my own, unless otherwise indicated. Where an existing translation has been modified ('tm'), the pagination of the consulted edition of the original is in most cases given alongside with that of the English edition, and the two are separated by an oblique stroke. For full bibliographical details the reader can consult the list of cited works at the end.

Abbreviations

Rancière

A	*Aisthesis: Scenes from the Aesthetic Regime of Art*
AD	*Aesthetics and Its Discontents*
AL	*Althusser's Lesson*
C	'The Concept of Anachronism and the Historian's Truth'
D	*The Disagreement: Politics and Philosophy*
DS	*Dissensus: On Politics and Aesthetics*
FW	*The Flesh of Words*
GF	*Et tant pis pour les gens fatigués*
ME	*The Method of Equality: Interviews*
MP	*Moments Politiques: Interventions 1977–2009*
NH	*The Names of History*
NL	*The Nights of Labor*
OA	'On *Aisthesis*' (interview by Oliver Davis)
OSP	*On the Shores of Politics*
PA	*The Politics of Aesthetics: The Distribution of the Sensible*
PP	*The Philosopher and His Poor*
SR	'La Scène révolutionnaire et l'ouvrier émancipé (1830–1848)'
SV	*Short Voyages to the Land of the People*

Althusser

ES-C	*Essays in Self-Criticism*
FM	*For Marx*
PSPS	*Philosophy and the Spontaneous Philosophy of the Scientists*

RC *Reading Capital: The Complete Edition* (coauthored with Balibar, Establet, Macherey and Rancière)

Lardreau

SO *Le Singe d'or*

Introduction: Spatiality, equality, intelligence

This book aims to make visible a core methodological gesture of Jacques Rancière's thought. This gesture makes operative a certain idea of spatial logic which serves to think modes of egalitarian coexistence. Such a coexistence contrasts first of all temporality as a form of ordered difference, be it based on teleology, causal successions or determined sequences in general, no matter what the principle or practice that orders them. To be sure, in wanting to radically challenge ideas of progress or those of linear evolution, Rancière is not alone. In the Marxist tradition neat linear developmental models of historical time, which make part of the orthodox Marxism, have been questioned at least since Walter Benjamin's statement 'that capitalism will not die a natural death'.[1] However, even if such schemes hold that 'temporality does not, as such, exist' but rather 'temporalizes itself', the ways in which time does this and the way the relations between the present, the past and the future are arranged remain the central concern for much of the Marxist and post-Marxist tradition.[2] Rancière enters this tradition as a student of Louis Althusser, one of the most original thinkers to challenge linear forms of historical temporality.[3] And, as Mark Robson puts it, 'Rancière's work is never not about time'.[4] In several occasions, Rancière has expressed an aim to rethink the temporality of politics, and the word 'time' or 'times' now appears in the titles of no less than five of his books. However, as Robson's phrasing might hint, there is something peculiar in Rancière's engagements with time. As I will argue in this book, rather than coming up with alternative forms of temporality in order to better grasp the schemes under which emancipatory political projects unfold, there is a logic at work in Rancière which tends to decouple emancipatory practice from questions of its overall temporal coherence. This logic is sourced from spatiality.

Hence, to grasp Rancière's rethinking of time, we need to shift focus from the concept of time to a certain spatial logic. The time of emancipation, rethought through spatiality, is a time which does not come with qualities that orient it or model it according to usual temporal qualities. As he says, he does not 'think of things in terms of radical novelty, of beginnings and endings, but rather in topographical terms' (MP, 130). A fundamental gesture of Rancière's thought includes an abstraction of the time of the present from the past and the future. As he has bluntly put it, time appears for him as 'the best medium of exclusion'.[5] He is uncomfortable with 'the idea of the future, of deferred [or differentiated] time [*l'idée du futur, du temps différé*] because it amounts to using "time as an interdiction"' (GF, 659). He says that 'the very simple separation of the present and the past' is a 'way in which time works as a principle of impossibility'.[6]

In this radical rejection of ordered temporal sequences one can see a certain rehabilitation of the Kantian rational subject as the subject of emancipation. While as a being of the world of sensibility, as Kant says, 'I am never free at the point of time in which I act', differentiations imposed by the forms of sensibility do not apply to me as a purely intelligent moral subject: 'reason, when it is a question of the law of our intelligible existence (the moral law), recognizes no distinction of time.'[7] To the extent that Rancière is first of all known for his preoccupation with the sensible, a comparison with Kant's noumenal being may admittedly strike as paradoxical. However, it is also true that Rancière's interest in the sensible is directed to disordering and levelling all forms of sensibility against attempts to organize hierarchies through them. This can be understood as a gesture aiming to make a Kantian-type subject effective in the sensible world; rather than placing it into a suprasensible noumenal realm, it is based on undermining the attempt to circumscribe possibilities through the sensible. Hence, for Rancière it is not a question of simply a realm beyond the sensible but a question of thinking egalitarian practice whose possibilities are not restricted by their situatedness in time (or in space, in the sense of specific location). Such an idea of practice is distinctively Kantian. It retains from Kant the rejection of time in its basic sense of ordered difference as something to which a universal rational being would need to accord. As Rancière says, in a highly Kantian tone, 'there is only one intelligence'.[8] 'There is only one kind of thinking being' which is in possession of the 'same intelligence'.[9] The equality which moves Rancière is that of such rational beings bypassing differences imposed by the sensible, first and foremost by time. The abstract spatial logic operative in Rancière's thought should then be seen as a methodological stand-in for a Kantian, purely rational being. It is a way to articulate a radically equal intelligent being into the configurations which make up the sensible, historical and social universe.

In this introduction I want to clarify and unpack this claim by first discussing the specific notions of space and time developed by Ludwig Feuerbach who, as I claim, is the source of Rancière's basic understanding of them. I will then look at Rancière's uses of the idea of demos in order to get a fuller sense of the abstract spatial logic at work in his oeuvre. After fleshing out this idea of spatiality, I will elaborate the Kantian moral dimension of Rancière's thought a little further. I will finish this introduction by outlining the chapters that follow.

Space as the first sphere of reason

In order to understand the significance of spatiality for Rancière, as well the sense in which it is contrasted to time, we need to see how Ludwig Feuerbach makes an ethical point with the two concepts. In 'Towards a Critique of Hegel's Philosophy' (1839), Feuerbach characterizes space in terms of inclusion, freedom and equality, defining it as a dimension of 'coordination and coexistence'. Space thus defined is opposed to the 'exclusive time', which in contrast appears as a principle of '*subordination* and *succession*'.[10] This conception of space and time is presented as a critique of Hegel's philosophy where time has a privileged and determining role. Hegel, as Feuerbach argues, concentrates on the 'differences of various religions, philosophies, times, and peoples' seen through 'progressive series and stages'. In doing so, he 'ignores the common, the same and the identical [*das Gemeinschaftliche, das Gleiche, das Identische*] in them'.[11] A certain conception of space allows Feuerbach to approach things in an egalitarian coexistence. In this way, temporally arranged differences, or different 'times', are approached from the perspective of spatial simultaneity which thus cannot be a temporally specific one. As Marx Wartofsky puts it, it is understood as a 'contemporary coexistence of *all* the stages' of temporal development.¹² Feuerbach does not deny that things appear in a certain temporal order, but he argues that the dimensional form through which they are put into relation with each other to make them meaningful according to equality does not adjust to temporal differentiation. Rather, it is sourced from the 'liberalism of space'.¹³

Thus, Feuerbach gives spatiality a certain independence of time insofar as what is in temporal succession is understood also spatially, in terms of simultaneous coexistence without temporal development. In his 'Principles of the Philosophy of the Future' (1843) time and space are discussed in more detail, and Feuerbach makes his point in clearer terms. He now appears to argue that spatial coexistence is logically prior to temporal determination. The former is the latter's condition of possibility, for 'only that which exists beside one another [*außereinander*] can also become understood as after one another [*nacheinander gedacht werden*]'.¹⁴ The target is again Hegel in whose system time is a superior dimension. 'Where there is no space,' Feuerbach claims, 'there is also no place for *any system*'.¹⁵ Although Feuerbach acknowledges a certain unity of space-time, he gives a logical privilege to one over the other: 'space is the first sphere of reason [*der Raum ist die erste Sphäre der Vernunft*]'.¹⁶

Feuerbach was the topic of Rancière's early doctoral research which after the events of May 1968 was (permanently) interrupted by 'the din of the street'.¹⁷ As Rancière has later acknowledged, however, he has retained something from Feuerbach's idea of space as an egalitarian principle as opposed to time as a function of subordination (ME, 148). Indeed, in addition to direct, if largely unqualified, references to Feuerbach's idea of space, clear echoes of it can be found in Rancière's work. Consider, for example, his recent references to Virginia Woolf. After defining progress in terms of 'the power that time exerts on space', Rancière explains how Woolf's understanding of modern fiction counters such a power with a 'time of simultaneity', which is a 'time of coexistence, obtained through the liberalness of space [*gagné par la libéralité de l'espace*]'.¹⁸ In clearly Feuerbachian terms (*Liberalismus des Raumes* in the latter's German),¹⁹ Rancière describes this time as one which 'does not reach toward any end but dilates endlessly, and includes, virtually, every other time and place'.²⁰ As we will see, in particular in my discussion of anachronism in Chapter 4, by serving as a form for virtual coexistence of times and places,

Rancière's Feuerbachian spatiality in a sense transcends any idea of historically specific social space. It includes all other times and places.

Similarly, we can think of several occasions where Rancière speaks of a determined temporal succession as opposed to a contingent one, understanding the latter in terms of a virtual coexistence of its stages. Regarding the 'time of emancipation' in Joseph Jacotot's anti-pedagogy, for example, Rancière states how it 'knows no definite order of stages'. It 'can start from any point ... extend in unanticipated directions by inventing its own connections at every stage'.[21] Rancière finds this logic also in, again, Virginia Woolf who contrasts 'to the tyranny of causal emplotment' 'sensible micro-events that happen one after another, but above all *alongside one another*, in the absence of any hierarchy'.[22] The idea of side-by-sideness as a framework underlying any temporal succession is, as we have seen, a Feuerbachian one. In the flow of time, it is not a question of novelty or becoming but an undetermined movement drawing on a virtual coexistence of its moments. As Feuerbach put it, underlying any temporally ordered sequence is a 'spatial side-by-sideness [*das räumliche Außereinandersein*]' of its elements.[23]

This book premises that space remains for Rancière a kind of 'first sphere of reason', to borrow Feuerbach's phrase. It is the first sphere of egalitarian reason. As a methodological principle, it is privileged by Rancière first and foremost over ways in which time introduces selective criteria for modes of action and thought available in specific historical and social conditions. The way Rancière uses spatiality can be understood as a form of topographical abstraction from such differentiating conditions. It reduces the temporal dimension to the present of egalitarian reason while avoiding to qualify this present with modalities that would introduce temporal structure to it. The simplest way to further clarify this logic of abstract space in Rancière is through one of his most central concepts, namely democracy.

Demos-space

While Rancière is famous for his defence of a specific notion of democracy, what has gone virtually unnoticed is the essentially spatial signification that he gives to *dēmos*, the Greek word for 'the people'.[24] His references to *dēmos* as space are relatively straightforward and relate it directly to the origins of the concept as well as the institution. The ancient Greek word *dēmos* does not refer only to 'the people' but also to a territorial unit, an area where a person is rooted. The spatial *dēmos*, or deme, gained a particular political significance after Cleisthenes of Athens's so-called democratic reform. In the pre-democratic period, different areas of the city were subjected to the rule of tribal groups and thus to the domination of kinship and familial genealogies, often fictionally imposed on an order based on wealth. Cleisthenes restructured what presented itself as a kinship order, according to artificial demes, that is, areas that no longer coincided with the old tribal divisions. By the same token the criterion of citizenship became simply a question of being enrolled in a deme, while also people of foreign origins and freed former slaves were included into the new spatially invented tribes. The sole criterion of membership to the new tribes of free men was birth or inhabitation in a particular deme, while larger political unities were formed out of demes which were not always geographically contiguous.[25]

In Rancière's take on Cleisthenes's 'strange reform', the function of spatiality in the making of the citizenship *abstracts* from the structures which have evolved in time and/or are presented as such, that is, inequalities through accumulation of wealth or narratives of family genealogies that serve to veil the economic basis of inequality. In affirming a 'fact of place' against 'the place's founding', it gives rise to an 'abstract place of the citizen' (MP, 43). Forms that *have become* to justify political action for a given person in a given place, and project this justification for the future, are replaced with another form of 'intelligibility [*pensabilité*]', namely 'an abstract and artificial space that was constituted as such'.[26] This spatial abstraction does not make temporal forms and narratives disappear but disturbs their capacity to maintain a specific social order in place. In so doing, it makes operative spatiality as a kind of minimally structured form to think egalitarian coexistence.

Rancière has made clear that he does not consider democracy an ahistorical principle; it emerges contingently in a specific time and place.[27] However, this does not prevent him from effectively treating it as an abstract form, a logic of spatial abstraction through which the historically emerged principle is turned into a method to think dissociation of historical conditions from their specific spatiotemporal situations. Consequently, the extent to which the actual historical example and the specific processes which condition its emergence can serve to think Rancière's notion of emancipation remains limited. What it demonstrates for him is simply a vanishing gesture of imposing a sphere where any place can be connected to or disconnected from any other place. Hence, a logical paradigm of displacement is abstracted from its historical conditionedness and turned into a framework through which Rancière consistently thinks emancipation and equality, regardless of where or when it may appear.

This spatial framework should be seen as the principle underlying Rancière's idea of the distribution of the sensible (*le partage du sensible*). The distribution of the sensible refers to specific configurations of perceived aptitudes, capacities and legitimacies, or lack thereof, attached to particular bodies and spatiotemporal locations. As Rancière says, a 'place that might be completely material' can 'at the same time symbolize a disposition, a distribution, a whole set of relationships' (ME, 58). Through this kind of inscription of symbolic functions into a concrete space-time, a person or group's 'social destination is anticipated by the evidence of a perceptive universe'.[28] Such an order is also what Rancière designates with the word 'police'.[29] It is this symbolic order and its social recognizability, ordered by virtue of being attached to material spaces and times, that the democratic reform replaces with an abstract space of its free reconfigurability. Hence, what matters in a distribution and a redistribution of the sensible is not the sensible as such but a 'form of (dis)connection' through spatial abstraction which brings the sensible coordinates in the 'same topographical unity' and enables their endless reconfigurations.[30]

Because 'democracy is this empty and abstract space', demos can signify an 'abstract people' made of 'those who are where they "are" not, where they "cannot" be', that is, where their condition is relocated into circumstances seen as incompatible with it.[31] Due to this link between the abstract spatial form and the notion of equality, space receives a role for Rancière which goes beyond any geographical and historical preoccupation with social spaces. This abstract sphere bypasses geographical or even historical unities. It transverses such unities by forming a 'space made of disconnected places'.[32] As a methodological framework, this abstract spatiality amounts to an atemporal possibility for reconfiguring anyone's identitarian coordinates by 'relocating, reshaping or redoubling' them.[33] In doing so, it mobilizes democracy as 'the principle of infinite substitutability or indifference to difference'.[34] This is how Rancière's particular use of spatiality serves to think equality. Fundamentally, it testifies to a commitment that there is 'no special place for the sameness of any of us', and it can be fully appreciated only if we link it back to Rancière's Kantian premises.[35]

Radical Kantianism

The way Rancière bypasses the questions of temporal ordering of equality or emancipation – as he quite strikingly puts it, 'we are already emancipated' – associates him more with Kant's commitment to extra-temporality of practical reason than with questions of temporal development towards an emancipated world with which much of the post-Kantian tradition is preoccupied.[36] Any reader of Rancière will be quick to notice that Kant is indeed among the most important philosophical reference points in Rancière's works. In particular, Rancière draws from the idea of 'aesthetic equality', however, as it appears in the *Critique of Judgment* and is further developed by Friedrich Schiller. Such equality is based on the nature of the aesthetic experience, and the mode of judgement related to it, which enables it to be dissociated from external purposes and, by extension, from predetermined roles of the subject of such an experience and judgement.

The equality related to aesthetics is present in Kant's concept of *sensus communis*. The *sensus communis* is a sensitivity due to which aesthetic experience is seen as universal without tying this universality to concepts. *Sensus communis* nevertheless gives rise to 'maxims of the common human understanding'. One of these maxims is formulated in terms of a certain virtual displaceability of the subject of judgement as a condition for their universal standpoint. It requires 'putting [one]self into the position of everyone else, merely by abstracting from the limitations that contingently attach to our own judging'.[37] As Rancière has stated, his principle of equality follows a similar logic of the universal. It 'functions fundamentally in the same way as Kantian maxims, as a form of universalizing the very conditions of a practice' (ME, 90/162, tm). The function of the spatial logic described earlier can be interpreted in terms of equality through abstraction articulated by Kant through the notion of *sensus communis*. It amounts to an abstraction from a given standpoint or a specific spatiotemporal situation. In accordance with the topographic logic outlined earlier, it opens to an infinite displaceability of qualities, relations and potentialities attached to a specific situation. This universal reconfigurability of the contexts of practice, for which the abstract space provides a methodological frame, is for Rancière the very principle of emancipation. This spatial logic is then also decidedly different from the Kant's definition of space as a form of intuition.

To the extent that *sensus communis* amounts to an imposition of an axiomatic equality which bypasses circumstantial differences, it bears an affinity with Kant's practical reason. Indeed, the aesthetic equality as it appears in Kant's concept of *sensus communis* accords with the form of his categorical imperative, a rule of morality which requires 'universal validity for every rational being'.[38] Seeing Kantian aesthetics from this perspective, I claim that it serves for Rancière first and foremost as a way to grant effectivity to Kant's practical reason.[39] Like the Kantian morality, Rancière's axiom of equality applies without being concerned with the specific effects that might follow from its application. For both Kant and Rancière, the moral principle applies unconditionally in every circumstance and is not based on what might be achieved by it.[40] It excludes in principle any consequential adjustments and remains always the same and indifferent to the requirements of a specific situation. The task for Rancière, as his every reader knows, is in any situation to posit and to immediately apply the axiomatic equality of anyone with anyone. This does not mean that it would always be played out in the same way in each concrete situation, far from it, but the circumstances in which it is demonstrated can in no way question the immediacy and unconditionality by which the principle itself is posited. From this perspective Rancière shows himself as an invariably rationalist thinker. He relies on 'a simple rule of morality' to always assume that a given mode of thinking remains essentially unaffected by 'the colorful prism of circumstances' (PP, xxviii). Such thinking is in permanent and principled revolt against all ordered difference that makes up the sensible universe. The aesthetic in Kant is then a way for Rancière to think the atemporal nature of practical reason differently, as a capacity to render spatiotemporal orders indifferent for emancipatory practice.

The continuity between the aesthetic equality and Kant's practical philosophy in Rancière's thought can be supported by textual evidence. Before engaging with Kant's aesthetics (starting from brief references in his 1983 book *The Philosopher and His Poor*), an axiom of universal equality has certainly been present as a practical commitment since his first monograph *Althusser's Lesson* and the Maoist politics close to Rancière after 1968, both of which this book will analyse in detail. Even earlier, however, Rancière was engaging with Kantian practical philosophy itself, in his *diplôme d'études supérieures* from 1963, which criticized it as the framework of Marx's early articles.[41] Although rejected as ideologically flawed in this youthful text, Marx's early Kantianism has later contributed positively to Rancière's perception of emancipatory practice. Let us thus see how Kant's moral philosophy may be indirectly spun into a leading thread of Rancière's thought.

In a chapter of his thesis called 'The Dialectic of Reason and Private Interest', Rancière analyses Marx's discussion of debates at the Rhine Province Assembly concerning legislation on theft of wood. Marx's moralist reasoning criticizes the Assembly legislators for allowing their legislating practice to be guided by private interest and neglecting their duty to act in accordance with the universality of the moral law. While Marx associates this legislative practice with the reality of feudalism as opposed to the 'epoch of general laws', Rancière argues that Marx is 'incapable of thinking a historical reality according to historical categories'.[42] That is to say, his argument is not based on 'a gap between two historical forms which would succeed one another in time, but between two essences which are mutually exclusive'.[43] His discourse is based on Kantian moral reasoning which simply judges a historical state of affairs according to the law of practical reason. It judges what is according to what ought to be opposing particular interests rooted in material reality, which is 'the reverse of the kingdom of ends'.[44]

At the time, the young Rancière was preoccupied with understanding the temporal development of the historical process, and Marx's early Kantian framework appeared as ideologically flawed to him. However, this Kantian moral logic later returns in a positive sense, most clearly in his 1990 book *On the Shores of Politics*. In it Rancière theorizes a 'syllogism of emancipation' to describe the discursive practice of the nineteenth-century workers. Rancière refers to his research of the workers' struggles after the 1830 revolution and how they were framed in terms of the Republican principle of equality inscribed in the new legislation. Based on the equality before the law the workers challenged actual realities in the workshop through a syllogistic logic. 'The syllogism is simple: the major premise contains what the law has to say; the minor, what is said or done elsewhere, any word or deed which contradicts the fundamental legal/political affirmation of equality' (OSP, 46). In contrast to Rancière's early critique of the young Marx, he now insists that the practice based on juxtaposing the universality of the law with particular conditions of actual reality is not futile criticism detached from any social power. Rather, it amounts to 'the workers emerging from their minority status and proving that they … truly communicate with all …; that they are not merely creatures of need … but creatures of discourse and reason' (OSP, 48). As Rancière has acknowledged later, this is a return to the 'Kantian moment' of the young Marx, but now it is seen as a framework of militant emancipatory practice, rather than ineffective moralism for which Kantianism has been criticized, including in Rancière's own youthful text. As opposed to criticizing 'the gap between the universal and the particular' he now understands the logic in terms of a 'political intervention as a discursive and practical montage which polemically ties together the universal and the particular, humanity and inhumanity, and equality and inequality'.[45]

To think a coexistence of two antinomic principles, Rancière uses spatial reasoning in contrast to a temporal ordering of emancipatory practice according to a futural orientation: 'not to find a counterpower susceptible of governing a future society' but rather to open a 'common space' which enables a practice of verifying equality and positing it against inequality (OSP, 49, 48). 'This space is virtual, which is not to say illusory' (OSP, 50). It is not 'real' in the sense of being a social or geographical construction. Rather, it should be understood in terms of a space which operates an abstraction from social constraints and offers itself as a standpoint for emancipatory practice. Indeed, it is not unlike Kant's kingdom of ends, that is to say, a sphere in light of which we all appear as bearers of the same reason, a 'common space of thinking' where we act, as Rancière puts it, 'as if we were all members of an already existing community'.[46] This is how the abstract or virtual space serves to think differently the Kantian idea of practice, as a methodological stand-in for Kant's purely intelligent being and the suprasensible sphere of such beings. What is retained from Kant is freedom's non-accordance with its temporal ordering.

Emancipatory practice thus resists 'historical categories' in the way the early Marx evaded them according to Rancière's critique: 'it is not a question of a positive dialectic which would give birth to something new, such as, for example, the dialectic of the state and wealth in *Phenomenology of Spirit*.' Rather, we are dealing with dialectic 'in the Kantian sense of the word'.[47] That is to say, a dialectic which is based on a juxtaposition of 'antinomic terms'. In Kant these terms were sourced from reason untied by the 'fetters' of space and time on one hand and causally ordered phenomenal world on the other.[48] In Rancière, they are equality and inequality. To be sure, there can be novelty in the form of specific inventions of emancipatory practice which verifies equality. The point is, however, that the framework for this practice is sourced from a virtual space of shared intelligence, rather than from ideas of temporal becoming or qualitive historical change. This is a decidedly different framework than the historicizing dialectic which characterizes the post-Kantian philosophy from Hegel to (the mature) Marx and various developments in Marxism and post-Marxism. Whatever the differences of such developments, they share an idea of specific historical circumstances as laying the conditions for emancipatory practice. Rancière rather wants to universalize such conditions by undoing logics that would fix them to specifical times and places. Methodologically, he leans on spatiality as the framework which enables such undoing.

For Kant practical reason famously leaves very little possibility for its material effectivity. As a being 'whose existence is determined in time' our action is tied to objective causal chains.[49] In light of the objectively determined world, then, practical reason risks becoming a mere point of view or a mere subjective attitude with very little capacity to disturb forms of objective time-determination.[50] One way to criticize Kantian ethics from the Marxist position is based precisely on this: the atemporal immediacy of Kant's moral principles dissociates its scope from the social realm and the structured mediations through which it functions.[51] For Kant, the only way to combine practical reason with space and time is in the form of a regulative idea of a transcendent future: 'We must assume the moral world to be a consequence of our conduct in the sensible world; and since the latter does not offer such a connection to us, we must assume the former to be a world that is future for us.'[52] This gesture paves way to Hegel's critical rethinking of Kant's first *Critique*, by approaching it as a concrete process of a dialectical becoming self-conscious of the Concept.[53] After Hegel, some aspects of Marxism are able to approach history as a temporal development towards communism through dialectics of class struggle. This approach notoriously comes with risks of being seen as an objectively determined, necessary process.[54]

The methodological privilege Rancière gives to spatiality serves as a way to avoid this path of giving reason a temporal form. As Louis Gabriel Gauny, one of Rancière's idiosyncratic worker heroes, puts it, giving perhaps the best summary of Rancière's basic intuition: 'I have lost faith in time.'[55] Rather than temporalizing emancipatory reason, Rancière, like Kant, sees time first and foremost as a principle of regulation, external to reason as such. For Rancière, it becomes the defining feature of 'the police', which is how he labels the social structure which orders reality on the basis of 'the denial of equality' (D, 35). The police is what keeps everyone in their determined places through a unified orientation according to the 'telos of community in all the activities of the different parts of society' (D, 64). Thus, the broad outline of Rancière's conception of emancipation can be based on a different reading of the Kantian framework, aiming at its political radicalization without concessions to temporalized horizons. Spatiality, in the sense of the methodological principle outlined earlier, becomes in Rancière a way to accomplish this. For Kant himself, of course, space could have no such role. As a form of intuition, it is subjected to temporal differentiation and is just as incompatible with the noumenal being as time is. But as we have seen, Rancière borrows his approach to spatial logic from Feuerbach and turns it into a principle of deregulating and disordering whatever temporality regulates and orders. Such a methodological ground motive nevertheless serves a position which remains Kantian in a crucial sense.

This framework places Rancière in the tradition of radical Kantianism, among the likes of Guy Lardreau or Françoise Proust. As we shall see later, Lardreau – with whom Rancière shares also, and perhaps more importantly, a radical Maoist background – is driven into a political impasse by an attempt to detach radical revolt from any temporalizing rationality. As for Proust, whom there is no space to discuss in this book, she rethinks Kantian freedom as a momentary appearance of a radical beginning in history.[56] What makes Rancière distinctive, if we accept my interpretation, is that he turns to spatiality as a framework to rethink the question of time. Emancipation is thus not a matter of temporal order, and it does not *succeed* the order of domination. Rather, it is articulated through an effectuation of connections and disconnections of a temporally oriented reality. It does not lean on configurations and reconfigurations of the sensible as such, however, but on a more fundamental framework which allows for (dis)forming them.

* * *

As a consequence of Rancière's methodological wager on spatiality, his thought leaves few tools for thinking temporal forms according to which reshapings of the sensible or social order are organized. As one commentator has recently put it, in Rancière's framework, organization remains an 'enigma'.[57] One aim of my reading is to show why this enigma is not accidental but a consequence of Rancière's basic methodological gesture. Spatial abstraction is incompatible with representable time or temporally determined process, be it objective, volitional or a dialectical intermediary between the two. To be sure, insofar as this framework bears some material effectiveness, there is always the time, the empirical duration that its operations takes. Yet, the way it is approached means that it cannot appear in an organized form. And fundamentally, this is the whole point. It is a question of egalitarian coexistence as such: People *are* equal. They do not need to *become* equal. The question remains, however, of how we can then persist on equality and enwiden its social effects in a way which enables strategy and organization, without cancelling its basis on equal intelligences.

Previous commentators who have discussed space in Rancière's work have not fully grasped this role of spatiality as countering forms of ordered time. For a telling example, Shapiro has tried to develop an understating of 'social space' in terms of dissensual political processes of reconfiguring it, based on Rancière. He briefly criticizes Rancière's model, however, for not properly allowing to theorize epochal differences in history. Shapiro suggests that Deleuze's work might be better suited for thinking social space with attention to such temporal differentiations than Rancière's.[58] According to my reading, this is not accidental, of course, but follows from the core logic of Rancière's thought where spatiality is *meant to* undo temporal differentiations – a claim that Rancière's own reading of Deleuze in fact supports.[59]

Mustafa Dikeç has done extensive and valuable work on Rancière from a spatial perspective. Dikeç wants to avoid distinguishing the concept of space too clearly from time and emphasizes that in Rancière the practices of redistributing the sensible are at once 'spatial and temporal practices'.[60] While there is an obvious sense in which this is true, it does not take into account how time itself is rethought by Rancière through space as an abstract principle which problematizes any socio-historical localizations of emancipatory action. Dikeç fails to appreciate Rancière's use of spatiality also as a principle of abstraction from temporal coherence. Because of the failure to see how Rancière in some sense *opposes* the principles of time and space to each other Dikeç views Rancièrian politics in terms of what 'starts or introduces something new', thus giving a temporally synthesized form to the rupture that emancipatory politics effectuates.[61] In my view this doesn't fully capture the nature of the rupture in question. Furthermore, in Dikeç's reading, this temporalized, 'inaugurative' space-time produces an implausible proximity between Arendt and Rancière.[62] Namely, Rancière has criticized Arendt in terms of *archē* precisely as a combination of a grounding principle *and* a temporal beginning (DS, 29–30). In Rancière, as I argue, spatiality as a way to model egalitarian coexistence serves precisely to *not* present the workings of the fundamental principle of emancipatory politics, that is, the axiom of equality, through a unified temporal form.

Thus, what distinguishes my interpretation of the role of spatiality in Rancière is its use to model a *non-* or *de-temporalized* egalitarian coexistence, before any 'concrete' space-time of political action. For Rancière space is the 'first sphere of reason', to use Feuerbach's phrase again, which serves to lay out the practical presupposition of equality without leaning on temporal developments, evolutions or becomings. No doubt the temporal dimension that such ideas imply is present in Rancière's writings, but according to the argument of this book, they are secondary to the dimension of equality for which temporal trajectories and changes articulated through them are irrelevant. At stake in Rancière is thus something like a logical break between time and space, or time as a principle of ordering difference and spatiality as a form of egalitarian coexistence.

* * *

I begin my first chapter with a discussion of the theoretical context where Rancière famously started his career, that is, Althusserian philosophy. I do not go immediately to Rancière's critique of Althusser, however, but will first look at the question of rupturous temporality of history central to Althusser's own project. Brief discussions of the historical contexts of the Chinese Cultural Revolution as well as the Maoist radicalization of Althusser's students before and after May 1968 allow me to move to a critique of Althusser by Guy Lardreau which precedes Rancière's own book-length confrontation with Althusserianism. Lardreau provides a philosophical formulation of positions embraced by the Maoist organization Gauche Prolétarienne, of which Rancière was a member between 1969 and 1972. As we will see, Rancière's own attack against Althusser in 1974 points towards a critique of this organization. His distinctive position already insists on a certain juxtapository conception of the present without addressing the question of post-May 68 political revolts through a break between temporal stages, or the past and the future.

The beginning of Rancière's original trajectory is thus situated in the context of the different ways to insist on rupture by Althusser and Lardreau and their relations to the political questions seen through the lens of the Cultural Revolution. Mapping out this context allows us to see Rancière in relation to the extremely problematic status given to time as a dimension of continuum where political action could be reflected upon. The first chapter then leaves us with a configuration of three different figures of rupture: (1) Althusser's complex theory of rupturous historical time; (2) Lardreau's Maoist insistence, contra Althusser, to affirm revolt in practice and a radical break with all past theoretical tradition; (3) Rancière's simultaneous break with both Althusser and the first Maoist break with Althusserianism. In a certain sense, as the later chapters will show, Rancière never leaves this configuration but, like any good heretic, stays with what he breaks with. These breaks are constitutive of his position, not in an intellectual-biographical sense ('they made him what he is') but in the sense of actual side-by-sideness or contiguity allowing different forms of (dis)connections.

While Rancière has later dissociated himself from the historical experiment of the Chinese Cultural Revolution, it is clear enough that the broad theme of intellectual equality was central to the movement, especially in the form it was received in France. Chapter 2 aims to formulate a specific way in which a certain positive relation to the Cultural-Revolutionary Maoism persists in Rancière's work. This is done by deepening the themes presented in Chapter 1 and relating them to the question of space. I will first consider this from the perspective of localized practices emphasized in the radical leftist Maoist circles where many young militants went to work in factories as *établis*. The localized approach to practices of revolt is addressed in reference to some elements in Rancière's work which, as I argue, attempt to dissociate spatial encounters from historical-temporal operators that would condition and orient them. This is read as an implicit critique and a rethinking of the way the leftist practice of revolt was framed and understood by divorcing it from temporal directionality according to a unified historical time or a historically established state of things. I then discuss this in relation to Rancière's concept of 'literarity' which serves to think intellectual practices in spatial terms in a way that confuses any identification of established historical state of affairs. This logic serves to counter the question of theory, or the 'book' in Althusserianism on one hand and in Maoist *gauchisme* on the other. I show how for Rancière both the Althusserian theory of reading and the *gauchiste* rejection of the 'book' were attached to the same underlying teleological reasoning. Finally, the elements are there to present a Rancièrian interpretation and defence of a specific logic of the Cultural Revolution, based on egalitarian practices of reading following the abstract spatial logic of literarity.

Chapter 3 sets out from the notion of 'stage' (*scène*) in Rancière as a term to capture the idea of the revolution. After suggesting that this 'stage' should be understood in opposition to the idea of 'stages' (*étapes*) of history important for French Maoism, I discuss the way the notion appears in an article 'La Scène révolutionnaire et l'ouvrier émancipé (1830–1848)'. In light of Rancière's later statements on the theatrical stage, I will show that the revolutionary stage should be understood in terms of emphasizing the space of revolution without linking it to underlying temporal schemes. I will then demonstrate how Rancière problematizes the attempts to unify the revolution temporally through a certain critique of the notion of self-reflection. The emphasis on space and the notion of the self allow me to move to develop a specific interpretation of Rancière's ideas concerning aesthetics in relation to Kant and Schiller. In respect to Rancière's thought of emancipation I suggest that he rethinks the Schillerian idea of escaping time in time through a gesture which overturns the Kantian primacy of time over space. The form of inner sense as the dimension of the states of the self is then replaced by an emphasis of a certain spatial-external anonymity.

Chapter 4 circulates around the question of time and the privileged notion in Rancière's positive account of it, namely anachronism. I aim to show that the use of this notion serves much less to acknowledge a specific form of temporality than a certain connection between time and a capacity to think – and to some extent to act – independently of temporal constraints. Hence, the ambiguity present in the ways Rancière discusses the relation between time and eternity, through a certain invocation of spatial metaphors: while in the first instance appearing to favour time in contrast to its 'eternalization', in the second instance he frames the emancipatory rationality by invoking a certain (temporally) undisciplined relation to eternity. This reading is reinforced with a view to what appears as a symptomatic link between Rancière's notion of anachronism and '*achronie*', or non-time, and suggests that Rancière's thinking is oriented towards an idea of an intelligent being as timeless or non-temporal. Insofar as anachronism relates to the idea of coexistence of multiple times, it provides an opportunity to return to this aspect in Althusser and to formulate Rancière's relation to him. Comparing Rancière to Peter Osborne, as an example of a thinker who has continued Althusser's project by theorizing historical *time*, I will state that Rancière's work embraces the Althusserian legacy in its very failure to think the unity of such time.

In the final chapter, I take the discussions of anachronism and eternity to a specific political context by looking at the French Revolution and Rancière's relation to its legacy. This allows me to deepen the connection between anachronism and the eternal. For, while Rancière's interest in anachronism is to some extent sparked by the French Revolution, we also know that for its radical current the question of *eternal* rights was crucial. By addressing the problem that time posed to the most radical current of the French Revolution, I will suggest that Rancière's thought can be seen as a specific way to solve this problem, although his solution risks rendering the revolution itself unintelligible by dismantling it as a *project*.

1

Can rupture be thought?

One aim of this book is to clarify Rancière's relationship to Althusser and Althusserianism, often simplified with a reference to a 'break' between them. As is well known, the young Rancière studied under Louis Althusser in École Normale Supérieure and was profoundly influenced by him. Along with a few of his fellow students, Rancière collaborated with Althusser and contributed a presentation to a 1964–5 seminar on Marx, published in *Reading Capital* (1965). The following years saw first a Maoist radicalization of some of Althusser's students and then the turbulent events around May 1968. In 1974, Rancière attacked his former teacher with a venomous polemic in his first single-authored book. *Althusser's Lesson* generally serves as a monument of the 'break' between Rancière and Althusser, and it is true that Rancière's early trajectory is an evolution from being one of Althusser's most ardent followers to becoming one of his sharpest critics. However, this sequence can hardly be captured with the word 'break', and, as I want to argue in this book, the Althusserian problematic has had a lasting positive influence on Rancière's work. In order to be able to appreciate the full scope and meaning of this influence, I will return to the question of the 'Althusserian Legacies' only later in the book. In this first chapter I want to map out the political and theoretical context in which Rancière starts his career. Just as much as Althusser's rethinking of the fundamentals of Marxism, this context entails Maoism and the Chinese Cultural Revolution in light of which May 1968 and the years that followed it were largely seen. It is these two elements, Maoism and Althusserianism, in light of which I analyse the beginnings of Rancière's career capturing it around the question of rupture, which was present in different forms in these theoretical and political contexts.

Althusser is a thinker of a revolutionary rupture. A leading thread of his Marxism is a theorization of historical time in a way which makes it impossible to understand history in terms of evolutionary progression or temporal continuity in general. Instead, it is to be conceived according to a discontinuous time thought in terms of *present* conjunctures or structures consisting of multiple coexisting times. This scheme constitutes an attempt to rid Marxism of the Hegelian understanding of history as a linear-teleological progress. Although Althusser's anti-Hegelian Marxism builds on a close study of the history of Western philosophy, one of its most crucial, yet most underappreciated, inspirations is to be found in the political and theoretical work of Mao Zedong. At the moment when the French Communist Party was following the Soviet Union in pursuing a policy of de-Stalinization, Althusser, in his theory, followed Mao's insistence on *revolutionary break* instead of notions of peaceful transition and their theoretical basis in 'evolutionism'. He develops an understanding of temporality not compatible with linear development, evolution or continuity. Thinking political change in terms of Mao's view 'On Contradiction', Althusser contrasts the idea of a temporal-linear 'passing' (*dépassement*) included in the Hegelian *Aufhebung* to a topographical figure of 'displacement' (*déplacement*).[1]

While history is a process made of displacements and ruptures, Althusser's discourse retains the broad idea of progress with scientific practice as its privileged site. True, science is not understood in terms of evolutionary continuity but according to epistemological breaks. Yet, these breaks are only so many steps through which science makes progress. Furthermore, revolutionary historical transformation towards communism can itself be guaranteed only if political practice proceeds under the guidance of the discoveries of science. It is due to science and its progress through breaks that a contingent functioning of social structures can be reconstructed in order to achieve a desired future. And it is such scientific education that Rancière and his peers start to eagerly promote within student circles.

Insofar as Althusser's discourse is based on an idea of consequential political action led by science, it no doubt retains some form of temporal continuity. This continuity, based on scientific practice and its authority, is challenged by the political practice of the Cultural Revolution and the way it is observed, interpreted and imitated in the Althusserian-Maoist circles. Boosted by the events around May 1968 in France, their Maoism comes to insist on rejection of inegalitarian relations between theoreticians and the masses, intellectuals and manual labourers. Continuous temporality gets now its second revocation through insistence on a radical break with all theoretical tradition in order to make room for anti-authoritarian mass revolt in the present. This idea is put forward in the practice of the Gauche Prolétarienne, a group whose member Rancière was. Before Rancière publishes his own book-length rejection of Althusserianism, the broad ideological framework of the Gauche Prolétarienne is presented by Guy Lardreau, one of the organization's initial core figures.

Lardreau's early position deserves to be discussed at some length, crucial as it is for understanding the politico-theoretical context of Rancière's early career, after its Althusserian beginnings. As we will see the two thinkers share a lot when it comes to critiquing the counter-revolutionary tendencies included in the Althusserian emphasis on theory. However, Lardreau's position takes him to an impasse later in his career, insofar as it leads him to reject all actualization of revolt and consequently to abandon the very political practice that he initially set out to defend. Keeping in mind this impasse, I will present a reading of *Althusser's Lesson*, first tracing the ways Rancière criticizes Althusser's discourse for retaining continuous temporalities and then discussing the problems he sees in the position of the Gauche Prolétarienne. After pointing out the methodological moves with which Rancière tries to avoid Lardreau's impasse, I will finish by looking into how these are reflected on Rancière's early discussion of Marx in terms of historical succession. While Lardreau's failure – if we can call it that – followed from his incapacity to think the present revolt without attaching it to a temporal logic of organized difference and a teleological historical project, Rancière sets out to find alternative ways to think the historical present and the ruptural practices in it.

Althusser: History, theory, rupture

Althusser's most distinctive theoretical project is outlined in *For Marx* and *Reading Capital*, both published in 1965. This project takes form in a particular political context, marked by new policies of the Soviet Communist Party on one hand and the Sino-Soviet conflict on the other.[2] While distinguished first of all by the autonomy it grants to theory or science, Althusser's intervention around this moment is also a political move towards Mao's revolutionary position, against the humanist line of 'peaceful transition' established after Khrushchev's so-called secret speech in 1956.[3] Althusser's attack against the post-Stalinist revisionism was in no way – any more than that of Mao himself – a call for a return to Stalinist dogmatism.[4] Rather, it was targeted against both Stalinism and its humanist critique launched by Khrushchev, both of which were fundamentally based on the same erroneous philosophy of history. Already in his 1937 essay 'On Contradiction', Mao had denounced 'evolutionism'.[5] The essay influenced Althusser's critique of established currents of Marxism which was aimed at dismantling the idea of linear time of history. Althusser found in Mao a genuinely anti-Hegelian understanding of Marxist dialectics which did not lean on teleological and linear temporalities.[6] For Althusser, it was such a temporality that underlined the two main currents in the history of Marxism which were broadly coined as 'economism' and 'humanism'. This interpretation enabled Althusser to see the contemporary de-Stalinization and the ideology of peaceful transition as nothing but another, humanist version of the conception of history which had enabled 'the mechanism and economism of the Second International' as well as its rebirth in the form of Stalinist dogmatism (RC, 269; cf. FM, 240; ES-C, 89).

Both 'economism' and 'humanism' were flawed because based on 'the ideological obviousness of the continuity of time', and a re-elaboration of revolutionary Marxism required a break with such a time (RC, 250). The rejection of such an idea of time amounted to a rejection of all philosophy based on 'lived experience' and placed Althusserianism in opposition to much of phenomenological tradition as well as thinkers like Bergson.[7] In a didactic essay on the concept of alienation, published anonymously in *Cahiers Marxistes-Léninistes*, the young Rancière extends this Althusserian criticism to the contemporary thinkers, such as Henri Lefebvre and Lucio Magri, along with the humanist Marxist views that were at the time dominating *Clarté*, the organ of the l'Union des Étudiants Communistes.[8] What was required was a radical break by revolutionary action and this was possible only through theoretical reconstruction of the notion of historical time itself, based on absolute rejection of any reference to the continuity as reflected in the experience of the human subject.

For Althusser, this ideological view of time underlying Marxist theories stemmed from Hegelian influences which placed Marx's historicization of economic categories within the framework of a teleological philosophy of the subject (as we will see later Rancière would throw back a similar critique against Althusser himself).[9] Thus, if in classical economy the 'field of economic phenomena' were, 'in origin as in aim, founded on' the needs of the human subject, in the standard reading, Hegel's philosophy allowed Marx to merely 'set in motion' economic categories (RC, 315, 239). In other words, instead of a naturalism of a *homo economicus*, Marxist theory would naturalize the movement of history itself, with capitalism as one of its stages. The inability to get rid of naturalization of history was due to 'the Hegelian idea of time [which] is borrowed from the most vulgar empiricism, the empiricism of the false obviousness of everyday practice' (RC, 243).

The ideological conception of time is structured by particular causal logics. The expressive or teleological causality, which characterizes Hegel's system, presents every phenomenon in a given historical present – 'a material or economic determination, a political and legal institution or a religious, artistic, or philosophical form' – as so many expressions of the same essence (RC, 241, cf. FM 103). It connects all historical events to the same origin so that the empirical givenness of time 'merely reflects the essence of the social totality of which it is the existence' (RC, 240). In his contribution to *Reading Capital*, Rancière follows these lines in criticizing the Feuerbachian humanism of the young Marx, stating that it is 'never concerned with anything other than a history of the human essence. ... Indeed, everywhere we must recognize the same history. Everywhere it is the human essence which is being expressed' (RC, 98, tm).

Another causal scheme underlying the conception of history in traditional Marxism is 'lineal' or 'mechanical causality' which connects every event to an object-cause that precedes it 'in the sequence of a given' (RC, 337). Merged together as a 'linear and teleological causality', Althusser sees these two causal schemes characterize the history of Marxism in its economist and humanist guises. While economism leans on 'the fatality of the advent of socialism' through a mechanical development of economic structures, in the subjectivist-historicist views the teleological essence of history is incorporated in the voluntarist action of the proletariat. The latter is humanity incarnated and the 'historical role of freeing man from his "alienation" [is] its destiny' (RC, 292). Hence, a genuine Marxism requires a break with the causal ideas which keep Marx's conception of history a prisoner of the 'false obviousness of everyday practice' (RC, 243).

From the current moment to the structural whole

For Althusser, a proper analysis of Marx shows that neither the construction of knowledge nor the functioning principles of historically existing society follow the experience of temporal continuity or the empirical succession of events. In the words of the young Rancière, it requires a 'constitution of an objectivity which does not coincide with a development of history' (RC, 145). This amounts to no less than dissociating the intelligibility of an object from uniform succession of time. The properly Marxist conception of history must be thought through a new notion of causality which is not attached to the frameworks of continuity. Althusser would call this 'structural causality' or 'absent causality', thought in analogy with Spinoza's immanent cause. Before labelling it with this name, however, it is thematized in a discussion of Lenin's notion of the 'current moment' in the now-canonical 'Contradiction and Overdetermination' and developed further in an essay 'On Materialist Dialectic'. In addition to Lenin, Althusser refers to Mao's 'On Contradiction', although, as I have implied earlier, the influence of this essay on Althusser is arguably wider and more profound that is apparent from the few references made to it. Indeed, its effect on Althusser has been recently described as a 'revelation'.[10]

Mao argues that the reality consists in a multiplicity of qualitatively different forms of a universal principle of contradiction. Thus, the universal contradiction exists only in the particularity of concrete contradictions and their interdependence.[11] Althusser produces a specific interpretation of Mao's emphasis on the particularity of contradiction according to which the contradiction is not understandable on the basis of its continuous existence across time. Thus, the universal is not an underlying origin to which the particular would retain a relation through the course of time, but its existence is thinkable only through separate articulations of the particular which are not in a relation of continuity or temporal uniformity with each other. The historical existence of the contradiction consists in a complex multiplicity divided into primary and secondary contradictions each of which is further divided into principal and secondary aspects (FM, 194, cf. 94 n.6). Structural complex of contradictions functions through varying relations of dominance and changes of (im)balance between these contradictions and their aspects. Its functioning is thus not intelligible according to any one contradiction which would retain its role as the primary force and allow to follow its development in 'uniform duration' of time.[12] Hence, it is not thinkable according to 'expressive causality' which would make secondary contradictions only so many expressions of the same historical present.

Althusser takes Lenin's analysis of the 'current moment' as an exemplary application of this idea. What is relevant here is the type of temporality implicated in 'the current conjuncture' thus conceptualized. For, although it refers to a specific historical moment (in Lenin's case that of the 1917 revolutions) it brings together elements 'which are radically heterogeneous – of different origins, different directions [*sens*], different levels and points of application' (FM, 100/98–9, tm). This means that its historical position does not give any specific historical meaning or direction (*sens*) to the elements which retain their radical heterogeneity. Its elements are not in 'the modality of a memory' which would show the present or its elements as something that was anticipated in the past (FM, 115). The current conjuncture is simply the present articulated without giving any explanatory value to its temporal position or the empirical succession of time through which it has come to be. It can be readily stated, however, that this view of things makes it difficult to see where the selective criteria for the elements constituting an intelligibility of a specific historical moment come from, as these are not offered by the empirical-temporal position of this moment.

In *Reading Capital* Althusser develops further the 'current conjuncture' and its relation to the wider historical context, and it is here that the term 'structural causality' is introduced (RC, 341–4). Such a context is an era as a particular mode of production, and it forms a structural whole as a framework of intelligibility of 'current conjunctures'. The latter now become functions within a more complex whole. The articulation of such a complex whole brings together 'different historical times which are never given in the ideological obviousness of the continuity of time …, but must be constructed out of the differential nature and differential articulation of their objects in the structure of the whole' (RC, 250). This whole is not understandable according to a presence of a specific historical 'moment', because in such a 'moment' '[t]he present of one level is [always] the absence of another. ... And, [w]hat is ... grasped as absences in a localized "presence" is precisely the non-localization of the structure of the whole' (RC, 252). The logic concerning the whole here follows the same scheme as in the current moment in that it is a question of an articulation of relationalities of absent and present times in order to make a given locality intelligible according to it.

What matters here is that a specific historical moment is not intelligible according to what is present, 'visible' or 'legible' in that moment, but its intelligibility can only exist as a unity of a complex trans-temporal whole. The 'presence' of this whole itself can only be thought through its articulation in theory, that is, it 'concerns the knowledge of the complex articulation that makes the whole a whole' (RC, 255). Such a theoretical articulation makes a present intelligible not as a moment in a linear time but as a specific variation of the whole which crosses different temporal positions.

It is not clear to what extent there is any understandable idea of 'causality' at work in such an articulation, however. Rather, it tends to point merely to an internal logic of this articulation as such with little connection to something like an 'objectively' determined historical reality.[13] Rejecting any reference to the experience of time, the rationality of the articulation which produces the intelligibility of the whole does not mirror any conceivable temporal course. For the same reason it cannot include in itself a relation of continuity to a further state and is thus incompatible with politics or ideologies of evolutionary development, progress or 'peaceful transition'. As we shall see, Althusser's endeavour was nevertheless premised on an aim-oriented political project, but the rupturous form of temporality his philosophy leaned on risked rendering such a project unintelligible. This contributes to the fundamental problem that Rancière will have with temporal orders.

Epistemological break and theoretical practice

As we have seen, the dismantling of continuous temporality in favour of a non-contemporaneous multitemporal whole amounted to a radical rejection of lived experience. Hence, it was necessary that the activity of knowledge detach itself from any pre-given object reflected in consciousness. Such theoretical practice was famously conceptualized by Althusser through what he calls the 'epistemological break', a concept originating in the thought of Gaston Bachelard.[14] This concept marks a point where a new science distinguishes itself from its ideological 'pre-history' through a conceptualization of a new object as opposed to an ideological pre-given object. '[T]his detachment, this "break" inaugurates a new form of historical existence and temporality' which is discontinuous with 'the ideological prejudgement of visible succession' (RC, 284, 249). The new form of temporality is 'only accessible in *its concept*, which, like every concept is never immediately "given", never *legible* in visible reality: like every concept this concept must be *produced, constructed*' (RC, 249).

Because the idea of continuity of the given is radically rejected the epistemological break cannot happen 'in one blow' in order to give birth to an object which would then carry on existing in time, but it has to be continuously produced by breaking with the ideological pre-givenness (FM, 36). In other words, its existence cannot be trusted on the nature of temporal continuity because it is the very idea of such a continuity that it rejects: 'we know that a "pure" science only exists on condition that it *continually* frees itself from the ideology which occupies it, haunts it, or lies in wait in it' (FM, 170, emphasis added).[15] There is thus a peculiar idea of continuity, which cannot be reflected upon any given object. The continuity of (theoretical) practice cannot represent itself in its object (or subject). The 'continual freeing' of the theory from ideology thus amounts to continual dissociation of time from any subjective and objective reflectibility. We could characterize it in paradoxical terms as continuity of discontinuity.

The radical rupture that Althusser set out to theorize against historicist views was then first of all one between theoretical articulation of the historical totality and the principles of its functioning, on one hand, and an ideological conception of history which coincided with the empirical succession of events, on the other. For theory, as Althusser says, '[t]ime is required – a great deal of it', but this was a time of theoretical training, a time of learning the functioning principles of the structure, a time of conceptual construction. Such a time came to replace time as passive reflection of the given (PSPS, 21–2). However, the time of theoretical work was assumed to be strategically linked to a practical horizon of pursuing political ends. As Althusser says, the time spent in theoretical labour 'permits us to define the appropriate means of action for "making the revolution"' (PSPS, 4). It is indeed striking how Althusser, when talking about this aspect, does not hesitate to use terminology which his theoretical anti-humanism wouldn't allow any conceptual pertinence. Thus, towards the end of his own contributions to *Reading Capital* Althusser declares how theory will allow 'mankind [*l'humanité*]' to square its 'tasks [with its] capacities' and to find the 'right means to produce and dominate its future' (RC, 345, 355). At the same time when the Enlightenment conception of history was revoked as 'a teleological and therefore idealist rationalism', a certain form of aim-oriented progress was articulated back into scientific practice which proceeded through epistemological breaks in order to allow for a political revolution (RC, 45). As Althusser very plainly puts is, 'no science in the world lives without progressing' (PSPS, 275).

It was this insistence on scientific progress coupled with aim-oriented political strategy which would provoke venomous criticism from both Rancière and Lardreau in the post-68 context. They both saw Althusser failing to think a radical rupture. As such, however, both of their projects can be seen as holding on to the Althusserian attempt to think such a rupture, in a theoretical-political horizon marked by Mao Zedong. However, this is only after Althusser's Maoist students' (failed) attempt to combine Althusserian theory with organized revolutionary action. I shall now go briefly through the relevant phases around this historical sequence.

Practical ruptures

A theory for militants

Scientific progress required patient theoretical training which alone could allow the communist movement to dissociate itself from spontaneous ideology, and the conceptions of history it produced, and to rationalize its actions. Until the scientific principles of Marxism were fully investigated and explicated, it remained 'at the mercy of any *philosophical* theory that happens to come along' (FM, 107). The 'urgent necessity' for revolutionary Marxism was thus to formulate these principles and to study Marxist science in the most rigorous and thorough manner, to cherish 'a high degree not only of Marxist culture … but also of scientific and philosophical culture in general' (PSPS, 20).

Young intellectuals close to Althusser at École Normale Supérieure ambitiously took up the task of theoretical development of Marxism. Rancière himself was a core figure of this Althusserian project. In the late 1964, from his initiative, a group of young Althusserians started a journal called *Cahiers Marxistes-Léninistes* (CML) to promote Althusserian-Marxist theoretical training as a precondition of revolutionary political practice.[16] This was also the period of the seminar on Marx's *Capital* at École Normale whose proceedings were published as *Reading Capital* in 1965. Along with Althusser and Rancière, it included presentations from Étienne Balibar, Roger Establet and Pierre Macherey. Following Althusser's notion of theoretically adequate Marxism included in Marx's mature works, Rancière's contribution included a rigorous articulation of an epistemologically incompatible relations between the young Marx and *Capital*.[17] Around the same time Rancière published two shorter and more approachable texts around the same topic in the issues 1 and 3 of CML, before leaving École Normale in 1965.[18] Soon some of the people associated with the journal started to emphasize more and more direct political action, and in the early 1966 they parted ways with those more interested in theoretical questions. While Rancière would remain associated with the former group, the latter, including people like Jacques-Alain Miller and Jean-Claude Milner, launched another journal entitled *Cahiers pour l'Analyse*. On its pages direct political engagement was stressed less, and its ultra-theoretical focus was drawing from a broad context of Western epistemological tradition.[19] The basic problematic, however, was the one central in Althusserianism, and the main questions studied in the journal were related to structural causality, or 'the action of the structure', to quote the title of one of its most significant articles.[20]

Provoked by the Maoist sympathies within the Althusserian theory, the authorities of the PCF expressed around the same time that the independence of Althusserian theoretical work from the ideological principles of the party should no longer be allowed to continue – an occasion which 'was as close to an official censure as Althusser could receive'.[21] In response, in 1966 the group around CML which had theretofore supported the party line in distinction to some other factions, broke with the PCF and its student organization and founded the openly Maoist Union des Jeunesses Communistes – Marxistes-Léninistes (UJC-ml). UJC-ml took Althusserianism into a direct connection to Maoist political practice, declaring openly the centrality of China for the world communism and basing its theory and practice on 'the Althusserian theoretical rigour *and* the Chinese Cultural Revolution'.[22] The main task consisted in the 'defence of theory against its liquidators', that is, the PCF.[23] While remaining in the Party, Althusser himself published anonymously an article 'On the Cultural Revolution' in CML, now the official political and theoretical organ of the newly founded UJC-ml.[24] Although the initial position of the UJC-ml was thoroughly Althusserian and swore by theoretical expertise, it soon ran into trouble adjusting this position with the practical fidelity to the events in China. In order to understand the stakes, I will now move to discuss the Chinese Cultural Revolution itself before looking more closely to the problematic practice of the UJC-ml and its aftermath triggered by May 1968.

The Cultural Revolution in China

The stated aim of the Cultural Revolution was to adjust the ideology, or the 'superstructure', of the Chinese society to the socialist principles and to thus secure the course of the revolution. After a period of prevalence of egalitarianism in the Great Leap Forward, socio-economic inequality was spreading again in the first half of the 1960s and the actual socio-economic conditions grew further apart from socialist principles.[25] Exploitative practices continued to affect the relations between people and to characterize bureaucratic structures, educational institutions and Party organizations. Hierarchical ideological structures of the old social order were maintained or re-established. The purpose of the newly launched movement was to get rid of these: 'Although the bourgeoisie has been overthrown, it is still trying to use the old ideas, culture, customs and habits of the exploiting classes to corrupt the masses, capture their minds and endeavour to stage a come-back.'[26]

Althusser's reading of the Cultural Revolution was based on his idea of structural coexistence of multiple temporalities and the discontinuous notion of historical time requiring conjunctural analysis. This allowed him to explain and follow Mao's insistence on the continuity of revolution, after political and economic revolutions. As there was no historical reason that would either join all the phenomena to one temporal contemporaneity and automatically 'generalize' the events taking place at one level or sustain a mechanical causal chain originating in one single change, different elements of the social totality 'have sufficient of their own consistency *to survive beyond their immediate life context*' (FM, 116). Consequently, every revolution was a construction on multiple fronts which did not coincide temporally, and the ongoing Cultural Revolution in China could be seen as the working of the socialist revolution at the level of ideology. The fact that revolutionary changes had been accomplished on the political and economic levels did not neutralize the risk of regression as long as the society had not transformed its ideology. 'The C.C.P. declares that in order to reinforce and develop socialism in China, in order to assure its future and protect it in a lasting way from every risk of regression, it must add a third revolution to the prior political and economic revolutions: a mass ideological revolution.'[27] As Althusser says, 'the C.R. is a considered, deliberate decision undertaken by the Party; it rests on a scientific analysis of the situation, and therefore on the principles of Marxist theory and practice.'[28]

What makes the Cultural Revolution particular, however, was the way it encouraged masses themselves to attack authorities in institutions from primary schools to the Party itself. To the extent that at stake was a mobilization of ordinary people or 'the masses' *against* the Party authorities, the Cultural Revolution indeed represents an extraordinary, even heretical moment in the history of communist movement where the Party had traditionally held the monopoly in political authority.[29] Being itself located in a 'backward' country, one of the characteristics of Chinese communism was a certain reluctance to distinguish between 'advanced' and 'backward' elements, not least when it came to the distinction between peasants and workers, or the countryside and the city, a fact which had always caused suspicion in the Soviet Party.[30] Furthermore, for Mao, the masses had always played an integral part in determining the way theory was to lead the revolution. The method to correct theory on the basis of mass practice was known as 'the mass line'.[31] The Cultural Revolution took the insistence on mass authority to a new level, however, by refusing to distinguish the *leading* elements from the *led* at the level of the relationships between people, between the masses on one hand

and the Party cadres, academic intellectuals or other authorities on the other. The masses were given initiative, and they were encouraged to take themselves as equal with the people in higher positions, to refuse to adjust with the social inequalities and to 'liberate themselves'.[32]

K. S. Karol noticed the unprecedented insistence on radical equality in China just before the Cultural Revolution was unleashed:

> What struck me ... was the extraordinary egalitarian purpose of the Chinese Communists, their goal of abolishing as quickly as possible the social distinctions inherited from the old order and preventing new ones from being formed over the heads of the masses. ... I repeat that these egalitarian ambitions struck me as extraordinary in the true sense; I had never seen anything like it in the socialist world.[33]

The Cultural Revolution was seen to reject or minimize any preparatory programs and to insist on immediate or near-immediate realization of full equality. The reality to which the launching of the Cultural Revolution gave rise in schools and universities, the main sites of its early stages, was an extraordinary experimentation of free improvised political militantism. 'The point was to demonstrate the hollowness of all authority, whether bureaucratic-administrative or knowledge-based instructional.'[34]

This aspect of the Cultural Revolution which consists in allowing and encouraging self-authorized and autonomous revolt of the masses made it a phenomenon which is not so easily put in the framework of a theoretically conducted project. Thus, although Althusser's take on the Cultural Revolution was on one hand in line with Mao's own views, on the other, it was difficult to adjust the privileged authority of theory with the 'wish to join all the comrades of [the] party to learn from the masses'. Mao insisted that the communist authorities, himself included, 'be pupils of the masses', 'be supervised by the masses'.[35] It was not 'extremely long, arduous and difficult theoretical practice' that was called for (PSPS, 14). Rather, '[w]hat [was] needed are determined people who are young, have little education'.[36] There was no such thing as purely academic sphere where knowledge-based hierarchy would remain justified but relations between people were everywhere directly political.[37] And, to realize this principle in practice 'it [was] necessary that the professors be overthrown by the students' when the former were 'still desperately trying to maintain their academic "authority"'.[38]

Nonetheless, the ambiguity was that the anarchic mass democracy at the level of actual movement was at the same time supposed to be 'under the leadership of the Communist Party'.[39] It is not, then, that Althusser's reading of the Cultural Revolution as a theoretically planned project authorized by those who know the general course of the revolution simply misunderstood its stakes. The ambiguity between self-liberation of the masses or immediate actualization of full equality, on one hand, and a broader unidirectional project, on the other, lies in the very core of the Cultural Revolution. This ambiguity is summarized in Mao's statement which tries to shadow one of its terms in favour of the other: 'Democracy sometimes looks like an end in itself, but in fact it is merely a means to an end.'[40] Yet, there was little sign that the anarchic reality of the multiple self-authorized revolts would take a unified direction towards *an* end.

In both Althusserianism and the Cultural Revolution there is a problematic relation between a unified time of an aim-oriented movement and a form which tends to disperse it into a multiplicity of contingent events and processes. In Althusser this follows from the radical rejection of the reflection of history on lived experience and the theoretical understanding of historical temporality as radically rupturous. In the Cultural Revolution it consisted in the lack of centralized mediation of the reality of multiple self-authorized revolts. While on one hand the principles of the method of the 'mass line' were retained, on the other hand the unifying mediation between theory and mass practice gave way to largely improvised expressions of revolt as such.[41] The French Maoist circles close to Rancière would tackle these ambiguities in their own way before and after May 1968.

French Maoism and May 1968

The UJC-ml, the organization founded in the circles around Rancière in 1966, started with promotion of Althusserian theory against revisionist ideology (as explained earlier). At first the UJC-ml worked among students and the youth, but soon its practice became more and more haunted by the Maoist emphasis on radical mass democracy. The organization leaned on a commitment to the universal truth of Marxist theory, and its practice was to be 'guided by the scientific theory and the principles of the mass line'.[42] After a trip to China (as well as to Albany and Bretagne) by some members of the UJC-ml, and inspired by Mao's insistence on the study of the concrete situation, the organization launched in September 1967 *enquêtes* among the working class in order to avoid intellectual spontaneism and produce concrete analysis of the situation in the society.[43]

A more concrete engagement with the masses raised the question of how to adjust the authority of the masses – central to Maoism – with that of theory learnt in the Althusserian School in the most concrete manner. The constant occupation with self-criticism in the texts produced by the UJC-ml is telling of this difficulty. *Enquêtes* appeared to be too much based on 'bookish theoretical training' aimed at educating workers.[44] They were simply serving 'to fill the loopholes in … knowledge'.[45] To overcome the theoreticist tendencies of this practice, the programme of *établissement* was launched to take activists to the factories and the countryside, not for a brief visit but to live with the workers. A 'real dispersion' among the masses through distinct groups of *établissement* was supposed to construct a 'real unity' as opposed to an external and abstract unity of theory brought from the outside.[46] The real concrete unity was supposed to allow a genuine direction of the revolutionary movement according to the mass line and the leadership by the masses themselves.

In general, *enquête* and *établissement* as ideas of connecting with the masses can be understood as differing degrees of emphasis on the authority of the masses. While *enquêtes* still insist on a more dialectical mediation between theory and mass practice, *établissement* emphasizes more self-authorized practice of the masses.[47] However, before May 1968, the *établissement* programme was still marked by a strong belief in the advanced position of the young intellectuals themselves and their knowledge of the movement of history: 'The most advanced revolutionary ideas and theories enter on a large scale first the students and young intellectuals. That is a law of historical development, which can be verified in France as in everywhere else.'[48] But 'the students and the young intellectuals cannot be the leading force of the revolution, even when some of them join the masses'.[49] That is why they are not supposed to take the lead but pass the 'avant-garde ideas' on to the workers so that the latter can constitute a genuine mass leadership. This did not stop the self-criticism within the UJC-ml: 'It became clear very quickly that to serve the people meant for [them] taking *control and the leadership* of the detachment which was organising itself'.[50] The ideas would instead have to arise from the masses themselves, it was now insisted, and the activists had to content themselves with raising 'an enthusiastic spirit in order to get them to work'.[51] We can see how the months preceding May 1968 were marked by a vexed relationship between the authority of theory on one hand and the authority of the masses on the other. As Jason E. Smith argues, this problematic ' "divorce" between the revolutionary ideas circulating among students and intellectuals and the spontaneous combativeness of the advanced elements of the working class' concerns directly the question of 'historical development'.[52] Where did the driving force of history lie, in the more or less academic knowledge or in the practice led by the working class? In May the question exploded when unanticipated revolts erupted in the streets of Paris taking the young Althusserians by surprise. Following the events of May, the UJC-ml split, the majority holding on to a more traditional avant-gardist position, many of them joining the existing Maoist Party. After the initial reserve concerning student revolts, the minority that had most emphasized the autonomy of the masses joined hands with the members of the March 22 Movement and decided to devote their activism to anti-authoritarian mass revolt in full scale. It was at this faction that the Althusserian group now found itself. To continue the moment when revolts had erupted without any relation to external theoretical guidance, they founded the Gauche Prolétarienne in the autumn of 1968.[53]

What happens to the question of historical development and its relation to the rupturous practice now comes to be seen in terms of an opening of the new in the present which operates a full scale cut with ideas belonging to the past. Theory or 'books' included nothing but 'ossified ideas'; Althusserianism was to be abandoned.[54] The new bore the name of Mao, which only stood for the masses' right to self-authorized revolt. Instead of planning the future on the basis of analyses of the past, one needed to put full emphasis on the present and build on it under the leadership of the masses themselves, to 'draw the lessons of May 1968 in the factories and in the street'.[55] The most important thing for the post-May *gauchiste* ideology was to struggle against the *old* – as a consequence of which the GP itself was soon dissolved in favour of an attempt to build a 'new instrument'.[56] The class struggle appeared first of all as a struggle for the authority of that which was new in the present: 'it was a struggle between the old and new ideas.'[57] The question of history was no longer about its broad course, but it was reduced to the present, where the dividing line between the old and the new needed to be drawn. This view should be seen against the background of not only the Maoist insistence on the authority of the masses but also Althusser's refusal to conceive historical reality according to the continuity of time while at the same time seeing his theory as a means to bring forth a desired future.

Having belonged to the radical Maoist Althusserian group which broke with the PCF in 1966 and earlier founded the *Cahiers Marxistes-Léninistes* which became its organ, Rancière was away from militant engagement until 1969, when he joined the GP as a grassroots militant and started to teach at the new University of Paris 8 (ME, 17). He published his famous critique of Althusser in his first single-authored book, *Althusser's Lesson*, in 1974, a year after the dissolution of the GP. While the book includes a critical position taken towards the organization, many of its emphases emerge from the collective Maoist practice whose leading force the Gauche Prolétarienne had been in the years after May 1968. To get a better sense of the stakes in *Althusser's Lesson* as well as Rancière's subsequent trajectory, I will first discuss another remarkable book which emerges from this context. This is Guy Lardreau's *Le Singe d'or* (1973) which is the most elaborated theoretical formulation of the philosophical framework of the Gauche Prolétarienne and the *gauchiste* ideology of the time.

The revolt of Guy Lardreau

The Althusserian-Maoist *Cahiers Marxistes-Léninistes* had printed on the cover of each of its volume Lenin's phrase '[t]he Marxist doctrine is omnipotent because it is true'.[58] The stakes of the post-May 1968 Maoism can be aptly summarized through the reversal that this maxim undergoes in Guy Lardreau's *Le Singe d'or*: 'Marx's theory is true because it is omnipotent' (SO, 189; cf. AL, 154). While the first formulation declares an overwhelming power that the Marxist theory can grant to revolutionary practice due to its scientific knowledge of history, Lardreau's formulation states that what is true in Marx's writings is sourced from the revolutionary struggle. The essential was crystallized in Mao's phrase 'it is right – or reasonable – to revolt', *on a raison de se révolter*.

Althusser had attacked the humanist critique of Stalin by stating that both Stalinism and its humanist opposite rest on the same belief in linear continuity of historical time which rendered impossible any adequate understanding of revolutionary break. Instead, such a break should be constructed by a patient preparatory work in theory. Boosted by the Maoist movement after May, Lardreau would claim that instead of enabling a genuine rupture the Althusserian logic itself was compatible with the continuity of systemic oppression. Thus, he saw the problem with Althusser to be that the latter was not able to follow the principle of rupture, but his theoreticist construction led him back to the position he wanted to leave. This was not, however, a specific conception of historical time per se but a continuity of theoretical practice itself, which established and sustained itself regardless of the historical events that took place in the present, first of all by continuing to imply a division between intellectual and manual labourers.

Lardreau does not develop his argument so much in direct reference to Althusser, but there is no doubt that Althusser was the main contemporary example of 'ossified Leninism', or the general theoreticist avant-gardism against which his book was targeted.[59] *Le Singe d'or* is to a large extent a confrontation with Althusser and Lardreau's own Althusserian phase. In contrast to Rancière, Lardreau is not so much occupied with a detailed polemic with Althusser's writings and their contemporary political reality, but he proceeds through more general and overarching theses. However, it is these very theses that would largely underlie Rancière's critique, too, and thus help understand it and link it to its context.

If the Althusserian conception of society, especially the contemporary capitalist society, was a complex whole which rendered any direct consciousness useless for understanding its systemic function, after May, and the Cultural Revolution seen through its lenses, 'things had become very simple' again (SO, 24). In essence there was only one thing to know: the age-old fact of oppression. The most basic manifestation of this fact was social division of labour, and the whole history of philosophy and science was for Lardreau a history of the factuality of this division. His critique of Althusserian theoreticism consists in assigning it to this history.

The division of labour went back to the antiquity and 'the division between Being and Thought' that occurred there (SO, 185). This conceptual division is not the origin of the first, though, but 'a re-ordering of an already-there', that is, a way in which the system of oppression, based on a particular type of division of labour, manifests itself in thought, in order 'to mask' itself (SO, 170, 72). Once thought has its independent existence, it can take the social and political reality as its object while remaining in its being neutral to it – precisely because it is Thought as opposed to Being. Consequently, 'because thought is no longer political, there is room [*il y a place*] for political thought' (SO, 177–8). Thought belongs to the realm which is separate from social and political life, and it can think such life without automatically becoming a part of it thus masking the social structure which conditions its existence. Those who dwell in the realm of Thought deal solely with the 'truth', and theirs is a '*bios*, a way of life of the one who is in search of truth' (SO, 71, 177).

By positing autonomous and objective scientific practice, as Lardreau argues, Althusserian Marxism remains in this tradition of masking the oppression. In accordance with this tradition, 'Lenin is not understood in relation to his time but through his relation to Marx' (SO, 86). In other words, Lenin is not rooted in the political reality of his time but rather in an independent history of Marxist theory. His contributions are not primarily contributions to his contemporary political context, and his motivations are not motivations arising from this context. As the Althusserian narrative has it, by applying the philosophy implicit in Marx's theory of history, Lenin had invented a Marxist theory of politics and thus accomplished a '*theoretical* revolution' (SO, 95, my emphasis).[60] Similarly, as we have seen, Althusser saw the Chinese Cultural Revolution primarily as a fulfilment of the Marxist theory. The Cultural Revolution meant that 'a Marxist theoretical thesis that up to this point remained in a theoretical state' converged 'with a new historical fact'.[61] It was an event with 'political and theoretical credentials' to be judged 'in the light of Marxist theoretical principles'.[62] The Cultural Revolution was thus part of the 'Leninist heritage' which is 'a heritage of true propositions'. It makes progress breaking with what appears as flaws, or ideological remainders, which, as Althusser said, 'haunts' every scientific practice (FM, 170).

Even if science makes progress through breaks, it still constructs those breaks on the basis of a history internal to the realm of science. If the very form of the independence of science leaned on the ideology of progress regardless of what its content was, this science could become that of discontinuous history while at the same time sustaining the idea of scientific accumulation and progress. This is the argument underlying Lardreau's attack against Bachelard's epistemology – which, as we know, was one of the most important precursors of Althusser's philosophy of discontinuity. Lardreau argues that the concept of epistemological break is conditioned upon a belief in the progress of 'the human spirit' in the realm of which science can proceed by separating itself from its ideological pre-history gradually purifying 'the desire of science' from ideological impurities (SO, 67, 76). Even if science proceeds through ruptures it has always already posited a separate realm of thought, or *'l'esprit scientifique'*, in which the rupture can occur, thus sustaining the division of labour or the division between *'le savant et l'ignorant'* (SO, 68, 66). In other words, there is a continuity of a certain realm in which the constant demarcation between science and ideology can occur. And, it is 'this continuity [… which] founds the series of discontinuities of science' (SO, 70).

Although Althusser's conceptual configuration, taken as such, seems to break with logics of continuity, its specific conceptuality forms a continuity of a certain form. The continuity does not lie within specific concepts through which science thinks time but in 'the very form of Science or, rather, [in] Science as a form' which constructs itself upon a social order based on the division of labour (SO, 64). Thus, Lardreau argues, the very existence of Althusser's theory is conditioned upon the position he is attacking, that is, a continuity of a certain social structure in the guise of scientific progress, as a consequence of which 'no absolute rupture is possible' (SO, 223). The continuity thus lies 'at the level of this constitutive affirmation' through which science sustains itself as independent and exclusive practice, constituting itself as *a historical continuity of the separation of science from history*. It is a continuity of a discontiguous relation between thought and life. If, at the level of content, the history of science is discontinuous, this is because it keeps reinventing itself in each new historical situation presenting itself in a new disguise, as it were, making progressive steps. By definition, science is a 'discourse which lies about its origins' (SO, 38).

This is also the lesson we should, according to Lardreau, draw from Foucault's archaeological and genealogical studies. Foucault's studies on the 'will to truth' in the early 1970s were preceded by investigations on the historical a prioris of knowledge, or 'epistemes'. The concept of episteme, explicated in *The Order of Things* (1966), refers to a specific structure which determines production of knowledge within a given era. Between different epistemes there is no continuity, and thus their history is a history of radical breaks or discontinuities.[63] When Foucault moved from this intra-scientific archaeology of knowledge to the genealogical approach, 'will to knowledge' or 'will to truth' took the place of episteme. Now, Lardreau suggests that these are parallel structures so that '[e]ach episteme … is marked by a [specific] desire of truth' (SO, 70). The factual continuity of science, that is, the continuity of science as a form, is at the level of this desire of truth, for 'there are forms of desire of truth only to the extent that' they are based on 'the desire of truth' as such (SO, 70). And, the latter is nothing else but a translation through masking of a social reality of oppression, that is to say, it is the will to detach thought and the lives of those who think from the historical reality into the level of disinterested truth, that is, 'the will of the discontiguity of science', in the form of a belief in progress (SO, 66).[64]

Seen from this perspective, Althusser – who in *Reading Capital* pays homage to Foucault's work of the early 1960s for contributing to the understanding of discontinuous history of science – completely misunderstands Foucault's lesson to the extent that he sees discontinuity as an epistemological problem and one into which scientific progress is articulated (RC, 45–6). If Foucault did not give *theoretical* explanations of the transitions between different epistemes, it was for a good reason. If the history of science is history of masking the system of oppression based on the division of labour, then its continuity/discontinuity is not to be looked for at the level of science itself but in the social reality. As Miguel de Beistegui puts it, in Foucault's 'effort to analyse the origin of the system of truth that underpins our epistemes, philosophy is going to be of no use.'[65] Rather, if Foucault presented the history of scientific thought as discontinuous, it was because he wanted to reveal the real continuity behind the institution of science. Hence the genealogical research which Foucault enters in the early 1970s. What we should find in Foucault's 'archaeological research' is not a specific mode in which science makes progress but rather the incapacity of science to sustain its independent continuity. To see in Foucault's theory an immanent problem of science, a conceptual problem of transition between epistemes, amounts to nothing but a reaction of science to his discoveries, where science once again tries to separate itself from social reality.

We can see how Lardreau displaces the question of continuity/discontinuity from specific conceptual structures to the continuity of the production of such structures itself. This continuity is not as such a specific philosophical conception but a 'way of life' of 'those who know' which allows them to conceptualize history regardless of the immediate historical situation in which these conceptions are created. This fact of continuity of science or scientific practice consists in a continuous denial of its absolute social and historical conditionedness. Thus, it does not matter whether science proceeds through breaks or not, for, to the extent that it is its own practice, it has to assume itself as continuous. It is a question of the way science constitutes the continuity of science by a discontiguous relation between *le savant* and *l'ignorant*. In this respect Lardreau see the question in terms that will be adopted by Rancière. But while Lardreau aims to bring *le savant* and *l'ignorant*, or science and ideology, into a relation of *contiguity*, his perspective remains focused primarily on temporal succession, in its continuities and breaks (cf. 49 n.1). As for Rancière, we shall later see that his work will be characterized by ways to insist on contiguity through a spatial logic rather than seeing rupture to concern temporal succession.

On a raison de se révolter, or How to read Marx

If independent practice of science renders any radical rupture in the social order impossible, the revolutionary potential of Marxism cannot lie in its theoretical content. As Lardreau argues, it has to be based on the way Marx rejects the authority of science, finding it instead in the revolting masses. While science relates to the social and political reality by masking the oppression in order to sustain its independence, Marx subjects it to the theses which arise from revolutionary practice of the oppressed. His discourse has its roots in the historical situation where, against the odds of the classical economy's naturalization of the order in place, 'the practice of the mass revolt' demonstrates 'the possibility of another economic and political order' and insists 'that there is nothing that could not be changed' (SO, 53, 42, 54). As the laws of economy are in this way forced into a historical horizon, the supposedly objective knowledge now shows to concern only a specific social order 'where capitalism is the obligation' (SO, 46). Marx intervenes, as Lardreau argues, in this situation with his historical science which justifies the mass revolts by attaching them to the movement of history. In doing so, he puts a new imperative against the bourgeois one by assigning the economic structures of society into a certain logic of historical transformation. '[S]cience shifts to the side of a new obligation, the truth becomes proletarian' (SO, 47). Insofar as Marx's discourse of history, as is the case particularly in the late Marx, leans on 'a scientific necessity', which is founded 'on the nature of things', he can certainly – just like Lenin after him – be incorporated into the bourgeois tradition of science, which tells the truth about historical phenomena from an external perspective (SO, 85).

However, Lardreau insists that '[w]hat renders possible the critique of the classical economy …, is not *first* a progress in thought, the transition of one form of discourse into another, but the de facto collapse of the necessity of capitalism' through mass revolts and a glimpse of another world to which they give rise (SO, 42). Hence, the crucial feature of Marx's discourse is not the content of his science but the fact that it 'adopt[s] the proletarian viewpoint of the revolt' and is conditioned by this adaptation – not in that it continues scientific discourse but that it opts to take that discourse where the revolutionary movement guides it, thus disrupting the tradition of autonomous and self-sufficient scientific practice (SO, 54). 'It is precisely because Marx has adopted this viewpoint, because he has moved into this sphere of the grant luminosity produced by the revolt, because of the very position from which he speaks, that he can speak the truth of extortion' (SO, 54).[66]

Thus, the Marxist theory itself is a consequence of a break in the social reality, not its condition, as Althusserian theoreticism would have it. True, to the extent that Marx leans on scientific necessity, it cannot fully acknowledge its own historical conditions but opens the door for reactionary readings. Nonetheless, we do not have to, and we indeed should not, forget 'what was the aim behind these concepts of progress and necessity as well as the science which guaranteed them: to assure the revolution, to authorize the deployment of the spirit of revolt by forging a reason for it [*en lui forgeant une raison*]' (SO, 222). We should not loose from sight the origin of Marx's discourse in the mass revolt: 'His whole science of the economic serves only to prove that: *on a raison de se révolter*' (SO, 83). In this Maoist slogan, then, the essence of Marxism as a discourse of revolt had come to light and crystallized.

Stage and era: Towards a vanishing present

Drawing from the practice of the Gauche Prolétarienne, Lardreau conceptualizes a certain minimal temporal scheme of the present. As we shall see, he later conceives even this to be too much, however, to express the rupturous nature of revolt. In *Le Singe d'or*, the form of the present is conceptualized through the notion of the 'stage' (*étape*) and the way it relates to that of 'era' or 'epoch' (*époque*). This is a key question in the post-68 Maoism which declared the novelty of the Maoist stage. While it was conceived as a particular stage of Marxism, its distinctive feature was a certain absolute nature it granted to itself. It was an expression of the revolt as such.[67] By the same token it amounted to a rethinking of all previous stages according to the absolute authority of the mass revolt that limited the scope of each stage of Marxism to a rupturous nature of a given historical moment or era. Because Marxist thought is not 'produced by philosophical research but by re-irruption of the masses on the stage (*scène*) of history', it cannot be in conceptual continuity beyond its present stage (*étape*) (SO, 24). Hence, each stage of Marxism has to be seen without relation of continuity with the frameworks of thought with which revolutionary Marxism responded to the past situations and thought past epochs. Marxism is merely a name for thought which sets out from and takes sides with the mass revolt (just like 'science' is only a name for thought which takes the opposite side).[68] There is thus a continuity, but it is nothing but a continuous will to break absolutely with the past.[69] It can therefore be understood as a counter-form to science which we should again refer to Lardreau's ideas of 'contiguity' and 'discontiguity': revolt is a continuous will to break the way the society establishes a discontiguous relation between those who think and those who work by building on its past (SO, 49–50 n.1).

Any theoretical constellation which draws from knowledge produced in different historical contexts only works against the present reality of the revolt, attempting to restore or sustain historical circumstances against which the masses struggle in the present. 'To think a historical epoch in terms produced by another epoch, is precisely to guarantee the impossibility of the revolution' (SO, 107). The radical 'heterogeneity of historical epochs' gets Lardreau to 'hope for amnesia' in order to annihilate completely the dangers of continuities within history.[70] '[H]umanity won't find anything good in its memories' (SO,

127). The dream of amnesia shows the stakes of Lardreau's Maoism in all clarity: it is a question of a radical reduction of the framework of revolt to the present and the absolute sufficiency of this present for revolutionary rupture.

As Peter Hallward puts it, in the early Lardreau, '[t]he only time of revolt is the present, and it proceeds by breaking with the previous present'.[71] Yet, this present is still one with a certain futural orientation – it aims to *establish* itself for the future.[72] It still has a temporal form, a temporally synthesized coherence of the era-stage couple, that is, a historical moment of the irruption of class struggle and the form it comes to take in revolutionary practice and thought. This coherence means that theory or knowledge only draws from the present struggle of the masses, but it still constitutes itself as the time of 'the recollection, concentration, as Mao says, of the partial knowledges of such and such strata of the popular masses who know' (SO, 122). The present 'stage' names the temporal form where immediate knowledge of the masses goes through a needed mediation to encounter the state (SO, 57, 123).[73] This will become the most important difference between the early Lardreau's *gauchiste* conception of revolutionary politics and Rancière who, as we shall see in later chapters of this book, in a way rethinks Lardreau's tentative idea of contiguity while avoiding structuring it in temporal terms.[74]

If *Le Singe d'or* still shows a certain affinity with Hegel, Lardreau later moves from Hegel back to Kant and gives up whatever there was left from the post-Kantian project of winding together freedom and temporal unfolding of history (cf. SO, 84). And, in separating freedom from the phenomenal world Lardreau aims to be even more determined than the Königsbergian himself, 'more Kantian than Kant', as he says.[75] The way to this radical Kantianism goes through a stage in Lardreau's work where revolt is still thought as taking place in the phenomenal reality, through the figure of 'the Angel'.

The Angel, which gives a title to a book co-authored with Christian Jambet three years after the publication of *Le Singe d'or*, is the figure of pure revolt without any mediated relation with the historical reality that it comes to interrupt. As we know, in the first book, there was still a minimal degree of mediation between the revolt and the historical reality – although it is true that already the brevity of the discussion of this aspect in *Le Singe d'or* is symptomatic of what will be affirmed in *L'Ange* (1976). This latter work radicalizes the tendency of pure revolt and marks an attempt to think the revolt in its absolute purity without any such mediation being established. The pure revolt is thought according to annihilation of power – be it in the form of sexuality or knowledge – to which any existing historical order attaches itself.[76] Yet, even the angelic revolt comes to realize itself as another *future*: the figure of the Angel is there to 'maintain the hope that another world, despite everything, is possible'.[77] This hope was accompanied by an imperative to 'stop oneself from knowing that which comes. To not foresee the new.'[78] But the new was to come nevertheless.[79]

Soon Lardreau (and Jambet) started to see also the angelic absolute revolt as too much attached to historical reasoning. Starting from their *Le Monde* (1978) the revolt starts to be conceptualized as belonging wholly to a noumenal dimension, and it is thus seen as something which is to be kept out of the historical reality altogether. Between the publication of *L'Ange* and *Le Monde* the horrors of the Cambodian revolutionary regime had come to light, boosting the shift between the positions of the two books: The Angel as the figure of absolute revolt now appears to lead to unbearable consequences as soon as it comes in touch with the worldly reality. The crimes in Cambodia did not prove of a failure of revolt as such, however, but in contrast showed what it means for revolt to realize itself in its absolute purity in the midst of this world. The mistake made in *L'Ange* had been to try to adjust revolt to a temporal project with even a minimum of continuity: 'This little gnosis that we prepared for ourselves, with its declamations of neo-Platonic knowledge – the Angel, the Rebel, the Soul – what else was it good for than for slyly re-establishing a continuum, for designating a point from which a World could come to existence [*d'où pouvait s'engendrer un Monde*]?'[80]

The radical Kantianism is elaborated more fully in Lardreau's *La Véracité* (1993). Following Kant, Lardreau draws from a strict distinction between the theoretical and practical interests of reason. In order for freedom to remain absolutely autonomous, for Lardreau all attempts for connecting these dimensions must be abandoned. Practical reason must not seek to transform the reality grasped by theoretical reason since this would require some degree of compromise with the latter. It would necessarily take a constructivist or technical perspective to the phenomenal world while trying to bring forth another reality in it. We are trapped in time, and any act of realization would have to adapt to its logic and thus to the laws of this world.[81] Practical reason can only exist 'as a denial of any theoretical proposition'.[82] If such a denial takes a sensible form it can only appear as *'pulsion de mort'* and end up in barbaric horror: the only way for our sensible world to have done with temporal reality is death. For the late Lardreau, a radical thinker of revolt has to give up any hope of fulfilment of justice, or of ending of oppression, simply because this would, again, require complicity with the laws of phenomenal reality. Thus, we have to give up 'the Idea of the *future* of Humanity'.[83] The only mark that this attitude leaves to the phenomenal world is none other than the present as such: 'There is … only the present, and no Humanity', that is, no future.[84] But this present is nothing but a vanishing gesture of an ethical attitude of renouncing the world, with no effectivity in it.

We can read Lardreau's work as a systematic attempt to detach the idea of revolt from any form of temporality, to the extent of retreating to the noumenal in a vanishing present. The gesture is a more or less systematic consequence of his endeavour to reject all logics of temporal reasoning, even the general desire to move from the darkness of oppression to a better future. My claim is that Rancière's trajectory can be best understood against the background of Lardreau's (failed) attempt to think the effectivity of revolt in reality without temporalizing it. The guiding question for my reading of Rancière is: How to follow Lardreau as far as possible while still affirm the realization of emancipatory revolt in this world? This is the question which drives the following chapters. In Chapter 4 we shall see that Rancière's attempt to think revolt can be understood as a certain rethinking of the Althusserian rupturous temporality where the Althusserian theory paradoxically returns to give form to revolt. In this first chapter, however, we will still see how Rancière starts his post-68 trajectory with a critique of Althusser just as furious as that of Lardreau.

Althusser's Lesson

Seven years older than Lardreau, Rancière had received a thorough theoretical training in 'the Althusserian School' by the time the UJC-ml was founded to promote such training. After the dissolution of the organization, Rancière became a member of the Gauche Prolétarienne, and in 1974 he published *Althusser's Lesson*, a critique of Althusserianism, whose framework shares a lot with Lardreau. To quote Rancière himself, it is 'a genealogy of Althusser's present discourse, to seize at its origin the relationship between politics and theory that his thought puts into play' (AL, xxiii). Following the post-68 radical Maoist norm, the criteria of the critique are not received from any interpretation of the course of history but from 'the uprisings going on today' (AL, xxi). As expected, Althusserian discourse does not pass the test. Its 'stakes are clear: preserve philosophy ... as the exclusive business of academically trained specialists by upholding a division of labour that safeguards its place' (AL, 11). The broad scheme is thus the familiar one. Against disruptive practices of the present, Althusserianism brings back continuity in the guise of the continuity of science or theory.

Yet, apart from a section written in 1969, *Althusser's Lesson* is a product of a moment where the position of the Gauche Prolétarienne no longer appears adequate to Rancière. This becomes clear from a few remarks which, albeit short and incomprehensive, make the overall message clear enough: the position of the Gauche Prolétarienne appears to have been based on 'the bourgeois ideology premised on the repression of revolt' (AL, 54). Hence, while occupying an anti-theoreticist position in many ways similar to that of Lardreau, Rancière at the same time wants to distinguish himself from it. What *Althusser's Lesson* shares with Lardreau is first of all the idea that Althusser's conceptualization of theoretical practice sustains historical continuity. This, as I will show, is a leading thread of Rancière's critique. However, as I will show towards the ends of this section, anticipating the impasse of Lardreau's position, Rancière's argument already in *Althusser's Lesson* proceeds more according to the logics of simultaneity and conjunctive and disjunctive relations than in terms of radical temporal breaks. To conclude this chapter, I will briefly show how an article by Rancière from a year after *Althusser's Lesson* addresses such logics in relation to the question of time itself.

Origins and ends: Althusser's clandestine theory of the subject

The last chapter of *Althusser's Lesson* is an essay which was first published in 1969 on the basis of a course given in the newly founded University of Paris 8, at first placed in Vincennes.[85] My reading here will show how the essay traces ways in which Althusser, despite himself, relies on the models of continuous time his project set out to criticize, in order to safeguard an independent place for theoretical practice and hence maintain social division of labour.

According to Althusser, as Rancière argues, ideology guarantees 'the cohesion of the social whole' as such (AL, 130). The structure of society 'is necessarily opaque to its agents', and ideology is what makes possible 'the expression of the relation between men and their "world"' in a way which is necessarily false and illusory in respect to the real functioning of the social structure (AL, 130; FM, 233). For Rancière, however, this goes against Marx's conception of ideology which exists only *within* the class struggle. It cannot be understood as a function of 'cohesion' because it exists only through class *division*. Thus, if ideology functions to dissimulate the relations of production, this is not ideology in general but the *dominant* ideology which aims to hide the oppressive nature of the capitalist society against which the dominated class struggles. 'Would the function of the ideology of the dominated class', as Rancière's rhetorically asks, 'be to keep the exploited "in their place" in the system of class exploitation?' (AL, 135). For Althusser, however, the class division at the level of ideology is only a supplementary layer 'superimposed' upon ideology as a guarantee of the social whole, and its analysis depends on the concepts of this 'general sociology', that is, on the theory of the more fundamental level of ideology as a function of social cohesion (AL, 132). Having rendered ideology as such into a function of cohesive unity, Althusser displaces the class struggle at the level of objective science. The class contradiction and the division between class discourses can then be organized 'into the realms of true and false, into the world of science and its other (opinion, error, illusion, etc.)' (AL, 136).

As Joseph J. Tanke has noted, Rancière's uses the verb *partager* to describe the division between science and ideology in Althusser in this early text. It would then give us an early instance of Rancière's topographical method of analysis: 'The *partage* in this case is Althusser's separation of material practices from the theoretical apparatus that discloses their truth.'[86] Tanke correctly describes this method as one aiming to deconstruct hierarchical divisions, drawing on the double meaning of the French *partage* as both sharing and dividing.[87] Although it is true that Rancière's point in the text is to abolish the qualitative distinction between science and ideology and bring them to a level of reality of a political struggle, here the term itself barely communicates this.

Rather, it is likely to stem from Althusser himself who uses it to describe a 'division [*partage*] between ideological knowledges and scientific knowledges' through their '*progressive* erection' (RC, 63, my emphasis; cf. AL, 136). Indeed, what is crucial for Rancière here is the linear progressive temporality on which Althusser leans in order to establish a realm for science as independent from social reality.

For, having as its object a *unified* social whole, as a more fundamental level underlying class divisions, Althusser's science needs a point *beyond* the struggles in the present. It thus grounds itself on a teleology, which resembles the one we find in Kant's regulative ideas, in order to displace the present into a futural '*focus imaginarius*'. In Kant, regulative ideas make possible 'connecting up things in the world in accordance with teleological laws, and thereby attaining to the greatest systematic unity among them'.[88] Rancière refers to this Kantian model connecting Althusser's thought to its teleological horizon, or to the 'myths of origins (or of ends)', as Rancière puts it echoing Althusser's own critique of Hegelian Marxism (AL, 134; cf. RC, 162). The divided field of ideology is here unified through a function it has in keeping together the human society: 'ideology will not be posited as the site of a division, but as a totality unified through its relationship to its referent (the social whole)' (AL, 134). Thus, instead of juxtaposing two contradictory terms – that is, bourgeois and proletarian ideologies – Althusser subjects the division appearing in the present to a teleological framework where phenomena are thought through a unifying function of the idea of reason towards which the reality is oriented and from which it thus receives its coherent temporal course. In so doing, Althusser submits all ideological phenomena under the same futural origin: 'Investigation of origins, under the "as if" mode', Rancière concludes, functions 'to mask division' (AL, 134/238).

The social whole thus functions as an organizing principle which bypasses ideological struggle by submitting it under a teleological direction. It justifies Althusser's science and the institutional order and establishes a temporal-continuous course beyond the present reality of the revolt while the latter appears only as superficial phenomena unable to get to the heart of the matter:

> The student struggle aims only at the effects of capitalist exploitation; similarly, grass-roots struggles in factories against hierarchy, automation

and harassment aim only at effects. The real target, however, is the cause of exploitation itself: capitalist relations of production. But only science – meaning the wisdom of the Central Committee – can pierce through to this dimension of the problem. The retreat of the structure thus becomes Kant's *focus imaginarius*, the inverted image, condensed to a point, of an endless future: France's peaceful march towards socialism. (AL, 190 n.10)

This teleological scheme is not the only form of continuous temporality which Rancière finds in Althusser in this early text. He turns next to Althusser's text on 'Student Problems' to argue that it leans on a conception of a necessary succession of modes of production. In 1964, this text of Althusser's set out to criticize a student movement that was demanding educational reforms and dissolution of the hierarchical relations between the students and professors at universities. In the face of revolting students Althusser defended the existing structure of the university institution based on the 'technical division of labour' which was to be distinguished from the 'social division of labour'. Whereas the latter was determined by class relations of exploitation, technical division of labour was based on inherent scientific criteria. However, while such a division can be found in Marx, Rancière argues, 'it is not a real distinction, but merely a *formal distinction* corresponding to two ways of conceptualizing the same process' (AL, 137).[89] The technical division of labour always coincides with the order of the reproduction of the social relations, which are class relations, but 'Althusser treats the distinction as a real distinction between places and functions, and he correlates each to one or the other division' (AL, 138).

In order to think technical division of labour independently of the class struggle, Althusser has to once again rely on an objective temporality of history for its justification, this time in the form of a necessary succession of modes of productions: 'technical division of labour corresponds to every job "post" whose existence is exclusively justified by the technical necessities that define the mode of production at a given moment of its development in a given society.'[90] Distinguished as it is from the social division of labour, the technical division is not referred to the class struggle where it serves one class and is resisted by another. It is thus not understood according to the social reality shared in struggle but according to an order of historical time. When it comes to the question of scientific practice and the existence of a scientific institution, as Rancière concludes, Althusser does not hesitate to think 'history in terms of evolution and linear development' (AL, 139).

The irony of course lies in how the critique of Althusser is here constructed in the very terms of Althusser himself, that is, continuous historical time in the guise of teleological and successive-linear logics. To add insult to injury, Rancière associates these logics, again following Althusser himself, to a certain philosophy of the subject of history, akin to humanist and existentialist Marxism. Althusser 'wants to fight against the anthropological ideologies that make a theory of the subject out of the theory of society. But the only subversive effect of his discourse is that it re-establishes the theory of science as the mediator that regulates the relationship between the two terms' (AL, 153). Thus, Althusser does not manage to get rid of the idea of the subject as a function underlying the course of historical time, of its origins and ends. All he does is to make scientific practice the privileged site of this function, instead of seeing it in the politico-ideological practice as the thinkers he was criticizing.

We can see then that the argument in this early text by Rancière is twofold. On one hand, it concerns the way in which Althusser establishes qualitative distinctions and in so doing justifies science as its own practice and sets up an unchallenged place for it in the society. On the other hand, its independent realm is safeguarded through a horizon of linear temporal order in the course of which science performs its function. The terms of this argument seem to represent a wider Maoist position of this moment, and we can notice their affinity with Guy Lardreau's *Le Singe d'or*, which makes similar points in a more general philosophical register.

Althusser's 'double game' and symptomal reading

In the chapters of *Althusser's Lesson* written in 1974, Rancière continues his critique and here, too, it concentrates on the way Althusser's theory serves to retain or re-establish uninterrupted continuities. What he calls Althusser's 'double game' serves to establish first of all a temporal structure which evades accounting for political reality in the present. It consisted in a 'long-term defence [of the revolts] *against the authority of the Party* [which] demanded, in the short term, a tactical intervention *in support of its authority*' (AL, 52).

The main lesson was that one had to 'learn to wait, to step back, learn to take the time of theory' in order to find the right means for a political break – in the future (AL, 57). The political lessons were not drawn from the actuality of revolts but constructed in reference to the tradition of Marxist politics and theory. The time of theory was constituted through 'a double relationship' with distinct political realities: 'local politics (French misery in need of a solution)' and 'distant politics (the revolutions of long ago or of distant places, whose specific dialectic had to be thought through)' (AL, 25). The latter worked for Althusser, through texts of Lenin, Mao and Marx, as a source of rationality to be articulated and applied in the 'local politics' – once the time would come. This non-coincidence of the 'two politics' enabled a temporality of purely theoretical work which in its turn allowed for an infinite deferral of the actualization of politics.[91]

The theoretical scheme that this model gives rise to is the notorious procedure of 'symptomal reading', a method of dialectical materialism explicated in *Reading Capital*. It is based on the idea that a given theoretical practice 'does not see ... what it *does*' (RC, 22/17, tm), and the task of philosophy is to articulate, or bring to light, concepts on the basis of a previous practice for which those concepts necessarily remain invisible. More precisely, a given practice produces answers to the questions which are invisible to itself. It thus cannot formulate the principle of rationality it puts to work, but a new practice is needed to articulate these questions. Thus, Althusser explains that when Marx read the classical economists he formulated the questions to which they answered without knowing it. In this way Marx produced the concepts of historical materialism.

Symptomal reading is a scheme which constructs continuity into an apparent discontinuity. As Rancière states in a later text, despite Althusser's willingness to think in terms of a break, 'symptomal reading thinks necessarily in terms of continuity' (FW, 135). True, there is discontinuity between the classical economists and Marx, in the sense that the discourse of the former remains in the realm where it is impossible to make progress because of the invisibility of the scientific concepts which belong to it. The science of history emerges when Marx produces these concepts by making them visible. However, despite the apparent discontinuity this scheme establishes a specific kind of continuity: a 'field of knowledge ... structured as a weaving of questions and answers that do not correspond to each other' but 'are still waiting to be matched' (FW, 133, 135). What is at stake is thus the way scientific practice sustains itself as a 'community of science' through construction of its inherent continuity (FW, 138).

Rancière also points out the difference between Althusser and Foucault in this context. Despite that fact that Althusser would like to connect his project with that of Foucault, in the latter any implicit continuity between epistemes or a (non)relation between given answers and unasked question would not be possible (FW, 135–6). This should remind us of the reference to Foucault and Althusser earlier, in the context of my discussion of Lardreau's *Le Singe d'or*. Namely, we can again see the issue here to be a misunderstanding or abuse of Foucault's model by turning the idea of discontinuity into an intra-theoretical question, that is to say, into the method of symptomal reading which works to construct a relation, and thus continuity, between terms that are posited as discontinuous. If, as I suggested earlier, Foucault wanted to demonstrate a certain discontinuity between knowledges of different epistemes thus opening a door for a genealogical or historical perspective to knowledge, Althusser theorizes the transitions between them within the unity of theoretical practice. In doing so, he sustains the continuity of the independent and self-sufficient existence of a community of science, or a community of scientists. Instead of a struggle rooted in class antagonism, we end up with a historical community of scientists in the form of continuity of theoretical work.

From theory to class struggle

In 1966, following the critique by the Party authorities and the subsequent resignation of the radical Maoist Althusserians from the Party, '[t]he double game of strategy and tactics had reached its limit'.[92] Not willing to go along with his young followers who in 1966 broke with the Party and founded the UJC-ml, Althusser 'was obliged to orchestrate his own retreat' (AL, 55) which came in the form of redefining his philosophy as 'class struggle in theory'. His new idea of philosophy was supposedly to solve the problem of overemphasis on theory (over politics) characteristic to his thought as outlined in *For Marx* and *Reading Capital*.

In his reading of the Cultural Revolution Althusser had emphasized the strategic importance of the ideological revolution – ongoing in China – and the 'class struggle in theory' amounted to understanding philosophical practice itself as ideological struggle. According to Gregory Elliott Althusser's 'politicism' was essentially a concession to Maoism whereas for Rancière Althusser was 'not enough of a Maoist', to borrow Elliott's phrase.[93] Both agree, however, that the change was for the worse, albeit for different reasons. Rancière argues that if anything Althusser's 'politicism' was less political than his original 'theoreticism' which had nevertheless left the door open to its (Maoist) radicalization and, if not produced, then at least allowed a 'real rupture' between his militant students and the Party.[94] Althusser's new way to see Marxist philosophy was only a consolidation of the separation of theory and theoreticians from political struggles: ' "Class struggle in theory", Rancière writes in 1974, 'represents philosophy's latest attempt to cement, once and for all, the division of labour that guarantees it its place' (AL, 115). It served 'to confine philosophical activity to a place where it would be sheltered from such accidents as those that had compromised it during the creation of the UJC (ML)' (AL, 57). While in the 'theoreticist' phase, the stakes lied still in principle in the present politics, be it that the judgement on it was infinitely deferred through a detour of tempor(al)ization, now there was 'no longer a question of the relationship between the time of theory and the time of politics' (AL, 59). Althusser was now 'proclaim[ing] the primacy of class struggle' without 'bother[ing] himself with any of the class struggles happening today' (AL, 112).

Althusser's new way to see philosophy as a practice which defends materialist theses against ideological ones in sciences and politics rendered philosophy '*political* only insofar as it is eternal, only insofar as it is the indefinite repetition of the same battle' (AL, 83). Everything was now thought through 'timeless tendencies' between materialist and idealist frameworks, but what matters to this reading is that in historical analysis these quickly translated into a framework of continuity of historical time beyond the rupturous present (AL, 105). The latter makes a return in the midst of Althusser's interpretation the 'Stalinist deviation', that is, a repetition of the humanist-economist ideological tendency of the Second International in the context of the Stalin era. Namely, in order to speak of 'deviation' Althusser needs to establish a historically continuous existence of that which deviates. In a passage that

Rancière quotes, Althusser states: 'there exists a continuity, in the history of the Labour Movement, of its difficulties, its problems, its contradictions, of correct solutions and therefore also of its deviations, because of the continuity of a single class struggle against the bourgeoisie.'[95]

Here the theory of discontinuous history cannot retain itself without bringing back the continuity of theory itself as a maintenance of the identity of the categories which it reflects on the political reality: 'Althusser wants a discontinuous history, "without a subject or goal(s)". But he also wants a philosophy able, with each object and each circumstance, to distinguish the *idealist* from the *materialist*, the *proletarian* from the *bourgeois*, the *correct* from the *deviant*' (AL, 105; cf. ES-C, 94–9). There is continuity in order for the 'same' to be recognized in specific differences, and its recognition is nothing else than the practice of science itself, of which the 'community of science' consists. Therefore, class struggle in theory 'postulates that history is discontinuous, only to reinsert strange continuities into it, like this "labour movement" that has the Second International and Stalinist politics as so many of its manifestations' (AL, 105). The aim of this understanding of Stalinism, based on continuous existence of general tendencies across time, is clear enough to Rancière: 'to obscure the present'.[96]

Beyond the Gauche Prolétarienne

As we know, the story of the UJC-ml ended with the events of May 1968 which came to surprise its members by autonomous mass mobilizations taking place independently of theoretical guidance. The UJC-ml was followed by the Gauche Prolétarienne which abandoned theoreticism with the aim 'to abolish the division of labour that separated intellectual from manual labour' (AL, 121). In the familiar Maoist vein, the new task of intellectuals consisted in 'abandoning their specific roles as intellectuals and joining the masses, ... helping the masses themselves to speak up and with fighting all the apparatuses – from unions to the police – that stand in the way of this free expression' (AL, 72).

If the earlier reading of Rancière's critique of Althusser fits the framework manifested in Lardreau's *Le Singe d'or* – which was in line with the positions of the Gauche Prolétarienne – I will now look into the way in which Rancière's discourse starts taking a different path from that of his fellow Maoist. Rancière states concerning the GP that 'the abstraction of the project yielded only a simple negation' (AL, 121). To have done with the 'memory' created by 'theoretical formation', on which the UJC-ml was based, it 'decreed the death of the book, and with it the futility of those struggles that stayed within the apparatuses of bourgeois ideology' (AL, 50, 121). But this simple negation could only be based on a certain positivism which 'countered the totalizing discourse of revisionism with its own totalizing discourse' (AL, 119). This risked bypassing the contradictions within the struggles: The Gauche Prolétarienne did not manage to fully get rid of the principles of the UJC-ml, but its 'history … is still weighed down by a *neutral* understanding of organization as the instrument for the application of a line founded on the positivity of a class ideology' (AL, 54). In other words, it still presupposed knowledge of how the course of history advances and wanted to adjust the struggles accordingly.

Rancière's critique of the Gauche Prolétarienne here reminds the one which can be found already in Lardreau's *Le Singe d'or* itself, namely in its 'letter-preface' by François Châtelet. Châtelet states that in positing the discourse of revolt against science Lardreau remains imprisoned in 'positivism', 'the one which took for granted that there is immanent knowledge in the society itself which has its "good" historical expressions. It is precisely this perspective which allows [him] to affirm that the "masses are never mistaken"' (SO, 10–11). In producing only an 'abstract negation' of the discourse of science Lardreau founds his own discourse on 'another subject of history supposed to know' (SO, 11). Thus, his 'anti-positivism is positivism' (SO, 12).

How should we understand this critique of positivism by Rancière and Châtelet? How should we understand it in relation to history and historical time? While declaring 'the death of the book' the Gauche Prolétarienne wanted an absolute replacement of the old with the new. In Lardreau's theoretical account of its practice, this took the form of absolute distinction between historical stages. A given historical stage, such as the present reality of the revolt, achieved its self-identity through a radical distinction of the preceding stage. In this way, through 'abstract negation', it reached a positivity of the present, on which an organization could be built in a 'neutral' way – that is, without confronting tensions which contradict it. Thus, despite the attempt to rid his discourse of all forms of historical reason, it did imply a temporal succession where the new follows the old, where the stages follow each other, while remaining separated by a radical historical break. This was not a continuity of historical time through evolution or gradual development, but it was a kind of negative continuity, in the sense that a historical stage was thought through that with which it was *not* in continuity with, remaining thus paradoxically in the framework of continuity.

It was Lardreau himself, however, who best formulated the problems of his early positivism and the politics of simple negation to which it would lead. As we know he could detach the revolt from historical reasoning only by reducing it into an unactualizable moral law. In *La Véracité* Lardreau states that the actualization of revolt, that is, the politics of 'positive destruction, [or] simple negation ... cannot help forming a historical fabric [*tissu historique*]'. It cannot help 'establishing *another* world', another society.[97] In doing so, it does not rid itself of historico-temporal reasoning but thinks revolt only as a means of realizing an historical aim. Furthermore, this means that it only allows revolt 'with the intention of a great establishment [*instauration*] which renders all future revolt as such illegitimate'.[98] In other words, it is impossible to think the actualization of revolt because this would amount to bringing forth a state where it would be no longer right to revolt. It could not be right to revolt against a stage which would *realize* revolt.

The problem here clearly follows from the fact that revolt remains to be thought in terms of replacing the world of oppression by fulfilling a historical goal and succeeding the old world in time, in a word, in terms of temporal *succession* brought about by the *success* of revolt. Insofar as the revolt accomplishes its task, then, insofar as it leaves behind the world of oppression, it renders revolt itself illegitimate. Thus, no matter how radical the break that the revolt is supposed to bring forth, as long as it is thought through a temporal sequence, where a stage follows another, it cannot get rid of suppressing or neutralizing the revolt by disciplining it through temporal differentiation. Any historical aim is aimed against revolt.

* * *

We can now start to understand what kind of problem Rancière was faced with at the time of writing *Althusser's Lesson*. Like Lardreau, he does not want to compromise the self-sufficiency of revolt in the present. However, already in this early work Rancière is less concerned with the ideas of break in time than a certain favouring of simultaneous juxtapositions, relations of disjunction and conjunction. If '[t]here is no world or society without contradictions', as Mao says, then revolt cannot to be thought according to any logic of historical resolution.[99] Thus, Rancière tries to think the positivity of contradiction as such, or 'to think *positively* the specificity of ... revolt', to think it not as a motor of temporal development, nor as a rupturous resolution, but through simultaneous disjunctive relations (AL, 121). This idea is the very point of departure of *Althusser's Lesson*, which sets out to '*juxtapose* what Althusser says with what Marx says' (AL, xxi, emphasis added). It aims 'to surprise [the] articulations [of Althusser's discourse] by forcing it to answer other questions than those posed by the complacent partners it had picked out for itself, and by reinscribing its argumentation into the concatenation of words used ... to articulate both the inevitability of oppression and the hopes for liberation' (AL, 123). Rather than simply revoking the Althusserian discourse with a discourse of revolt, he wants to produce its 'staging' [*mise en scène*] which 'echo[s] the expressions through which the struggles and questions of our present seek to give voice to a new freedom' (AL, 124).[100]

The way this method of reading Althusser is linked to Rancière's understanding of historical time can be clarified through an article published a year after *Althusser's Lesson*.[101] In it Rancière criticizes the positivist tendencies in Marx and Engels. According to Rancière, the latter two blame the working-class idea of emancipation for leaning on bourgeois utopians' 'reactionary nostalgia of a pre-capitalist order', whereas in reality the great industrial development is in the process of bringing forth the conditions of the workers' self-emancipation.[102] Rancière questions this understanding of the nostalgic bourgeois utopianism on one hand and the industrial development as the motor for workers' future self-emancipation on the other: 'Is the relation of this working class idea of emancipation to the utopian *programming* really that of temporal succession? Is the reformist utopia a prehistory of an idea of self-emancipation?'[103] He goes on to explain that 'in many respects the ideas [*la pensée*] of the utopians are after all advanced in relation to those of workers [*cette pensée ouvrière*]'. While the latter insist on qualified work and resistance to the industrial order of capitalism, it is the former which is oriented according to 'the capitalism of the future'.[104] Rancière's point, however, is not to argue for a reversed temporal order. He questions Marx and Engels's temporal-historical analysis in order to argue that these different discourses and practices exist simultaneously and their relation is not determined according to any historical tendencies. He refutes the construction of the present into a historico-temporal narrative which 'turns the two terms of the contradiction into two stages [*étapes*] of a development'.[105] The point is thus to displace the perspective from the temporal ordering of the struggle to the contradictory forces in the 'present based on which two futures are equally possible'.[106]

The division is not between knowledge and non-knowledge concerning what is to be the order of the time but between 'the power' concerning the question who gets to determine the organization of workers' lives in the present, the workers themselves or the bourgeois utopians.[107] It is not a question of history but a question of who gets to decide what is to be done. Before any argument concerning what is going to be, there is the question of whose 'knowledge' of what's going to be will prevail. Before there is historico-temporal determination, there are contradictory wills in the present.[108]

Yet, this view of things tends to lock the present into a suspension of contradictory aspirations towards possible futures while not allowing to trace the trajectories leading to them. A simple suspension of the present does not seem to allow to grasp the reality of the struggles which are after all directed to desired futures. A proper grasp of these power struggles would nevertheless seem to presuppose an understanding of where they are directed and what objective elements in the situation their directednesses are attached to.

However, alongside with this problem, Rancière's article already points towards an idea that will deepen in his future work and that will allow him to dissociate his framework from the problem of the divisions of power trapped in a specific historical moment. This different break with ordered succession stems from 'another ... function of time' in the workers' struggles. This concerns free time as opposed to the bourgeois utopians' visions characterized by a 'total grip from above of the time and the space of workers' life'.[109] The workers' idea of emancipation in contrast was based on an 'absolute distinction of the time reserved to work and the time reserved for leisure'.[110] Whereas the bourgeois theories were drawing on a totalizing vision of the life of the utopian community, the workers insisted on free time not subjected to any planning. As one of them describes the *proletarian* utopia: 'The philosopher will be a builder, a shoemaker, a tailor, a painter, etc. He will have time to be both without being dependant of his fellow man, the same will go for all professions: after having done what is useful, everyone will have time for what pleases her.'[111] Here we find an acknowledgement of Marx who 'stood the closest to the workers' view of things [*la perception ouvrière*]' precisely on this point.[112] Rancière is of course referring to Marx's famous description of communism in *The German Ideology*: while in the present social order 'each man has a particular, exclusive sphere of activity, which is forced upon him and from which he cannot escape ... in communist society ... nobody has one exclusive sphere of activity but each can become accomplished in any branch he wishes'.[113]

In Marx, however, the possibility to divide one's time rather than to be subjected to an order from above prevailed only in the *future* society, whereas Rancière sees it operative in the present, in 'workers' optimization of possibilities of freedom given or conquered in the present of the struggle'.[114] This conception of time shows the contradiction of which the struggle consists in a very specific way. Namely, it is the very idea of time in which the contradiction is located. Thus, it is not a question of a change which takes place in time, in the process of transformation from the order of exploitation to communism, that is, a movement between different historical stages. It is precisely the function of time as *ordering* of difference that the idea of free time contradicts. If such a contradiction is itself ordered temporally (present exploitation differentiated from the future communism) the *determined time* of exploitation has always already prevailed over the free or *undetermined time* of communism. It is a question of time as a principle which orders terms successively, and time which is free from such ordering.

Yet, here the undetermined time still overlaps with the time of the power struggles over a specific future, that is, a world where such undetermined time could prevail. It is rooted in the social order where the workers struggle to make space for it by distinguishing it from the 'determined time' of work. There is the function of undetermined time in the present *and* the struggle for power in the social reality which aims to consolidate the conditions for freedom in the future. As the rest of my chapters will argue, rather than insisting on these two perspectives, Rancière will invest more fully in cutting freedom off from the social space-time in order to affirm emancipation as such in the present, without any necessary need for changes in the social order to be *achieved*. This method gets consolidated in his 1981 *The Nights of Labor* which Rancière has often referred to as foundational for his peculiar way to think emancipation. The idiosyncratic history of nineteenth-century worker activists is premised on the idea of time which is extracted from the normal cycle of days devoted to labour and nights devoted to rest. This 'empty time' enables the workers to escape their condition into the equal universe of thought. Space as a dimension different from temporal succession is emphasized by Rancière in thinking the equality of this empty time. It allows Rancière to both break and stay with the positions he attacks. Thus, as we will see, his rupture with the Gauche Prolétarienne allows him to retain a fidelity to the *gauchiste* practices in another way (Chapter 2). Likewise, his break with Althusser comes with a realignment with certain aspects of theoretical practice as well as Althusser's understanding of history (Chapter 4). Rather than moving on from these positions, his break with them should be understood in the very terms he has later described May 1968: 'a rupture with neither past nor future [*sans passé ni avenir*]'.[115]

2

Rancière's literary Maoism

In the previous chapter, we saw that Althusserian theory as well as the post-Althusserian Maoism, both in their own ways, put a certain emphasis on the rupturous present. Rancière has never stopped insisting that it is *here and now* that emancipation has to form itself.[1] Yet, everything depends on how this 'here and now' is understood. In this chapter, the ruptural present continues to be the focus of attention. However, it will be argued that such a present in Rancière is no longer a temporally qualified one, but it is thought through a more radical detachment from historical continuity/discontinuity. This detachment is played out with granting a central role to spatiality. Therefore, in Rancière the rupture does not figure as a cut, in time, separating two stages or two sequences from each other. Rather, the ruptural 'here and now' appears as a break *from* temporality in the sense of a unified orienting horizon.

Continuing the contextualization produced in the previous chapter, I will argue that this position arises as a critical engagement with the Maoist discourse and the *gauchiste* practice in order to rethink this practice and the logic of the Cultural Revolution in particular. I will start with a discussion of Maoist militant practice of *établissement* and the discourse around it. This discourse concentrated less on temporal evolutions than on spaces of revolt. For Rancière, as I will show, the spatial perspective of this practice remained problematically attached to a historico-temporal rationality keeping it within an anticipatory-teleological framework itself based on a certain logic of origins. Furthermore, such a framework was in continuity with the Althusserian 'bookish reason' and was bequeathed to *la nouvelle philosophie*. As I claim, Rancière takes as his task to rethink spatiality as a sphere of revolt in a way which resists getting absorbed into historical temporalizations. Instead of an oft-occurring theme of 'burning books' in Maoism, this spatial logic is developed through a certain emphasis on textuality, developed by Rancière through the concept of 'literarity'. Literarity goes together with the figure of 'ignorant schoolmaster', introduced in a book with the same name. This book forms an anti-thesis to traditional pedagogy which persisted in Althusserianism. To finish this chapter, I will use the concept of literarity as well as the figure of the ignorant schoolmaster to present an interpretation of the Cultural-Revolutionary logic and the constitutive role that Mao's Little Red Book played in it.

Étape and *établissement*

In the beginning of *Le Singe d'or* Lardreau plays with the resemblance between the words *étape* and *établir*. He recounts that the Althusserian understanding of 'the peculiar time according to which [the Marxist theory] develops' readily pointed towards the concept of *étape* that would gain importance later in the militant Maoist discourse. However, Lardreau continues, in the Althusserian phase, 'we didn't really have in mind to *establish* [établir] something new, but rather to *re-establish* [rétablir] the Marxist philosophy in its original purity' (SO, 23). In other words, Althusserianism remained stuck within the continuity of theory and thus the old order of things. It was not in accordance with the radical novelty of the Maoist era. Although the word *établir* is in common usage in French, and although Lardreau emphasizes it here in order to draw a link with the word *étape*, we should mark its particular weight in the French Maoist discourse of the time. As was explained in Chapter 1, the notion of *établissement* refers to the practice of going to the masses, that is, 'establishing oneself' – the French verb is the reflexive *s'établir* – in factories and other working-class sites. Settling in factories was the strategy through which the French militants aimed to provoke and assist workers' revolt.[2]

To establish something new was intimately linked with the practice of *établissement* which was *the* mode of fidelity to the historical novelty of the Maoist era and the third stage of Marxism, the Maoist *étape*. History was no longer framed in science and its continuities or breaks; it was not to be found in universities or theoretical studies but among the masses. This displaced the *temporal-historical* question to a certain *spatial* framework; or, the interest in the problem of historical temporalization per se was downplayed in favour of the problem of localization. As Rancière has explained it later in an interview:

> In the Gauche Prolétarienne, *établissement* of the militants in factories or activism in the workers' cafés and other living sites aimed first of all at a presence in the working-class milieu, that is to say, it aimed at once at a legitimacy, a knowledge of the milieu, and a capacity to release its potential for struggle.[3]

The Althusserian project of theorizing the complex mechanics of historical time was changed in a certain sense to a question of a localized presence of epochality or an epochal rupture. That this localized perspective seemed to come at the price of the study of historical temporality was the target of the critique of *gauchisme* by a different Maoist position at the time. As one such critique has it, the ideology visible in *La Cause du Peuple*, once an organ of the Gauche Prolétarienne, 'does not consider the relations of capitalist production, but only the relations that exist in the factory'. Thus, it ignores 'the phases of capitalism', 'the historical … circumstances' which should 'orient' the struggle. And, 'generalizing the reality of one determined period' it substitutes the 'relation[s] at the place [*lieu*] of production' for the temporal development of the 'relations of production'.[4]

However, if the *gauchiste* militants no longer claimed to possess the science of history, their ideology tended to lean on the working class as a force which was in itself a sufficient function of orientation of the struggle for a new historical era. As one ex-*établi* puts it, 'The working class was the carrier of History.'[5] In an interview concerning his book *Le Singe d'or*, Lardreau tries to separate the two possible meanings of the phrase '*sens de l'Histoire*' from each other, stating that one needs to distinguish *sens* as 'signification' from the 'detestable idea' of *sens* as orientation. While abandoning the latter idea, he embraces the *sens*-signification of history which is simply 'the struggle against oppression'. Due to this struggle, however, historical multiplicity 'organizes itself into a single [*unique*] driving force [*moteur*]'.[6] Thus, although Lardreau insists on disclaiming the orientation of historical time, he nevertheless takes as pregiven a force whose revolt is to establish a new historical epoch. For, as he writes in *Le Singe d'or*, '[i]f there is no History, if chance leads the world, it is always wrong to revolt' (SO, 227). Hence, the oppressed class remains for Lardreau the carrier of history which is why he hardly avoids presupposing historical orientation. The double meaning of *sens* persists, and it appears to be less about dropping the idea of history with an inherent vector of orientation than rejecting the possibility of scientific knowledge of it.[7] As opposed to such a knowledge there was a class with the readily given potential for epochal transformation. 'The force was presupposed', as Rancière has later characterized the position of the Gauche Prolétarienne.[8]

To the extent that such an orienting force for the new Maoist era was expected to be found in the working-class sites, the notion of *étape* as the operator of historical time can be understood to have been tied to that of *établissement*, the localized practice among the masses. Politics was, as Sartre summarizes the *gauchiste* framework, a question of 'realizing *local* actions whose *origin* is always found in the masses'.[9] This idea of the masses as the origin of epochal action, to be found in factories, is in accordance with the logic of *archē* to which Rancière has later made reference in multiple occasions, to posit against it his conception of *dēmos* as the divided subject of politics. The Greek *archē* signifies both commandment and commencement. The double meaning is present in the idea of *archōn* as the one who walks ahead and thus begins and leads the way. To draw here on Rancière's later discussions, in the *gauchiste* discourse the masses were 'in possession of the power of the *archein*, understood as a power to begin' and to lead (DS, 29/227, tm). The figure of the worker was a figure of 'the one who precedes, the one who walks ahead, the one who was there before'.[10] The working-class sites were sites where the leading force of history was waiting to be found.

Yet, the experience of *établissement* taught to many militants that things were not so simple. Instead of a unified force with an inherent capacity to lead one found a disoriented multiplicity. This experience is well described in Robert Linhart's famous account of his time as an *établi* in 1968–9, published in 1978:

> Seen from outside, *établissement* seemed clear: you get hired and you organize. But here this entry 'into the working class' disintegrates into a multiplicity of small individual situations among which I can't find a solid footing. These very words, 'the working class' don't have the same immediate meaning to me as they did in the past. Not that I've come to doubt that they

hide a profound reality, but the variety and mobility of this population of *ouvriers spécialisés* into which I've been thrown have upset me, submerged me. Everyone here is a case. Everyone has her own history. Everyone chews over her tactics and in her own way tries to find a way out. How can I find a direction [*Comment m'orienter*] in this kind of semi-penitentiary, indefinitely provisional universe ...?[11]

The question was, then, how to find a direction to realize the historical novelty once the localized practice was no longer reflected upon knowledge concerning historical time. How was this orientation to emerge in the ruptural present? We can see that for Linhart such an orienting force nevertheless exists, even though it was not immediately visible.

If I have interpreted the *gauchiste* problematic through a specific relation between the historical novelty and localized practice – *étape* and *établissement* – it is because I think that this interpretation provides the terms in which Rancière's work is best read when it comes to his relation with the history of *gauchisme*. What is specific in Rancière is that, after an initial attempt to identify the 'true' working class, he will not seek to find an orienting force or any rationality of historical directedness. If Linhart still believes in the 'profound reality' of the working class, Rancière will try to dismantle the opposition between depth and surface.[12] In so doing he wants to persist in Linhart's 'indefinitely provisional universe', as the stage where egalitarian politics is played out. A meaningful emancipatory intelligibility is to be found in this disoriented spatial coexistence not reducible to a unified orientation. This is what I will now set out to argue.

From spatialized time to disoriented space

The problem of spatiality attached to the irruption of a historical break at the same time when this break manifests itself in epochal terms informs a lot of Rancière's writings. His work can be read as insistence on the spatial perspective – the idea of displacement, of leaving – while dissociating it from overarching temporal-historical reasonings or making spatial displacements clash with such reasonings. In this sense, his work is about dismantling what he has called 'spatialized time' while retaining a certain kind of spatial logic as an emancipatory function that escapes or disturbs temporal determinations (NH, 82/165). Such a spatial logic favours multidirectionality and simultaneity of disjunctive or contradictory elements indifferent of their successive orderings. As 'spatialized time', in contrast, space is readily subjected to temporal orientation and made into a manifestation of a unified historico-temporal moment. Rancière's work aims to put spatiality to work in a ruptural function in relation to temporal coherence. Strictly speaking, this kind of rupture is then not a rupture in a temporal continuum but rather a logical rupture between temporal coherence and the spatial logic which is at odds with it. It is a question of encounters or coexistences which do *not* come about as epochal historico-temporal events, a spatial coexistence which is not subjected under temporal determination or unification. In a sense this is a way for Rancière to sustain his fidelity, in its own way more persistent than anyone else's, to a certain idea of *établissement* and to radical Maoism in general.[13]

Gauchisme and seismology

In one of his most representative and yet least discussed works, *Short Voyages to the Land of the People* (1990), Rancière encourages rather explicitly – and untypically for him – a contextualization with the Maoist framework of the late 1960s and early 1970s. To meet 'the proletariat in person', Rancière explains in the introduction, '[s]uch was the flower once promised by a text of Mao Zedong's to those who agreed to leave, to go see outside the city and the books, to get down off their horse and pick up [*cueillir*] the living reality' (SV, 2/8, tm).[14] And, Rancière goes on:

> More than the analysis of oppression or the sense of duty toward the oppressed, the core political experience of our generation may have well been to go on such a voyage, discovering by ourselves this recognizable foreignness, this shimmering of life. (SV, 2)

It is to address the experience of the Maoist generation then that Rancière, in this book, turns to discuss journeys and encounters lived by past poets, workers, Saint-Simonians or movie characters. Throughout these accounts the book shows how spatial encounters are teleologicized, taken as 'the return to the origin' or as 'the arrival in the promised land' (SV, 1/7, tm). For instance, Rancière recounts how William Wordsworth witnesses during the French

Revolution a spatial inscription in the landscape of 'a time of beginning that is also a time of fulfilment' or how the same Wordsworth experiences an encounter with someone who incarnates 'the profound meaning/orientation [*sens*] of the era [*époque*]' giving it 'its visible form' (SV, 11, 24/16, tm). Likewise, Rancière follows Saint-Simonians 'in search of the people of the future', witnessing a 'scene visible from all sides' manifesting 'an end and a beginning'.[15] Rancière then starts with enthusiastic descriptions which capture the essence of an era and turn the landscape into a force of historical orientation. The way they do so is described by Rancière through a certain idea of cartography: 'This is the meaning of travel: to establish [*établir*] at each step ... the immediate correspondence of the lines on the map and the undulations of the ground [*territoire*]' (SV, 36).

A map is something which allows to plan and anticipate a journey, something that secures that one finds what was expected to be found. The reference to cartography draws the attention to an earlier text, co-authored with Danièlle Rancière and published in Les Révoltes logiques in 1978. The article attacks a new figure of intellectual authority which had emerged after the anti-authoritarian movement around May 1968. Here these *nouveaux philosophes*, André Glucksmann as their leading figure, are named as 'cartographer-intellectuals'.[16] The latter appear as justified to speak for the reality of the masses, because they 'have – in Maoist terms – *come down from the horse*': 'immersed in the midst of the masses, [they have] seen the truth in its materiality'.[17] At stake is a legacy of the logic which saw the figure of the worker as the carrier of History, a cartographer-intellectual being, the one who has seen this figure and is thus in the position to follow in its footsteps. This amounts to acquiring knowledge of where historical time is heading. Even better than with 'cartography' the idea is expressed with another metaphor used alongside it, namely 'seismology'.[18] A science which studies earthquakes and develops methods of predicting them by reading the signs occurring in the space of earth serves well to mark a form of thinking which subjects space under time, inscribes space to a temporal rhythm or, as the Rancières put it, turns it into 'grids of time' (*grilles du temps*).[19] In the hands of seismologists, then, the Maoist activist experience could turn into 'a work of re-coding ... that defines the direction [*sens*] of a history ... and confers titles of inheritance'.[20]

Time as a principle of spatialization

Rancière's discourse on the journeys to the people then relates to the transformation of the Maoist practice into yet another form of historico-temporal reasoning through a logic of turning space into an operator of such reasoning. This line of thought is developed extensively in Rancière's reading of French historiography in *The Names of History*. In it Rancière investigates Jules Michelet's project which aims to democratize historical science by including the speech of the people – the 'chatter of the poor' – in it while not allowing this speech to disturb his view of history as a 'progressive triumph of freedom', to quote the historian himself.[21] There is no need here to go to the detail of the procedures that Michelet's new historiography consists of.[22] It suffices to say that they are designed to state the meaning of a given historical document directly through Michelet's voice. Instead of focusing on quoting documents as such, as Rancière argues, Michelet monumentalizes them by describing them in their materiality and subsuming what they say to his own 'discourse-narrative'.[23] Thus, he shows the reader 'not their content but the meaning/orientation [*sens*] of their content' or 'not their content but the power that causes them to be written' (NH, 57, 48/100, tm).[24] This style, where speech is kept in reserve through showing it in its material location, allows its *sens* to be 'read … in the materiality of … objects' or shows this *sens* 'inscribed in the texture of things' (NH, 57, 60). The historical actor becomes a 'silent witness of the tomb' whose passage in the materiality of space allows Michelet to speak for her, to state not what she said but what she *would* say if she were speaking: 'Guardian of the earth, man's monument, the tomb contains a silent witness who would speak as needed.'[25] 'The silent voice of the conditional is that which can come back to us only through the tombstone or the cries of the rocks' (NH, 57). The scheme of the 'silent witness' allows Michelet to include the intentions of historical actors directly into a unifying narrative thus managing to give it a unified meaning (*sens*) and subject it to a unified orientation (*sens*) of historical time.

Thus, the unification of historical temporality functions first of all through turning *space* into its carrier, a procedure where Rancière sees Michelet's core invention. As Rancière puts it, Michelet gives 'a place for speech' where 'a way of thinking about the tomb and a way of thinking about the ground [*sol*] are tied together' (NH, 65/133). In so doing Michelet invents 'a theory of space as an inscription of meaning/orientation [*sens*]' (NH, 65/134, tm). This 'geographic "basis"' of history invented by Michelet is inherited by the Annales historians the most important of which for Rancière's study is Braudel and his canonical *The Mediterranean and the Mediterranean World in the Age of Philip II* (NH, 62). Following the logic of Michelet's 'founding narrative', for Braudel the Mediterranean can serve as 'a surface of inscription of time as a producer of meaning/orientation [*sens*]' (NH, 82/166, tm). With Michelet's help the 'scientific' history of the Annales School is able to retain the unified historical time in the democratic age, that is to say, in the age when 'kings are dead as centers and forces of history' (NH, 11/27). The task of the new historians becomes, as Rancière puts it, to 'offer kings a good death, a scientific death' (NH, 23). Such a good death amounts to constituting 'the conditions of succession, that make the Mediterranean a subject of history *in place of the king*' (NH, 83).[26] Despite Michelet's democratic aspirations, the gesture tends to cancel the regicide by inscribing the uniformity of historical orientation – which used to be carried undisturbedly by the succession of dynasties – on the space of coexistence of historical actors.

Kristin Ross has argued that Rancière's *The Names of History* is at odds with ways of thinking that give privilege to space as opposed to time.[27] However, what the historiography based on spatialization of historical time in fact does is to neutralize the possibility of a *spatial* coexistence which remains undetermined by temporal qualifications. It can be stated that in *The Names of History* space actually has a suppressive function *only to the extent that it is subjected to a temporal coherence*. Rancière has in fact commented on Ross's argument reminding us of exactly this function. As he states, '[d]isciplinary thinking uses time itself as a principle of spatialization. It makes time a place that encloses and defines those who are in it.'[28] To some extent this works both ways, but what is crucial, I think, is that space works as a certain indifference to directionality characteristic to unified time, and that as such it enables to counter structures based on ideas such as advanced and backward, leading and being led. Instead, it keeps things in 'the uncertainties of conjunction' (NH, 94/190).[29] It is only when the unity of space as a sphere of coexistence is qualified through a temporal coherence that it becomes a realm of unified orientation as opposed to a field that allows radically multidirectional, or non-directional, dimensionalities.³⁰ Hence, my claim is that while it is true that, as Ross argues, Rancière is embracing a certain idea of temporal multiplicity as opposed to unified spatialized time, the crucial point is that Rancière uses space as a dimension of coexistence regardless of temporal differentiations or directionalities. For him, space allows temporal qualifications to be challenged, mixed and blurred in favour of a less determined form of egalitarian coexistence. Let us now pick up our discussion of *Short Voyages* in light of these claims.

Disintegration of maps

As we can see, Rancière sees the Maoist practice of going to 'the masses' to have been linked to an idea of cartography as a new kind of knowledge of historical directedness. This idea of space which lends itself to a construction of an orientation of historical time then develops into an extensive critique of French historiography. However, along with the critique, there is also an attempt to rethink the *gauchiste* practice in a positive manner. Therefore, the epochal encounters described in the *Short Voyages* need to be followed through to the point where they disintegrate. The teleological experiences need to be put next to the experience where they break down and pave way for a certain cartography of disorientation. The actual problem of *Short Voyages* is then the disintegration of maps, which makes space incompatible with temporal orientation. Thus, in Rancière's account of Wordsworth, the latter does not witness merely the spatial expression of a futural orientation but in Paris has to face a 'space of the revolutionary city in which the noise of speech and the agitation of factions did not allow the people's achievement to be reflected in the landscapes and spectacles of a new world' (SV, 18). The point is, however, to persist in this coming apart of the epoch-making experience and the teleological function of cartography. Hence, Rancière shows us how Wordsworth reworks the writings of his youth as an older man forced to draw other conclusions from his past travels: 'Nature … does not symbolize in its spectacles any future [*avenir*] for the community' (SV, 21).

The clash between spatiality and temporal orientation becomes especially clear in the sections devoted to Michelet and Rainer Maria Rilke, respectively. As we know, Michelet would become an important interlocutor for Rancière's historiographical studies. What is interesting in Rancière's first discussion of Michelet in *Short Voyages* is that here the historian's occupation with spatialization of historical time in his scholarly work is shown to clash with a spatial togetherness in his private life. While Michelet composes his historical work based on the idea of progress, Rancière reads this undertaking in light of the inspiration which conditions and yet fails it. It is Michelet's maids, renamed by him as Barbara and Rustica, that 'reveal to him precisely the rustic, barbaric origin of the French nation' (SV, 71):

> Day by day a whole series of equivalences ... identify the return to the far of historical source with the nearby satisfactions provided by the relationship with his serving woman. ... The acquiescent body of the rustic or barbarian is also the subject of history deciphered. ... The same *subject* satisfies the man's desires and the requirements of new science. (SV, 72)

'[I]nscribed in the movement of returning to the source', Michelet's exploitative coexistence with the maids is akin to a teleologicization of history (SV, 76/100, tm). What Rancière wants to show is how the togetherness in space nevertheless resists the subjection of the maid to her master, which is also a subjection to a historical progress. Thus, while Michelet manages to write a history of the French nation as 'the passage from primary maternal rusticity to civilization, progress, and democracy ..., the distance from contemporaneous simplicity, there under one's own roof, remains insurmountable' (SV, 76–7). This insurmountability of the contemporary distance, or disjunction, names Michelet's failed attempts to educate his housemaids. The failure is nothing else but the impossibility to inscribe his coexistence into a narrative of organized temporality of progress. The spatial coexistence of these incompatible beings signifies resistance to full submission and to unifying temporalization.

This resistance is even more visible in Rancière's discussion of Rilke's short love affair with a young working girl Marthe.[31] Rancière describes Rilke's experience of her: 'She is "futureless" [*sans avenir*]', and her 'hands were unable to hold together the end and a new beginning' (SV, 93, 102).[32] Therefore, it is 'impossible ... to advance in the path of common knowledge and language', and the only thing that remains 'possible is to grant the other some space' (SV, 94). Yet, Rilke remains unable to affirm this space as such, unable to put this relation into words, until his encounter with Marthe is over. And once this is, retrospectively, the relationship appears as fulfilment, as an authentic *origin* inspiring and giving meaning to *Duino's Elegies* that he has finally been able to finish. The spatial togetherness thus appears as a 'nonplace', as an impossibility which insists on being subjected to temporal consistency in order to be taken into account (SV, 101).

In *The Names of History* Rancière uses the term 'nonplace' repeatedly. There the notion marks the exclusion of speech and its capacity to render meaningful an event or a reality. It is speech which threatens to disturb the established consistency of historical reality and its uniform time. It is speech of the poor insofar as 'the poor do not represent any defined social category but rather an essential relation with nontruth' (NH, 18). While historians from Tacitus to François Furet rely on an explicit exclusion of 'nonplace' in order to invalidate such excessive speech, it is precisely Michelet who manages to invent a specific way to include it in the historical narrative.[33] As we have seen, this inclusion nevertheless dismisses it, insofar as the 'speech of the poor' is included merely as a 'silent witness' inscribed on geographical space, allowing Michelet to present it through a unified *sens* and thus include it into a progressive temporality. Rilke's retrospective account of his encounter with Marthe bears similarity to Michelet's gesture. After a period apart from her and looking forward to a reunion, Rilke writes: 'I shall soonest be able once more to heal the ruptured surface of my former life; Marthe's hands will hold the fractured end and the new beginning tenderly against each other.'[34] As Rancière concludes, 'To find the thread, the poet, like the historian, will have to dismiss the woman of the people' (SV, 101). They have to reject to acknowledge a coexistence whose form resists putting it into a horizon of a unified temporal course.

Rancière nevertheless finds in Rilke also an understanding of the kind of coexistence which is not dismissed through a unifying temporality. He describes it in another text, interpreting the eleventh of Rilke's *Sonnets to Orpheus*, as 'the union of two who go together without meaning or intending the same thing as their journey's aim; the always sufficient and forever disappointing schema of the bond'.[35] This is a striking passage, insisting on the sufficiency of that which cannot be held together through time. It is a togetherness in space without a shared temporal horizon but which is nevertheless affirmed as such. If the Micheletist concern can be captured with what Rancière calls 'spatialized time', then this temporally non-unified space is characterized with disorientation. Such is the sphere which serves for Rancière as a field of emancipatory action: a 'disoriented space of pathways and dead ends where people searched not long ago for what rebellious workers and dreamers called "emancipation"' (PP, 147). The 'disoriented space' should be understood precisely as one whose temporality remains discordant and which is as such the opposite of 'spatialized *time*'. The revolting workers who insist on their capacity to think are understood through this kind of space which is resistant to its temporal ordering: 'The proletarian philosopher does not use logical time according to operators such as "at first" and "at the same time" [*temps logique des "d'abord" et des "en même temps"*]. ... In his path there are only flexions. He can only go where his steps take him.'[36]

In Rancière's reference to 'logical time' here can be heard a polemical statement against Alain Badiou's *Theory of the Subject* where the latter theorizes a processual-historical ontology of the subject, through an immanent critique of Lacan's notion of 'logical time'. Badiou supplements Lacan's 'logical' account of time through 'speed' as a qualitatively different element of subjective intervention, in order to turn the function of logical time into a process of historical transformation.[37] The argument contributes to the book's overall task to develop a theory of the subject as a revolutionary process based on a dialectical relation between structural dialectics on one hand and a certain intervention of force in it on the other. Rancière rejects this attempt to think the temporality of revolutionary action through its dialectical relation with objectively structured time. He presents such action rather in terms of open-directed spatiality which dissociates the milieu of action from any operators that would direct or orient it in time.

In the last chapter of *Short Voyages* we find this logic of spatial disorientation understood in terms of an unguided walker. In it Rancière discusses Rossellini's film *Europe 51* and its heroine who 'takes a step to the side, losing her way' (SV, 117). After having gone to see the proletariat in its proper milieu with her communist cousin – who represents the Marxist savant – she returns there alone, 'without her guide'.[38] Her journey is now seen as the excess of non-place being forced upon the coordinates of the place which in the first visit had confirmed an anticipating reasoning: what we witness is, as Rancière puts it, a 'material inscription of what has no place in the system of reality' (SV, 129). This inscription is thought in terms of disorientation which leans on spatial dimension: 'All of a sudden space becomes disoriented' (SV, 116). It is a question here not so much of a break in time but of a break between the logic of temporal anticipation and that of spatial disorientation, or spatiality which clashes with a 'spatialized *time*'. Rancière's core gesture then includes using spatiality as a sphere which remains as such without orientedness and where temporal directedness or temporal differentiality disintegrates.

Getting lost in spatial disorientation marks a norm whose semantic design echoes the Maoist *on a toujours raison de se révolter*: 'The walker is always right to walk [*le marcheur a toujours raison de marcher*], one is always right to go out [*on a toujours raison de sortir*], go see something to the side, continue to walk where ever one's own steps – and not those of others – lead' (SV, 157). Hence, the 'step to the side', and the framework of the disoriented space, can be seen as a continued reflection on the Maoist theme of reason in revolt. Unlike revolution, revolt is not understood as a temporally managed project. To make use of the shared etymology of both terms – something that the figure of the 'step to the side' might invite us to do – we could suggest that while 'revolution' marks a turning point and a redirection of historical time, 'revolt' signifies a deviation from the temporally managed reality itself. Space as an omnidirectional openness serves as a sphere where such deviation can be figured. In a certain sense, it is a revolt against historical time as such, understood through spatiality as a counter-form against temporal coherence. Hence, as opposed to the earlier chapters of *Short Voyages*, we have no more failed or fulfilled promises, no return to the origins, no expectations, no retrospective rationalizations. All we have is the norm which 'oblige[s] us' to keep '[w]alking under the sign of interruption' (SV, 118). There is thus a certain duration of interruption, but this duration is not temporally uniform.

The duty of the book

Literarity

Rancière's idea of 'disoriented space' as opposed to 'spatialized time' can be properly understood only as a kind of middle space between 'words' and 'things'. One of the most central notions of his philosophy is reserved for thinking such a space. This notion is *littérarité*.[39] Literarity is a capacity through which the human being 'undoes the relationships between the order of words and the order of bodies that determine the place of each' (D, 37). It is what makes the human being a political being: 'Man is a political animal because he is a literary animal', that is, 'a being capable of embracing a distance between words and things' (PA, 39; OSP, 51).⁴⁰ This distance is characterized as 'an open space of infinite promenades and aleatory encounters, a space which is in a sense empty, but also populated by spoken and written words [*paroles proférées ou écrites*]'.⁴¹

It is an 'empty and abstract space' which is empty of any readily identified beings or rather empty of objective mediations between bodies and symbols which enable to identify them (FW, 104). Such a space renders equal different configurations between 'words' and 'things'. The empty space of distance between 'words' and 'things' hence rejects any *established* state of affairs that would exclude other states of affairs. As such it needs to reject *time* as an ordering principle, for any determined 'description of a "state of things" gives a major part to time. There is a simple reason for this: a "state of things" presents itself as an objective given that precludes the possibility of other states of things.'⁴² The emancipatory spatiality is rather a space which renders possible the articulation of an indefinite number of different states of things simultaneously by allowing their constitutive elements to overlap in contradiction. Thus, it does not allow them to be consolidated at the price of the possibility of others. Leaning on 'supplementary words', or a homonymic 'excess of words', it renders mutually contradictory configurations equally possible at the same time (GF, 550).

As Rancière has said, it was the *gauchiste* practice of going to see the proletariat in person, which taught him the nature of political being as a 'literary being'. It taught him the distance between words and things and the disoriented and empty space that this distance inhabits:

> I think that there was something important in the *gauchiste* voyage. It was a question of saying that all these words, 'workers', 'factory', 'proletariat', etc. . . . must mean something. There is a place where one must verify what it all means, what is the body of which it all consists. The voyage was important for undoing [*défaire*] the incarnations.⁴³

Undoing of incarnations formed another idea of travelling, one which effectuated the undetermined space as opposed to the place where one knows what one is going to find:

> [T]he foreigner ... persist in the curiosity of his gaze, displaces his angle of vision, reworks the first ways of putting together words and images, undoes the certainties of place, and thereby reawakens the power present in each of us to become a foreigner in the map of places and paths generally known as reality. Thus the foreigner loosens what he had bound together. (SV, 3)

The *gauchiste* militant experience was thus important because, putting words in direct contact with reality, it introduced a certain heterology to them. This precisely allowed an understanding of another kind of subjectivity to emerge – which Rancière names the 'proletariat':

> 'proletariat' is a word which has a weight of truth even if it is to be found nowhere in person. The truth of the word consists of being an interval [*intervalle*] of multiple bodies, a singular crossing between designations and knowledges, of multiple ways in which words forge ties with things and knowledges, with things and actions.[44]

The 'proletariat' is thus the name for a non-identified and unidentifiable subject occupying an empty space of equality where the question of the milieu of one's action becomes a question of how one articulates it and how one (dis)identifies oneself in it. 'The channels for political subjectivation are ... those of "literary" disincorporation' (PA, 40/64, tm).

As we know, the Maoist era was seen as a distinctive stage which broke with the past, and *établissement* was a form of consolidating the new stage. As it broke with the past, it also broke with *theoretical* account of reality – first and foremost with Althusserianism. As Jean-Pierre Le Dantec tells us, 'we no longer read anything.'[45] Or, as Christian Jambet states, 'to read, *ça ne se faisait pas*.'[46] But this also meant that action was considered to relate to a self-identical reality which it was possible to identify with clear historico-temporal qualifications. One was engaged with 'the world in its transparency.'[47] Moving from universities to factories meant dropping the book in order to face reality and action as such. The 'rejection of books resonated with an aspiration to return to the "real life".'[48] Reality thus negated theory just like the new negated the old. Rancière's insistence on literarity, or the empty space between words and things, rejects the idea of a 'transparent world'. It refuses to make a distinction between 'reality' and 'books' and wants to think an uncertain space between them. In this way, he rejects any possibility for an *established* presence and *established* state of things associated with epochal action.

However, as I will argue, Rancière insists on the uncertain between-space because there was a *continuous* thread leading from the Althusserian emphasis on theory and the *gauchiste* rejection of the bookish reason in favour of practice in the 'real world', and neither of them managed to properly break with historical continuity. Furthermore, Rancière's between-space in no way goes beyond the Maoist horizon but if anything gives a sharper account of the Cultural-Revolutionary paradigm by thinking through the role textuality played in it. Before discussing this paradigm, I will look more closely at the theme of 'burning books' present in the *gauchiste* activist circles and the way this theme may have stemmed from the Althusserian theory itself.[49]

Burning books

In 1978 Benny Lévy, who had been the leader of the GP, discusses the theme of burning books and switching to action, attaching it to a certain Western literary modernity:

> I think that this crisis of the book in the origin of our youth, that is, of our will to action in the 60s, this crisis of the book lies at the heart of Western modernity. Ever since the latter half of the 19th century, books have been written in order to have done with the idea of the book. ... Surrealism which, as we know, had a great importance in respect to 68 and the GP, was the most spectacular attempt to burn the book in the book. In such a context, which had become insupportable, we said 'no' to the temptation of irresponsibility [*la tentation de l'irresponsabilité*]. In other words: if we must finish with books, let's do it for good.[50]

According to this statement, the idea of 'burning books' and moving to 'action' was related to a certain form of writing them. Rancière will argue that it is exactly because the idea of breaking with theory draws from a certain tradition of writing (and reading) that it remains within continuity of what it wants to break with. There is a logic of writing which aims to leave the writing for reality or, in biblical terms, aims to find flesh for its words. Therefore, within the book there is an idea of leaving the book by making the book *true* or fulfilling the task of the book: 'to project the book toward a reality that is not the one it speaks of, but the one in which it must become an act, a power of life' (FW, 2/10, tm). In this sense, the rupture expressed by abandoning the book is what was anticipated in the book itself. The act plays the role of fulfilment of that which the book was lacking and which conditions the book as something which is able to be true. In this context, the practice of going to the masses appeared as the incarnation of the word: 'Travelling is making the book true out of itself, in the *hic et nunc* which is its negation and has to become its confirmation.'[51] Consequently, 'the space of voyage' came with a certain 'readability' which readily teleologicized it. The present that it founds or finds in space is one that breaks with the past and establishes itself as an opening of a future. In this spatialized time, the '[r]outes of the future', as Rancière describes the journeys of the Saint-Simonians, were 'already written somewhere' (SV, 38/52, tm). It does not matter where they were written or what exactly was written, for what is meant is simply that the reality appears under a general framework of anticipation, as *that which was meant to be*, and thus allows it to be captured into a historical reasoning. The reality which is encountered is what was waiting to be encountered.

The readability of space was thus linked to a certain temporal-anticipatory rationality inherited from an ideology of bookish reason, that is, knowledge of that which is coming to be. If the books were no longer needed, it was because what was coming to be was finally here: 'Reality was there, denouncing the vanity of books, and yet just like what the books led us to expect, what words led us to love' (SV, 2/8, tm). The proletariat that the militants were going to meet in person was 'long time searched for and immediately recognized, in its very foreignness, corresponding to that which has already been said, read, heard, dreamt' (SV, 2/8, tm).

For an illustration of this anticipatory logic, consider the following lines that Robert Linhart wrote, at a very crucial moment, in a letter to his wife: 'My love, yesterday we visited a popular district. I had been waiting for that since 1964, and it is just as nice as we imagined it.'[52] The letter arrived from China where Linhart had travelled in the summer of 1967 following an invitation from Mao's administration.[53] At the time, he was the leader of the UJC-ml, and it was after this trip that the organization launched the program of *établissement* and that the role of theory started to clash with the emphasis on practice. The flaws of this anticipatory attitude are twofold. First, it was able to lead to an abandonment of politics at the moment when the supposedly fulfilled promise suddenly appears to have been deceived or when the spatial incarnation of what had been dreamt or read beforehand disintegrates. This flaw is described by Linhart himself in a work published almost ten years later:

> In France, shortly before or after 1968, I saw young intellectuals '*s'établir*' among the workers and entering factories with the religious fervour of the one to whom the absolute truth will finally be revealed. Then, after some difficult experiences and failures, I saw them abandoning '*établissement*'.[54]

Second – and especially if the visit to the people is short enough to not prove the expectations wrong (or worse, if it has not been made at all!) – the anticipatory framework can confirm itself and endow the activist with knowledge of social reality and the direction it is heading. This is Rancière's point in his critique of *les nouveaux philosophes* discussed earlier, where the latter are labelled as cartographer-intellectuals or seismologists legitimated by their activist experience. The experience is not that of getting lost in a disoriented space but rather one of witnessing the people in a neatly framed place, allowing a foreseen conclusion: 'The people in person is there, we've seen them, and theory is right. A certain use of sensory certainty … fulfils the desire to know' (SV, 114). After such a fulfilment, *les nouveaux philosophes* can then, as Benny Lévy says in his own account of them, continue to 'compose books as if nothing had happened, … as if we had not wanted to burn the books'.[55]

However, if the decision to burn books never actually broke with the logic of composing them, then the emergence of *la nouvelle philosophie* with the same old bookish reason was no wonder. The problem lies not in whether to write and read books or whether to burn them but in the underlying logic of such activities, the logic which makes them serve as functions of historical rationalization. As we know, one specific logic of writing and reading was particularly familiar to many of the militants within the ranks of UJC-ml and GP. This was the logic developed in Althusserianism. A part of my reading of Rancière's latent rethinking of Maoism is to argue that this theme of the rejection of books is itself in continuity with the Althusserian theory of reading. Let us thus return to Althusser in order to understand the stakes.

To the extent that the framework of travel is that of the 'incarnation of the concept', or spatialization of the previously written truth in its sensibility, it could seem that if anyone, it would be Althusser himself who was the most eager critique of such an idea. It was for him a question of the Hegelian scheme of facing 'the presence of the "abstract" essence in the transparency of its "concrete" existence'. Furthermore, it amounted 'to treat[ing] nature or reality as a Book' and thus implied an 'idea of *reading* which makes a written discourse the immediate transparency of the true, and the real the discourse of a voice' (RC, 14). Such reading was the one that belongs to the Hegelian empiricism and the everyday obviousness of ideological continuity of time. As became clear in Chapter 1, this is the primary target of Althusser's philosophy of discontinuity. Theory, which was able to produce the concept of history as discontinuity, was the realm of opacity, the opposite of transparency of historical reality always already caught in the continuity of time. It would seem then that the *gauchiste* ideology was nothing but a retrogression, after Althusser's critique, to naïve empiricism.

However, Rancière does not merely repeat this Althusserian critique of Hegelianism and present it to the anti-Althusserian Maoist practice, but, in a familiar vein, his move is to argue that Althusser's critique itself is conditioned by the very structure it is targeting. 'Rejection' of the religious myth of reading, of the Book, as Rancière states, allows Althusser to constitute his own reading along the lines of a kind of 'negative theology', that is, by retaining the religious idea of the Book and making 'its *absence* [be] shown openly in presence'. In a quite clever move, Rancière argues that the Bible – which is the paradigm here – was never a pure presence of truth. According to an image in St Augustine, its worldly readers were only ever able to see its reverse side while the living Word was turned towards the Father and his angels (FW, 130). The myth of the Book was then never about the presence as such but about the promise of a *future* presence, the movement *towards* the appearance of the Word. The function of Althusser's initial rejection of the Book is then only to fix the opaque theoretical field into a certain relation with a *coming* transparency. It assures that there is something like 'the Book', and that theoretical work is needed to wipe off the dust from its everyday readers' ideological eye. In this sense Althusser 'creates a dramaturgy of writing' which prefigures 'the passage from text to reality' or the point 'where literature [i.e. the merely written word lacking the presence in flesh] leaves itself' (FW, 5, 138/168, tm).

As we saw in Chapter 1, this Althusserian dramaturgy orchestrates first of all a theatre of deferral. But it is structured by an underlying believe 'that there is a "plain of history"', a plain which secures that aims eventually meet their ends and that theoretical work serves a 'people still to come'.[56] The whole scheme of symptomal reading is structured according to the relationship between the intellectual and the proletariat, haunted by the former's desire to rejoin the latter when the moment is ripe: 'By this ... strategy one can in fact buy back the debt, identify the movement of someone who "leaves" – who pays the debt of not having been born a proletarian.' In writing these lines, Rancière no doubt has in mind not only Althusser but also the generation of his students, Rancière himself included, who saw this textual practice, caught in the strategies of deferral, as blatantly insufficient.[57] However, their break with Althusser was prewritten in the Althusserian script itself: 'At the point where theory encounters politics, it reintroduces what it had initially rejected: a great Book of reality, a great book of history' (FW, 144).

In this sense this logic of Althusserianism absorbs the *gauchiste* political practice to the same structure of anticipation. *Gauchisme* interrupted the time of theoretical labour only to realize an aim which had been anticipated by this practice and which had constructed a view of reality that is in accordance with its aim-orientedness. They reached a presence of action but did not break with the anticipatory model of history so eagerly criticized by Lardreau, for example (as shown in Chapter 1). After such a logic, the practice of the GP, understood within the framework of breaking with theory for good, of 'burning the books', could only appear as a predetermined gesture. And the space of struggle in the present, in the here and now, was captured into this temporalizing rationality. To the extent that such a model persisted, it allowed the *nouveaux philosophes*, or the intellectual seismologists, to return to the position of those who know where history is heading.

The desire to burn books was only a symptom of the bookish reason, and it spoke of the theoretician's anxiety shared by (the supposedly anti-) Althusserian Maoism. It was 'anguish of speech that does not get through, ... of people that neither speech nor time ties together into a subject of history' that was driving in different ways both Althusserianism and *gauchisme* (FW, 139/169, tm). If there is a paradigm of 'speech that does not get through', of speechless and timeless speech, it is to be found in a written text. Writing, for

Rancière, forms a space where textuality does not reach the reality as it is, that is, a self-identical reality, but has always already broken its uniformity, opening the dimension of the disoriented between-space.

Before moving further to show how such textuality plays a constitutive role in the Cultural-Revolutionary revolt, it should be noted that Rancière's gesture nevertheless resembles that of Althusser himself. For, the latter had precisely produced a combined critique of a certain bookish reason and an anti-bookish attitude. He argued that 'the same ambiguities of formulation which fostered' the reading based on 'the fatality of the advent of socialism as if in a Bible' also produced the Gramscian voluntarist (and historicist) reading based on the idea of the revolution against *Capital* (RC, 269). In 'The Revolution against *Capital*' Gramsci writes that Marx's *Capital* was used in Russia by the bourgeoisie to argue for 'the necessity that events must take a certain course in Russia', that is, that the society has to go through a bourgeois development before a proletarian revolution can become possible. The Bolshevik revolution had nonetheless proved to be one against this determinist vision of 'the canons of historical materialism' insisting on the capacity of the masses to both develop their consciousness and voluntarily redirect the course of history.[58] This does not dissociate Gramsci's discourse from a certain fatalist conception of the Russian revolution, however, to the extent that it retains such fatalism as *Capital*'s 'deeper message which is its lifeblood'.[59] In line with this message the struggles of the proletariat in Russia show to be 'a testimony today to a world yet to come'.[60] This allowed Althusser to present determinism and voluntarism as the two sides of the same coin, both based on a belief of a uniform direction of history. We can see that Rancière's combined critique of Althusser and *gauchisme* that I have tried to reconstruct follows a similar pattern.

If Althusser tried to replace a certain biblical paradigm of reading with another kind of reading, rather than simply reject 'the Book', also Rancière retains an idea of reading in order to avoid the *gauchiste* 'simple negation' (AL, 121). For Rancière, to burn the Book of the bookish reason is to embrace another book, which is not reaching for a determined future presence but which for this very reason is free from the constraints of such presence and does not allow itself to be fixed to a specific historical reality or serve as a foundation (or establishment) for any *epochal* action. Such a book enables words to circulate without attaching themselves to any particular speaker, to any particular place or any particular time while being nevertheless put in relation with the reality in the here and now by 'the one who is emancipated and walks and walks, moving around and conversing, putting meaning into circulation' (OSP, 51/94, tm). Leaning on this logic of literature, the emancipated one releases the here and now from historical-temporal directedness putting emphasis on free circulation in space.

Rancière understands this idea of the written text and literarity in polemical relation to Plato's notorious critique of writing in *Phaedrus*. In it Plato criticizes the written letter in favour of the living word, arguing that writing has no control over its own transmission. 'Not being a *logos* guided, accompanied by its father,' as Rancière explains, 'it sets off anywhere at all, without knowing to whom it should and should not speak.'[61] As David F. Bell has noticed, 'movement through space is crucial to Rancière's reflections' of literature precisely because of the positive use it makes of Plato's critique. 'It shifts the focus of who is speaking and how' to freely constructed relations in space.[62] The spatial open-directedness allows to think an unguided circulation of meaning available to different overlapping configurations. As I will now move to argue, this spatial circulation of writing and meaning should be seen as an interpretation of the textuality operative at the very core of the Cultural-Revolutionary practice.

Education à la Lin Biao

As Rancière writes in *Althusser's Lesson*, 'Althusserianism is a theory of education' (AL, 52). In the Althusserian theory of reading, there is a certain idea of a teacher at work (FW, 133–5). The function of the teacher is to control the opacity of the text in the present and its directedness to the future realization of meaning. It makes sure that the student waits, that she does not leave too soon, while guaranteeing that the Book will eventually let its meaning become visible, and that in order for this to happen one needs to follow specific procedures – *which take time*. When the Maoists interrupted the infinite deferral of the Althusserian pedagogic machinery, they merely renewed the model of mastery, identifying the new master with the figure of the worker.[63] The truth no longer had to wait to be pronounced but was incarnated in the here and now of the sites of struggle. As Virginie Linhart puts it, for the *établis*, 'the worker is the one who speaks the truth'.[64]

In one of his most renowned books, *The Ignorant Schoolmaster* (1987), Rancière presents a full-scale critique of pedagogy through texts of Joseph Jacotot. Much of the work addresses the function of traditional model of education and the figure of the master included in it to establish an infinite temporal continuity in the vein of Rancière's critiques of Althusser (as we saw also in Chapter 1).[65] Jacotot, however, finds himself acting as an alternative figure of the master, an ignorant one, who is no longer a guide endowed with the knowledge of the underlying, not-yet visible truth beneath the text. This is due to him finding himself teaching French to Flemish students without knowing or learning any Flemish himself. The students need to make their way between the two languages, in a bilingual edition of François Fénelon's *Les Aventures de Télémaque*, without help from a superior intelligence. Jacotot himself appears merely as someone who is able to concentrate the will of his students, to urge them to read the text *without* guidance, that is, without giving them a direction which would lead towards the revelation of its meaning, without knowledge which would be withheld by the teacher during the progressive process of learning. Learning is not subjected to 'the speech of the master' but to 'the authority of the book' (IS, 5, 7). This authority amounts precisely to an authority of writing as it was criticized by Plato, that is to say, the authority of the letter which addresses itself to anyone whosoever: 'the privilege that the Jacotot method gave to the book … was the exact reversal of the hierarchy of minds that was designated in Plato by the critique of writing' (IS, 38).

The Ignorant Schoolmaster is often discussed as an intervention in the pedagogical debates in France at the time of writing it both by Rancière and his readers.[66] However, this Jacototian authority of the book brings to mind one specific book, which was indeed *not* to be dropped at the time of Maoist movements. I mean of course the little red one, edited from Mao's writings and learnt by heart by millions of militants, not only in China but all over the world. The logic Rancière traces in *The Ignorant Schoolmaster* is in my view clearly inspired by the couple formed by Mao and his *Quotations* during the early stages of the Cultural Revolution.[67] Rancière's book is best read as a rethinking of this couple and thus as a rethinking of the logic of the Cultural Revolution itself.

The immediate background context of the compilation of Mao's Little Red Book and the emergence of the 'cult' surrounding it can be seen in the debates over the educational methods to be applied in the People's Liberation Army in the late 1950s and early 1960s. One view emphasized 'systematic study' of Mao's thought with reference to the canonical works of Marxism-Leninism to enable understanding of the complicated theoretical surroundings of his writings.[68] The other view, held by Lin Biao, insisted on a slogan-driven method based on 'constant repetition' and 'learning to cite only the most important sentences' as the appropriate study of Mao's work.[69] It is this latter view which prevailed and helped shaping the form and use of the Little Red Book which would soon spread vastly outside the army context.[70] This Lin-Biaoist educational framework would then define much of the specific logic of the Cultural Revolution, albeit that the latter exceeded his original purposes, as will be explained later. This method, based on repeating catchphrases and citing quotations by heart connected to their lively application, is essentially linked to the formation of the image of the Cultural Revolution as a brutally irrational and chaotic movement where leftist principles were blindly followed and put in action in most absurd ways.[71] After Mao's death, the form of the Little Red Book, a fruit of Lin's controversial educational method itself apt to create the delirious manifestations of the Cultural-Revolutionary revolt, was blamed for 'vulgarization' of Maoist and more generally Marxist theory.[72]

It is a strikingly similar method, however, that we find Rancière polemically defending throughout his little book on Joseph Jacotot, against traditional and conservative views on education and learning. As becomes clear, Jacotot's is a method based on learning '*by heart*', repeating '*like a parrot*' (IS, 24, 69; cf. 3, 22, 101, 114; NL, 165). This method is constantly insisted on against the Old Master for whom 'to repeat is not to know' or against the idea that 'those who repeat ... are not intelligent enough to *understand*' (IS, 25, 22). There is no profound rationality of understanding which would require explicative methods that go beneath the supposedly superficial procedures of imitation or repetition. Challenging traditional pedagogical schemes, Jacotot's students 'moved along in a manner one shouldn't move along – the way children move, blindly figuring out riddles' (IS, 10). Rather than any explicative procedure of the savant, the most appropriate paradigm for emancipatory learning is thus that of children who never stop to 'imitate and repeat' in learning their mother tongue (IS, 5).[73] For there are 'no words underneath words, no language that tells the truth of language' (IS, 24).

What is at stake is to detach thought and discussion, reading and application, from an external rationality that would oversee, lead or direct them. Such an external rationality concerns knowledge of the 'depth' that conditions the correct interpretation of that which is visible in the 'surface'. The traditional 'pedagogical logic appears as the act that lifts a veil off the obscurity of things. Its topography is that of top to bottom, of surface to depth.'[74] What is crucial in the relation between the depth and surface is that 'this topography itself implies a certain temporality. Lifting the veil from things, bringing back the surface to its depth and bringing all depth to the surface … supposes a certain temporal order.'[75] Against such a temporalized topography, Rancière posits another idea of space, one that consists of 'horizontal ways of the self-taught who move from proximity to proximity, comparing what they don't know to what they do know'.[76]

The tendency of classical pedagogies and master–discipline relations 'to substitute the spirit to the letter' is played out through the temporal topography of the depth and surface, while the Jacototian horizontal model is based solely under the authority of the book (IS, 7/17, tm). Such a Jacototian-Lin-Biaoist method went directly against those Chinese Party cadres for whom 'the important point was to develop the *spirit* of the work and not just be able to recite' it.[77] While Lin's critics were worried that the readers of Mao's quotations were not able to understand the meaning of the text and thus required external explicators – be they teachers or explanatory texts – the absence of external rationality as well as any need for such a thing is the core lesson of *The Ignorant Schoolmaster*: 'Everything is in the book' (IS, 23). This does not mean, however, that the book wouldn't relate to what is outside of it – be they other books or discourses, objects or events. In contrast, it means that there are no limits or a pregiven framework for the book's meaning and applicability. Each word is, as Jacotot states, open 'to all directions'.[78] Like Fénelon's *Télémaque*, Mao's Little Red Book served as a tool for 'learning everything and expressing everything' (NL, 165). As Rancière captures the Jacotot-method: 'Learn something and relate everything else to it.'[79]

The horizontality, or the simultaneous openness to 'all directions', marks the logic of disoriented, abstract space. This omnidirectionality means not only that any word or phrase or other unit in the book is capable of referring to all the others but also that the book itself as well as everything in it can be connected immediately to anything else. One can refer to the book from anywhere and refer anywhere from the book. This means also that the particular consequences that might be driven from it cannot be *anticipated*, or can never be *established* as the right ones, because that would amount to annihilation of the specific rationality of the book, that is, its omnidirectionality. It allows to legitimize any particular application neither in advance nor retrospectively. Rather, the disorientedness and omnidirectionality are never cancelled by the conclusions that might be drawn from it, and the relationalities drawn from the book can be indefinitely rearticulated while the multiple articulations can exist at the same time.

The form of the Little Red Book was apt to effectuate such an omnidirectional spatial logic as opposed to coherent temporal orientation. As Daniel Leese describes it:

> The decontextualized utterances eased memorization and group recitation, but also allowed for near-infinite recombination and thus provided the fundaments for creative exegesis. The lack of coherent philosophical framework permitted free association of the quotations, even within contradictory arguments.[80]

With a notable similarity Rancière characterizes the practice of reading in the Jacototian intellectual emancipation with 'an infinity of ways that can be tried, an infinity of possible connections'.[81] Spatial omnidirectionality thus allows to think a sphere where one can 'combine study with application' more freely from restrictions.[82]

The spatial logic of the book is articulated within the geographical space where its applications are produced. In this respect, Rancière mentions the centrality of 'mnemotechnics' in Jacotot's method (IS, 38). This is another kind of spatial inscription of meaning which is not that of temporalizing presence but of omnidirectionality. Such a structure should be seen in relation to the Cultural Revolution, where free circulation of the Red Guards and rebels throughout the country was encouraged and rendered possible. Public transportation was made free of charge, and free accommodation and meals were offered to the travelling youth. Mao's writings offered, just like Fénelon's *Télémaque* among Jacotot's students, a 'thing in common' for the discussions and arguments.

The sameness of the book blurred distinctions of places, and the differences between places introduced varied meanings to the sameness of the book (IS, 2). In schools and universities the geographical space was doubled with textuality in a very concrete sense when 'big character posters festooned every available surface' defending conflicting interpretations of Mao Zedong Thought.[83]

The logic of spatial crossovers between texts and geographical space also mixed the differentiations of specific historical contexts from which Mao's fragments were extracted. '[T]ravelling seemingly without effort across … temporal boundaries', they were all made available for use in the present. As Andrew F. Jones well puts it:

> For what is the function of the quotation, if not to remove a textual extract from its original context, and allow it to *circulate* beyond the original and particular historical circumstances in which it was produced, rendering it available for reuse, recitation, and re-contextualisations? The *Quotations* achieve precisely this function, bringing together words spoken or written from the mid 1920s to the mid 1960s, torn from the often quite specific and complex tactical situations for which they were crafted, and offered instead as trans-historical scripts for revolutionary praxis.[84]

This spatial logic then brackets time, as it were, which does not mean that the flow of time would somehow stop or that the produced arguments would not draw from different temporal contexts. Rather, it means that to approach this reality of revolt from a question of a historical temporalization would amount to misunderstanding and cancelling its specific positivity which is best captured by the idea of application which leans on unrestricted omnidirectionality and is indifferent to historical contextualizations.

In his conceptualization of the book Rancière implicitly defends Lin Biao's exhortation to 'creative study and application' while offering the most radical interpretation of it through the story and writings of Jacotot.[85] In doing so, he joins Lin in rejecting those who feared that 'if the basic truths of Marxism-Leninism had not been understood' this would lead to 'wrong application' of Mao's texts.[86] What Rancière calls the authority of the book does not recognize the idea of 'wrong application' or wrong understanding.

> [A]ccording to Jacotot, … words are like orphans. They are not carried by the master of the word or by the person who is able to put them in the right

way in the soul of the student. So, there is this idea of writing as a certain status of words when they are made available to anybody for any kind of reading.[87]

The authority of the book is thus not about the knowledge of the correct or incorrect consequences drawn from it, for what it authorizes is omnidirectionality, a disoriented space where 'it is a matter of daring to be adventurous' (IS, 27). Rather than offering knowledge the book is meant to provoke 'confidence' and empower its readers.[88] The wider availability of Mao's quotations starting in the army in the early 1960s likewise provided the servicemen and servicewomen with a certain power against the Party cadres in cases where the actions of the latter were thought to contradict the word of the chairman. This empowerment exploded during the Cultural Revolution when the masses were encouraged to autonomously challenge their leaders. In vain did the authorities then try to stop people from self-authorized reading without a supervision of an explicative reason. As Kiang Shu-ying, a student in Peking at the start of the Cultural Revolution, remembers:

> [W]e began to ask our teachers and the school management why they weren't acting in accordance with Mao Tse-tung Thought. ... They forbade us to read Chairman Mao on our own. There must always be a responsible teacher with us, they said.[89]

Rae Yang writes in her memoir that 'up to that point, all my education told me that the teachers were always right'; 'they forced us to be stupid, to be "the teachers' little lambs"'.[90] The Cultural Revolution, she tells us, 'exhilarated me because suddenly I felt that I was allowed to think with my own head and say what was on my mind'.[91]

The *Quotations* and the exhortation to their self-authorized use established a 'thing in common' which flattened the hierarchical relations between teachers and students (IS, 2, cf. 13). 'Mao's sayings offered ample opportunities to substantiate opposing viewpoints once they were no longer applied within a hierarchical setting.'[92] Mao's thought remained the ultimate authority, but it was expressed in the 'mute speech' of the written word which allowed contradictory interpretations and paved way to what can be characterized by Rancière's specific notion of disagreement.[93]

'Disagreement [*mésentente*]', as defined by Rancière, 'is not the conflict between one who says white and another who says black. It is the conflict between one who says white and another who also says white but does not understand [*entend*] the same thing by it' (D, x). This seemingly simplistic definition goes to the heart of Rancière's philosophy. It is a question of the irreducibility of homonymy. As Rancière explains, in 'disagreement' it is not a question of ignorance (*méconnaissance*) or misunderstanding (*malentendu*).[94] This means that the discrepancy is not incorporated into a logic which would allow to exceed it over time through either clarification or additional knowledge of the situation. It is rather a certain idea of persistence of the conflict. To refer to another signature concept of Rancière's, *le partage du sensible*, it is a question of sharing which is also a division, that is, of *partage*. *Sens* can be both divided and shared because its structure is double: there is always a sense perception or sensible matter and the sense that one makes of it. The phrase *le partage du sensible* thus repeats in each of its members the form of homonymy, which itself is the form of disagreement, or, as Rancière's own and more adequate translation has it, *dissensus*. But, as was the case in Rancière's *The Names of History* discussed earlier, *sens* should also be understood as direction or orientation. Consequently, it is unidirectionality which is always already cancelled in disagreement or sharing of that which cannot *proceed* in the same path. Whereas the notions of 'ignorance' or 'misunderstanding' mark a temporary confusion which can be overcome to restore a common orientation, in disagreement it is the very impossibility of such an orientation which is shared. What is shared is a disoriented space, then, and it is in such a space where emancipatory practice is played out.[95]

It would be misleading, however, to not address the differences between the framework of Lin Biao and the one that Rancière constructs in reference to Joseph Jacotot. Namely, if the idea behind making the quotations available, first to the servicemen and servicewomen, and then to wider masses, was to give them confidence, it was never to be independent from unifying guidance and direction that was to accompany this confidence. As Lin says, the point in the availability of quotations is that 'every soldier at any time, under any condition can immediately receive *guidance* from Chairman Mao's thought'.[96] Such guidance was first meant to be offered 'from above' in group citation sessions in the army.[97] If Mao's word could be trusted on independent study when the Cultural Revolution broke out, it was partly because of an underlying belief in the unidirectionality of history.[98] It is due to the strength of such a belief that the explanations of the 'goals' or 'anticipated outcomes' of the movement could be left unexplained, 'vague and open to multiple interpretations'.[99] The most turbulent phase of the Cultural Revolution could then break out, as '[a]lternative interpretations and information gathering activities among Red Guards developed in previously unthinkable dimensions and temporarily broke the uniformity of the directed public sphere'.[100] The idea of empowerment stemming from the pre-Cultural-Revolutionary education and then the exhortation to revolt while not stating the concrete aims created the specific positivity of the Cultural-Revolutionary revolt. It is this positivity, preventing all 'progress' of the movement, that Rancière appears to affirm by thinking through 'the authority of the book', or 'the thing in common', which does not allow any unified direction to be deduced from it.

Surely, had Mao given specific instructions to the Red Guards and rebels, many would have likely been most willing to follow the living word of the Great Helmsman. The point is, though, that the characteristic feature of the Cultural Revolution was that any specific directions were *not* given. Among the most paradigmatic scenes of the Cultural Revolution are the ones where Mao appeared on Tiananmen Square, overall to millions of Red Guards and rebels waving copies of the Little Red Book in their hands. In those occasions Mao himself said very little if anything at all.[101] And the message of the speeches given by other leaders of the movement is captured in Lin Biao's assurance to Red Guards that 'whatever they did was right'.[102] It would be hard to think that Rancière was not inspired by this imagery when he described how Jacotot withdrew 'his intelligence from the picture in order to leave their intelligence to grapple with that of the book' (IS, 13/25, tm). Again, for Mao, the revolt as such was enough because of the belief in the movement of history underlying its launch. In a certain sense this shows the belief in the 'plain of history' at its purest, exactly because it does not present a spokesperson who would need to explicate its rationality. Hence Mao's oft-quoted statement in a letter to Jiang Qing according to which '[g]reat chaos will lead to great order'.[103] By the same token it ends up demonstrating the absence of history's unidirectionality, which absence caused the failure of the Cultural Revolution in respect to not only its aims but to aimfulness as such. Rancière appears to embrace precisely this failure or rather the logic that produced it. To put it another way, the means of the movement contradicted its aims, but Rancière insists on this very contradiction while generalizing it and turning it into a more radical principle. Emancipatory reasoning, or reason in revolt, does not lean on specific aims: 'Reason begins when discourses organized with the goal of being right cease, where equality is recognized' (IS, 72/123, tm). Equality rejects historical time as a directed and differentiating movement of collective reality. It rejects not only an overarching Historical Time, however, but also time as a coherent sequence specific to a particular revolutionary process.

The intelligence of the book imposes disorientation and multidirectionality upon the practice of its application, throwing its readers in 'this forest of signs that by themselves do not *want* to say anything [*ne* veulent *rien dire*]', that is, which will not lead to any specific direction or which does not *will* to direct (IS, 67/115, tm). The will needs to be brought to the intelligence of the book from the outside: 'The two faculties in play during the act of learning, namely intelligence and will, had ... been separated' (IS, 13). This gives a specific meaning to the ignorant master's command: 'It commands absolutely a subject whom it supposes capable of commanding itself' (IS, 38/67, tm). Commandment was an imposition of the will of the master upon the will of the students to do what they want with the book. The cult of personality formed around Mao interpreted according to Rancière's scheme should be understood in terms of imposing a will without guidance of where it should take those subjected to it.

However, the distinction between will and intelligence can be seen precisely as an attempt to render possible an organizatory unity compatible with equality of intelligences. It would be the will, then, which imposes direction to the omnidirectional field of equality, while such direction would not originate from any prestructured course of things or specific knowledge concerning it. In line with this idea, Andrea Cavazzini states that with the equality of intelligences Rancière posits inequality of wills which allows to retain the figure of the guide.[104] Yet, the idea of a particular guide does not fit well with Rancière's Jacototian Maoism and is profoundly problematized in it: 'there is no accredited guide because there is no right point of departure, no right order.'[105] The commander of emancipation 'is not the guide who leads the student's way'. The emancipatory master is 'purely the will who tells another will to find its way and thus to exercise its intelligence to find this way all by itself' (GF, 412). Thus, the idea of guidance can barely be used here in any positive sense, and it is indeed in opposition to this term that Rancière conceptualizes the Jacototian practice (cf. IS, 9, 29, 59, 120).

Even if we think that an orientative unity would be one introduced by the will, the latter must be coarticulated with the omnidirectional logic of equality which readily cancels any specific path that might be constructed. The logic of disorientation thus introduces a constant rupture into these paths, throwing them 'under the sign of interruption' (SV, 118). Such paths are not developed in relation to mechanisms which would safeguard their internal unities – something any organization would require – but only in relation to a logic of dispersal. In order for the omnidirectional community of the book to remain effective, the emancipatory movement cannot be brought under guidance which would necessarily tie it into a principle of direction and have to make use of some kind of ordered temporal unity. Hence the paradoxical nature of the egalitarian commandment: 'whoever emancipates doesn't have to worry about what the emancipated person learns. He will learn what he wants, nothing maybe' (IS, 18). The Maoist political will modelled according to the commandment of the ignorant master is thus best understood as a will to the omnidirectional equality as such. Such a will does not lead or direct; it is simply imposed.

This is not simply a question of a failed attempt to think organization but speaks to the ultimate orientation of Rancière's thought. If it can be characterized by the idea of guidance, it is guidance by equality as such, by the 'maxim of equality' (ME, 90). Much like the Kantian moral law, the will is then determined by this maxim as such. But the specific feature of the Rancièrian maxim of equality is that no specific consequences follow from it and that to insist on any specific course of things is to break against it. For, equality cannot be an aim. It is an axiom which breaks in advance with the idea of a determined aim.

The specific feature of the Cultural Revolution as it was received in France at the time was that it sought to implement social equality 'as quickly as possible'.[106] In this expression time features mainly as an obstacle, and it posits the task to allow a minimal amount of temporal mediation. Rancière's understanding of equality can be seen to present a qualitative switch to the notion of equality where it no longer depends on any amount of temporal mediation. But this problematizes any attempt to legitimize specific temporal processes through emancipatory aspirations and makes Rancière's discourse fundamentally problematic in any constructive, organized political use. I argued in Chapter 1 that Guy Lardreau's attempt to think through the rupturous logic of revolt, which would have done with mechanisms of temporal orientation, led him to the other side of the sensible world in the form of a 'purified Kantianism'. We could now suggest that Rancière is able to keep his other foot in its realm by playing spatial disorientation against temporally coherent orientation. Yet, there remains something of the tendency of his fellow Maoist towards an uncompromised notion of freedom, unrestricted by the fetters of time.

3

Politics of staging and the primacy of space

Scène, 'stage' or 'scene', has become a central notion of Rancière's work and signifies both its method and the 'object' to which this method serves to do justice. For Rancière, emancipatory practice is thought in terms of 'staging', *mettre en scène*. The English 'stage' – which can be used to translate *scène* – has an advantage in forming a homonymous relation with what is in French called *étape*. The reader has become familiar with this latter notion in the course of Chapters 1 and 2, but let me recap the stakes. The *étape* was a central notion for the French Maoists. As my discussion of Lardreau in Chapter 1 made clear, the particular feature of Maoism, as a stage of Marxism, was its will to break with historical continuity, to not draw from the past but to establish (*établir*) a futural present that breaks with it absolutely. Lardreau was driven into despair because, thus conceived, the revolt still leaned on an order of historical succession and could not be extended to counter this order itself. Instead of a radical rupture, it was a vehicle to organize historical time into stages (*étapes*). This, as I suggested in Chapter 2, was the framework behind the localized practice of the *établis*.

As I have argued, Rancière's trajectory begins with tackling the problem which made Lardreau give up any hope for the actualization of revolt and adopt Kantianism which leaned on the noumenal dimension as a merely internal ethical attitude. In Rancière revolt comes to be understood according to the present which would not be ordered as a stage in a historical process, as I tried to show through the reading of the Cultural Revolution in the previous chapter. Rancière's is then a revolt against coherent temporality, against a unidirectional or orientative ordering of not only historical time as a whole but also specific historical sequences. It is in this context that we need to see the role of the 'stage' or 'scene'. If for the early Lardreau 'the re-irruption of the masses on the stage of history [*la scène de l'histoire*]' took the form of a new historical *étape*, then Rancière's project is characterized by rethinking the notion of the *scène* as a function which dissolves the temporal coherence of *étape* (SO, 24).[1]

I will start this chapter by discussing an article published at first in 1988, entitled 'La Scène révolutionnaire et l'ouvrier émancipé (1830–1848)'. In it 'stage' is a word through which Rancière thinks the revolution, in particular the period in France which runs from 1830 to 1848. I will focus on how Rancière contrasts 'stage' with the concept of 'process' as well as the concept of 'the self', arguing that stage should be understood in terms of spatiality which resist its subjection to a temporal form exceeding beyond its presence. I will use the concept of the self to then enter a discussion of Kant and temporality which enables me to develop a particular interpretation of Rancière's use of Kantian aesthetics as well as Schiller's reading of it, again based on a certain idea of space that is not subjected to a temporal form.

Staging revolution

Rancière's 1988 article starts with a clear distinction of the notion of the revolution from an ordered temporality of a *process*: 'There is no revolutionary process. There is a revolutionary stage' (SR, 49). While acknowledging that one can surely find in a revolution 'all kinds of actions and chains of action' that may be called processes, he argues that the specifically revolutionary logic cannot be properly grasped with the term 'process'. Although in his later work Rancière often speaks in terms of political processes or processes of political subjectivation, it is telling of his position that here the logic at work in emancipatory politics is defined in opposition to the notion of the process. In light of this earlier text – as well as my general argument – I would claim that, although it is perfectly possibly to call 'chains of action' with this name, the term 'process' draws too much from an idea of coherent temporal sequence in order to capture adequately the emancipatory political logic as it figures in Rancière. The emancipatory paradigm is scenological, that is, it concerns staging, *mettre en scène*, and the notion of stage is defined through its distinction from 'process'.

In the text at issue here, Rancière does not give a clear definition of the stage, however. It is simply associated with 'a widened space of visibility to which the political will be for some time identified' (SR, 49). We can note here first a reference to (visual) appearance and second an indeterminate temporal duration as characteristics of stage. Regarding its time, the stage does not involve 'recognition of the right means to pass from the present situation to the one that will be' (SR, 59). Neither does it draw from any 'historical evolution', be it an objectively determined one or one that would use the present to articulate a trajectory leading to a desired future. Such temporally structured forms are not used to produce any differential structures according to which the revolutionary stage would *proceed*.

The unstructured and undisciplined temporality of the stage relates directly to it as a certain disordered appearance. Rather than an emergence of a force concentrated enough to redirect the course of the social order, the revolutionary stage operates 'a dispersion of the symbols of power and the representations of bond [*lien*]'. More precisely, it amounts to a decoupling of specific 'forms of saying and of showing' allowing 'any combinations of the one with the other' to be formed 'in whatever place, in whichever subject' (SR, 50). What constitutes the appearance of the revolution is then disorganized and reorganized in undetermined and unanticipated ways, as 'divisions and doublings multiply in every place' (SR, 69). Due to the dismantling of the forms of appearance which constitute the normal state of things, the reactionary logic renounces the revolutionary stage as nothing but 'theatre' (SR, 69, cf. 50). As we shall soon see, the notion of the stage is intimately linked to theatre. Thus, the logic which characterizes its actors is a capacity to imitate, that is, 'the power of the double', the power 'of representing anything whatsoever or being anyone whosoever', as Rancière has stated elsewhere (PP, 10). This is the capacity at work in the revolutionary staging which disperses an order of stable subjects.[2]

According to Rancière, there are two figures, the politician and the historian, who insist, in contrast to the statement that revolution is a stage, that 'the revolution is a process or it is nothing' (SR, 50). In order to present the revolution as a process, they need to 'establish a consistency to the change' by presenting order underlying its space-time (SR, 50).

> There is a spatial direction [*direction*]: finding behind the spectacular events, discourses and parades, the forms which bring them into visibility, the forms whose respective weights, compositions and conflicts

> define the revolutionary situation: the class forces and the social groups which are definable according to their fundamental proprieties, their evolution, their situation, and their aspirations. And there is a temporal direction: determining the causes behind the visible rupture which occurs during some hours and days of street clashes (July 1830, February 1848): the evolution of situations and relations of force which renders this rupture necessary and probable, which determines the forms that it can take, and the possibility for the politician to lead it, and for the historian to represent its leading thread. (SR, 50)

Rancière describes here how the surface of the stage is pierced and connected to determining factors underlying its visible space-time. In this way the spatial presence of the revolution can be brought under a processual orientation by articulating these factors into a movement of time and constituting what is apparent in the stage as a moment in a temporal continuum.[3] A spatio-temporal consistency and continuity then neutralizes the revolutionary stage by turning it into a process and projecting hidden 'evolutions' and 'aspirations' upon what is apparent.

Establishing such forms and modalities which underlie the visible space-time is then necessary in order to construct a temporal continuity of which the staging appears as a moment. Indeed, as a reference to Rancière's later discourse on the notion of the stage in relation to theatrical art will show, his attempt to dissociate the space-time of staging from a processual coherence tends to be presented as a dissociation of the spatial from a time which extends beyond it, into the past as well as future. Hence, when Rancière discusses the transformation of theatre in the course of nineteenth century in one of his more recent books, he characterizes it in terms of a shift in the relation of primacy between the spatial and temporal dimensions of theatre. Whereas the dominating Aristotelian scheme was based on 'the submission of the space of representation to the time of dramatic action', in the nineteenth-century theatre there emerged a rupture with this order.[4] The spatiality of the stage now received new importance. In an interview 'On *Aisthesis*' with Oliver Davis Rancière discusses this shift in reference to Aristotle's *Poetics* and unwraps a point made in his then most recent book: 'Aristotle referred dramatic action to the textual chain of causes and effects by subordinating to it what he called *opsis*, which is the disposition of bodies in the scenic space;

aesthetic logic, by contrast, privileges that disposition of bodies' (OA, 217; cf. A, 116).

The Greek *opsis* refers to sight or seeing. In the English editions of Aristotle's *Poetics* it is normally translated into 'spectacle', but it refers to 'everything that is visible on stage'.[5] According to Rancière, in classical drama spatial configurations were produced through subjecting the *opsis* to a narrative temporality while the overturning of this order amounts to dissociating it from such a narrative. Abstracting what is visible on stage without conceiving it as a segment of time is the basic idea behind the notion of the stage as Rancière understands it. It serves to think about revolutionary rupture in terms of what is taking place as such. This taking place has an extension in time but its temporal extension does not reach beyond what is present in space. Rather than a rupture understood in negative terms in relation to what precedes it, *scène* is a space-time which has its independent positivity, unrelated to stages – now understood in terms of *étape* – which precede or follow it.

What makes the revolutionary stage as a *scène* should then be understood in terms of action and actors *in space* without subjecting them to temporal schemes that enable us to associate them with broader evolutions, subject them to futural orientations or see them as results of past developments. The space of their action is not approached as being subordinate to processual reasoning that goes beyond their presence (SR, 54). The revolutionary stage is not measured against that which lies before or after it and which would allow to select between forms of action and subjects that make sense in the broader currents of historical and social reality and are rendered possible by them. This gives a certain sovereignty to what takes form in the space of revolution as such, allowing any actor to *appear* in principle with any kind of social qualifications and thus to be an *actor* also in the theatrical sense of the word.[6]

The 'question, by which politics is tied to the theatre, is not to know how to exit the dream in order to act in true life. It is to decide what is dream and what is true life.'[7] The revolutionary stage is oriented only towards itself, as an emancipated space open for such decisions. This does not mean, however, that the stage would be directed towards the reconstitution of a stable 'reality'. Emphasis on space bracketed from broader temporal sequences allows appearances to take shape which transcend the normal coordinates of the social order. For the July and February Revolutions this space is called the

Republic, and it does not have 'other end than the Republic itself' (SR, 53). It is, as Rancière describes it, 'a place [*lieu*] where everything is possible, the infinite form of its own transcendence' (SR, 63).

I will now continue to discuss this spatiality in relation to another notion which threatens to neutralize the logic of staging, that is, the 'self'. In the article 'La Scène révolutionnaire', the question of the self is raised in relation to the problem of representation. This, as I will argue, imposes a form of reflexivity with a unified temporality and as such destroys the logic of the revolution as stage or staging.

The self and the representation

Rancière has made it very clear that for him 'politics is not an enactment of ... the self of the community'.[8] In the text at issue here, he deals with the self as a concept incompatible with that of the revolutionary stage. The self should be seen as analogous to the process in that both the self and the process are notions which link the space of revolution to a temporal coherence. The problem is framed through the question of the self-representation of the people that emerges after the (re)introduction of universal male suffrage in 1848. This, according to Rancière, imposes 'an enigmatic reflexive relation' on the revolutionary stage (SR, 66). While 'an emancipated worker is ... an intellectual being, an individual who reflects on what he does and communicates this reflection to others', the problem arises when self-reflexivity comes to structure the collective space of the revolution (SR, 57; cf. IS, 57).[9] This happens when people are supposed to elect representatives for itself among emancipated individuals and 'the relation between the emancipated individual with the people [mingles with] the relation of the people with itself' (SR, 66).

The internalization of an external relation brings forth a problem of a temporal discrepancy between an individual and the collective. Rancière asks: 'to what extent, in what way is the emancipated worker a contemporary of the revolution?' (SR, 64). The question is somewhat rhetorical, and there is no relation of contemporaneity between them insofar as this would require a temporal unification of the revolutionary stage itself. As we know, the revolution itself is not a process but a stage which means that it does not have a temporal consistency upon which a reflexive relation could be established. Hence, also the relation of the emancipated individual to the collective milieu of politics cannot be approached from a temporal coherence. The individual emancipation draws its singular trajectory from the openness of the revolution. But the trajectory cannot coincide with any uniform time of the revolution, and its collective actor, for such a uniform time is precisely what the revolution as staging dismantles.

Therefore, the temporal unification brought forth by the idea of the people's self-representation comes with questions that are fatal for the very form of the revolutionary stage: 'How to guarantee that the people remain identical to itself [*semblable à soi*]?' (SR, 64). How to guarantee that 'the people', as it was witnessed in its emblematic revolutionary moments, 'the people of the barricades', continues to be what it was (SR, 65)? The essence of staging is to enable people to abolish the social order, which renders them recognizable as bearers of specific identities with specific interests. The question concerning the maintenance of the particular configurations through which the people appear reintroduces the very temporal-processual rationality that the revolution came to revoke. The people as the emancipated subject of the revolution does not exist in a unified time that could allow *its* course to be reflected on. Rather, revolution and collective emancipation mark the collapse of such a time.

The tendency present in the idea of *self*-representation gives rise to educational projects in order to produce 'men [*hommes*] of a people *to come*' modelled according to their idealized revolutionary presence (SR, 68). Soon faith is lost in the possibility of consistency of the revolutionary actor: 'The people will never know itself, it cannot be a place of a self-*reflection*' (SR, 71). If the people as a political *actor* is impossible to identify, an ideal of workers' association comes to replace it aiming at 'the future of a civilization of the workers' only to constitute a present through an 'infinite distance' to the desired future (SR, 72).

Rancière has written a lot about emancipation from the perspective of an individual, a 'reasonable being who reflects on himself' (IS, 57).[10] Nevertheless, political subjectivation is for him always a disidentification where one appropriates the role of another, a role which one is not supposed to have, thus imposing the democratic principle of substitutability upon the social order. This relation breaks a structure of reflexivity and the self. The words through which Rancière has distanced his position from the late Foucault's occupation with the idea of the 'care of the self' are telling in this respect: 'It's the reflexivity I don't like.' And, he goes on to link the question to that of space: 'The important thing is to construct the space where you are' (ME, 119). The spatially oriented question of the ' "where" is opposed to a certain idea of the "self". Emancipation is the discovery of an "individual" capacity which is at the same time the experience of sharing a common and impersonal world, belonging to everybody.'[11]

As we can see, to think the individual within this impersonal world requires a certain primacy of space. If Rancière posits such a view against Foucault's late lectures, it is worth remembering that it was Foucault himself who had earlier made the point about modelling the social sphere spatially in order to avoid imposing an internal temporality upon it. Emphasis on time over space, as he explains, amounts to 'erecting a great collective consciousness as the scene of events. Metaphorizing the transformations of discourse in a vocabulary of time necessarily leads to the utilization of the model of individual consciousness with its intrinsic temporality.'[12] Rancière's discussion of the stage dissociated from a processual coherence of a process as well as from the structure of the self hence bears some fidelity to Foucault's characterization of the differences between temporal and spatial modelling of things.

In order to better understand these relations between space, temporality and the self underlying Rancière's thinking, however, I will now move to discuss Kant and Rancière's use of Kantian aesthetics. I will begin by briefly discussing the relation between the self and temporality in Kant, in order to construct a more systematic framework for the concepts discussed earlier, and then use it to develop a particular interpretation of the Kantian aesthetics as it appears in Rancière's work. More specifically, I will claim that for Rancière, Kant's aesthetic amounts to a similar primacy of spatiality as opposed to temporal coherence than what we have seen in our discussion of the revolutionary stage. As such the aesthetics reverses the terms that Kant sets up through the relation between temporality and the self, based on notions of activity and passivity.

Rancière and Kant

Activity and passivity

In Kant time is the form of inner sense, which means that whatever is determined in time is determined along with the states of the self: 'Time is nothing other than the form of inner sense, i.e., of the intuition of our self and our inner state.'[13] Now, this self-intuition comes with a certain division between activity and passivity. Kant addresses the division in 'Transcendental Deduction' of the first *Critique*, as a 'paradox that must have struck anyone in the exposition of the form of inner sense' in 'Transcendental Aesthetic'.[14] The paradox consists in the way time 'presents even ourselves to consciousness only as we appear to ourselves, not as we are in ourselves, since we intuit ourselves only as we are internally affected, which seems to be contradictory, since we would have to relate to ourselves passively'.[15] He then goes on to explain this paradox as following from the division between the (determining) faculty of understanding and the (determined) faculty of intuition to which time belongs. Understanding, Kant says, 'exercises that action on the passive subject, whose faculty it is, about which we rightly say that the inner sense is thereby affected'.[16] Time is experienced as a relation between the active and passive within the same self. Temporal experience is thus defined as a structure where activity is reflected upon passivity.

Rancière's philosophy is concerned with how this division of the passive and active is played out within the social reality when the latter is structured according to uniform time. He has described the issue through a

> hierarchical square, which is defined by two traditional oppositions: there is the opposition between active people (those who are able to define and pursue ends) and passive people (those who are confined to the universe of means); and there is the opposition that sets the people of leisure (free people living in a time subtracted from necessity) against working people (people living in the mere alternation of activity and rest). In the hierarchical square, 'passive people' manifest their passive condition by their very activity – the activity of production of means of existence – whereas active people are also recognized by their way of not doing anything, by their monopoly of leisure. The hierarchical square structures representational logic just as it structures social domination. (OA, 210–11)

According to Rancière this division between active and passive people gets transformed into a division between different parts of the soul already in Plato, and as the faculties of understanding and sensibility in Kant – or, as Rancière also calls the latter, between 'a faculty that offers the given and a faculty that makes something out of it'.[17] This is one form of what Rancière calls *le partage du sensible*, which can be here understood as a division of the sensible reality into distinct elements or aspects. In this particular judgemental structure, the sensible is given through the passive and active aspects, and for Rancière these aspects correspond to a division between the active and passive people. In a unified society, there are the active people who are seen as playing the role of the understanding and the passive people whose lot is that of passive sensibility. The active people are recognized by determining and making sense of what appears in time. They are not themselves within the realm of that which is temporally determined but are characterized with leisure, or 'time free from necessity', because they have the monopoly on determining or interpreting the course of time. What comes to the people of sensibility their activity is a mere *object* of reflection which, according to the structure of the self, cannot but appear passive regardless of what they do. In this way, as I would argue, the society is *temporalized* into a unified structure, according to the structure of Kant's inner sense.

This reflection of the passive and active faculties on the social reality is found also in Kant himself.[18] But for Rancière the key reference in this respect is Friedrich Schiller who follows this translation of the faculties 'into anthropological and political propositions'. Hence, the division between the faculties is precisely 'a difference between two humanities', two classes (AD, 31). Schiller discusses the stakes in light of Kant's third *Critique* which introduces a new type of judgemental structure, one concerning the beautiful, where the understanding no longer determines the sensibility but enters into a 'free play' with it. In his letters *On the Aesthetic Education of Man* Schiller saw this notion of the beautiful as a means to overcome the imbalanced division between the understanding – or the intellectual side of the human being more broadly – and the sensibility and to bring forth a complete and harmonious humanity.

Time of the aesthetic

In Rancière's own conception of emancipation, the aesthetic takes a different form than in Schiller. As I will argue, Rancière nevertheless shares the tendency in Schiller to use the aesthetic in articulating a certain form that resists its temporal ordering. Schiller rearticulates the Kantian faculties into a 'form drive' and a 'sense drive', and the beautiful produces a non-hierarchical relation between them, which Schiller calls the play drive. What the play impulse aims at is, in his words, 'the extinction of time *in time*'.[19] At stake is another way to think the Kantian extra-temporal freedom. It aims to introduce freedom within the sensible reality and think the effectivity of non-temporality within time itself. In an ideal form of aesthetic experience, as Schiller states, there is 'no unprotected part where temporality might break in'.[20]

While not quoting directly Schiller's determined rejections of temporality, Rancière often refers to this aspect in Schiller in the latter's brief discussion of the statue Juno Ludovici in the Fifteenth Letter. In the appearance illustrated through the statue the free play signifies not only 'an activity without goal', but it operates what Rancière describes in another context as a 'subtract[ion] from time' as such.[21] To this aesthetic atemporality Rancière has given a direct political meaning by linking it to the idea of general strike 'where stopping one's arms is no longer the instrument of a particular negotiation but a global secession with respect to one sensible order'. The same paradigm structures the idea of barricade 'which starts by transforming the instruments of circulation (carts at the time [of the Paris Commune]) into elements for building a roadblock and constituting a certain theatrical presence of the worker collective – presence that in itself is anti-strategic' (OA, 211).[22] In line of what we have seen earlier in this chapter, such a theatricality should be understood in terms of stage or staging, which amounts to a presence in space which dismantles the coherence of a process. Now we can see that Rancière associates this to Schiller's idea of play which for the latter signified an 'extinction of time in time'.

However, according to Rancière Schiller is a metapolitical thinker, which means that he conceptualizes a displacement of the logic of emancipation from its existing reality to an underlying rationality.[23] I claim that this is because the introduction of non-temporality within time fails and remains subjected to another temporal scheme. Namely, for Schiller the aesthetic extinction of time is not possible in the present, but it has to be prepared through an educational project oriented towards the future. The metapolitical displacement is first of all a temporal scheme which is supposed to lead to such a future. For Rancière, this stems from Kant's 'Analytic of the Beautiful' itself. Rancière argues that already before its reading by Schiller Kant's theory of beauty expresses a certain fidelity to the idea of equality which would be declared in the French

Revolution of 1789. The traditional view of the society as divided into a class of intelligence and a class dominated by its sense drives cannot offer a framework where equal rights can be granted to both classes. Kant's aim was to articulate a form of intelligibility where such equality would be possible. As Rancière's formulation of the question behind Kant's endeavour stands: 'through what means can an equality of sentiment be brought about that gives the proclaimed equality of rights the conditions of their real exercise?'[24] However, asking for the conditions for bringing about equality sets this project upon a false premise, as it hints that equality is not, and cannot be, applied in the present. As Rancière describes the Kantian-Schillerian gesture, it is '[a] fiction of the possible responding to the fiction of the impossible'.[25] In other words, by the same gesture that equality is being acknowledged, its possibility is placed in future. As two commentators have observed, 'the big difference with Kant', of course, and the latter's Enlightenment predecessors and Romantic heirs is that', for Rancière, the demonstration of equality conceptualized as the aesthetic is possible 'here and now'.[26]

There is no space here for a detailed discussion of Rancière's multiple studies in art and aesthetics, but examples of the cases where Rancière targets his implicit or explicit critique on a certain temporalizing order are not difficult to find. At times this risks being missed, however, as happens in Oliver Davis's otherwise commendable reading of Rancière's study on Mallarmé. Davis emphasizes the logic of 'anticipation' as the democratic core which Rancière detects in the poet's work. As Davis says, 'Rancière tries to save Mallarmé from the "myth" of anti-democratic aloofness ... by insisting on the anticipatory character of Mallarmé's work and the paradox of its solidarity-through-separation with the democratic community to which it looks forward.'[27] More caution would be in place, however, regarding where the ideas of anticipation and forward-looking risk getting entangled with metapolitics. For, to the extent that this anticipation is really taken *as anticipation* it implies an imposition of a futural orientation on the reality to which it relates. As such it appears as a logic of 'preparing the "festivals of the future"' which Rancière sees explicitly as a metapolitical tendency in Mallarmé, that is, one which tends to reject the emancipatory logic in the present.[28] To the extent that Rancière appreciates Mallarmé's anticipatory configurations, he needs to abstract them from properly temporalized forms in order to avoid subjecting their present to a logic which directs them in time. Another example of the same problem Rancière finds in Deleuze and Guattari. After commenting approvingly their characterization of a certain sensible rupture, he is critical of the way this comes '*en vue de* – with a view to and in the hope of – a people which is still lacking'.²⁹ The rupturous present is thus not a manifestation of the capacity of dissensual figures in it but 'a mediation ... for a people to come'.³⁰

Although Rancière speaks of emancipation in terms of anticipation, his simultaneous rejection of any form that would direct or mediate its dissensual present towards some aspect in the future which this present is lacking risks rendering the very idea of anticipation unintelligible.³¹ The concept of anticipation thus marks a tension in Rancière between the basic logic of his thought and the application of that logic to the actual conditions of social and political practice. The answers he gives to questions concerning our contemporary world in one of his more recent books are symptomatic of this: Emancipation, Rancière explains, 'has always been a way to live in the present in another world as much as – or if not more than – to prepare for a world to come.'³² A little later, he states that 'the only way to prepare the future is to not anticipate it, to not plan it but to consolidate forms of subjective dissidence as such'.³³ This is a strange distinction to insist on, and an actual practice of consolidating forms of struggle hardly begs for ignorance to questions of planning or anticipation. Can we really understand our preoccupations in the present by cutting them off from the trajectory leading to a future we desire? And how many of us would be willing to embrace a lack of vision for any such trajectory, rather than consider it a problem?

The core of the emancipatory logic as Rancière sees it, however, cannot be captured in terms of temporal synthesis implicit in the idea of anticipation but rather in terms of a certain 'extinction of time', to quote Schiller again. His consistent rejection to approach any present from the perspective of the futural orientations in it testifies to an attempt to rethink this extinction without Shiller's metapolitical project of humanity's self-education, aiming to 'redeem the fragmented society' (PP, 209). This rethinking amounts to resisting attempts to bring this spatiality under a temporal coherence and is in line with his revocation of the self as an emancipatory framework. To argue this point further, I will now return to the Kantian question of the faculties and Rancière's discussion of them.

Conjunction and disjunction

As mentioned earlier, Rancière's signature concept, *le partage du sensible*, is often defined by him as consisting of a division within the sensible between the sense and the sense that is made of this sense. There is no sensible as such but it is always coupled with the intelligible in which its meaning is given.[34] Thus, the sensible reality comes with a division into two aspects and it is the relation between them which structures reality. The Kantian judgemental structure defined this relation as a relation between the active understanding and the passive sensibility, until such a hierarchical or determining relation was dismantled through the experience of beauty in the third *Critique*. To the extent that the relation is interpreted at the same time as a division between active and passive parts of humanity, the reality, while being shared (*partagée*) by both, is divided (*partagée*) in that it grants some an active and others a passive role within it.

Insofar as Kant defines the experience of time through the hierarchical relation between the faculties within the self, and insofar as the aesthetic problematizes this relation, it problematizes also the structure of temporality itself. I will now argue that Rancière rethinks the aesthetic through introducing disjunctive relations to the aspects or parts whose hierarchical ordering normally renders possible their temporalization.

Rancière sees the different Kantian judgemental forms in terms of conjunction and disjunction: 'The relation is conjunctive when it obeys a certain order of subordination between faculties.'[35] This amounts to determining the object of experience as an object of desire (sensibility) or an object of knowledge (understanding). In social terms this is interpreted either as the leading class subjecting the lower class under its rule or the lower class overturning the relation of domination in a rebellion driven by nothing but its instincts. The only model it thus gives to the revolution is the overturning of the relation between the leaders and the led. If we understand this in terms of the structure of time whose experience Kant describes through reflection of activity upon passivity within the self, conjunctive relation of the faculties or classes allows the structure of time to sustain itself.

Rancière explains that the aesthetic judgement introduces another type of configuration between the faculties/classes where their relation is no longer conjunctive but disjunctive. The disjunctive relation dismantles the passivity-activity relation on which the hierarchy of the conjunctive relation is based. 'This rejection of the hierarchical relation between the faculties that make sense involves a certain neutralization of the social hierarchy' by neutralizing the relation between activity and passivity.³⁶ Following my interpretation in terms of temporality, disjunctive relation is by the same token such that it cannot be brought under a uniform time. It is thus an articulation of a rupture through a coexistence which is not ordered according to the economy of inner sense. By the same token, it produces a form which it is impossible to conceive as a self.

There is one example of this disjunctive relation to which Rancière always returns. This is a joiner Louis-Gabriel Gauny's description of his work day as a floor-layer, written in third person and published in a workers' revolutionary journal during the 1848 Revolution. It is a passage relating an aesthetic experience in the midst of his work, which Rancière reads as a paraphrase of Kant's third *Critique*.

> Believing himself at home, he loves the arrangement of a room so long as he [*tant qu'il*] has not finished laying the floor. If the window opens out on a garden or commands a view of a picturesque horizon, he stops his arms a moment and glides in thought [*plane en idée*] toward the spacious view to enjoy it better than the possessors of the neighboring residences.³⁷

After including this passage in an edited collection of Gauny's writings, Rancière quotes it for the first time in *The Nights of Labor* (1981). When the passage appears in his next book two years later, it is referred explicitly to Kant's third *Critique*, as it would be many times to come.³⁸ According to Rancière, Gauny demonstrates his capacity to free contemplation which does not have a place in the normal configuration of the society where free contemplation belongs to the men of leisure, whose privilege it is to reflect on the ends of the social order.³⁹ As for Gauny, the activity of his class belongs to the realm of means and 'passive' realization of predetermined ends.

Gauny's aesthetic experience signifies for Rancière a disjunction within an activity formed through a nexus of determined ends which forms a unified direction of the social order, modelled according to human soul. Gauny's eyes no longer follow the same end as his body; his experience operates 'a disruption which begins with the disconnection between the activity of the arms and that of the gaze'.[40] '"This is what "disinterestedness" or "indifference" means: the dismantling of a certain body of experience that was well suited to the ethos of the artisan."[41] Such an ethos of the artisan is determined through a structure where the worker subjects his actions to specific ends. At the level of the social order these ends were further subjected to higher ends that were determined by the higher class. In the normal order of domination

> [t]he artisan knows of his condition as the condition of those who have to use their technical knowledge for making objects of needs and desire, thereby leaving to the others the privilege of knowing what the end of making and consuming objects of need and desire is in relation to the superior ends of knowledge.[42]

This passage makes use of the different types of ends according to which an object can be determined, as they are explained in the beginning of Kant's 'Analytic of the Beautiful'. There is the good which is immediately good and the good which is good only as a means to something else. The work of the artisan is occupied with the latter because he belongs to the class for whom it is not possible to have an immediate relation to the good as such, that is, the moral good. As Kant says, '[i]n some human beings there are such strong incentives that it is hard for his intelligence to discipline them.'[43] The only immediacy they are capable of is what Kant calls the agreeable, that is, that which is good for the sense, which pleases the senses.[44]

The artisan thus belongs to the passive class whose activity needs to be subjected to the ends determined by the class of intelligence. Hence the nexus of relations of determination which can all be placed in different ways within the Kantian economy of the determining judgement. What matters to the interpretation I am putting forward here is that the nexus allows a unified temporal direction through reflective relations between activity and passivity – understood as determination of ends and being determined through these ends. This is what establishes the self of the community as well as its uniform existence in time, in which the temporal structure of the artisan's activity follows the overall orientation of the social order. This is where the activities and meanings given to them are in relations which Rancière calls conjunctive.

The aesthetic introduces a sphere which is not in conjunction with determined ends within the existing economy of activities. Gauny enters this sphere while performing at the same time a task designed to fulfil a predetermined end. What matters is the disjunctive relation between a determined activity and the consciousness which accompanies it, whose conjunction normally orients the worker according to a unified social temporality and maintains discipline among the lower classes. The aesthetic disjunction disturbs the class hierarchy by no longer enabling to distribute activity and passivity between them. Rancière interprets Kant's notion of the 'finality without an end' through this disjunction:

> This is what the Kantian 'finality without an end' may mean: a rupture in the chain of the ends and means which is also a rupture in the hierarchies of science and desire. The 'disinterested' look at the palace and the look of the floor-layer through the window disrupt the set of relations linking what people see with what they do, what they do with what they are, and what they are with what they can do and be.[45]

This disjunction is thus a reconfiguration of relations in a way which enables them to escape their determination according to the hierarchical structure of activity and passivity, understanding and sensibility. By the same token, they escape the temporal structure which goes from the reflection of the highest end to the realm of means, all the while stopping the class of sense drive from turning active. In doing so, as I argue, they dismantle the form of time as a structure where activity reflects itself on passivity. While Gauny's experience mixes undetermined reflection with determined activity, his body is no longer the place of passivity upon which the ends of the social order are reflected. Rather, the aesthetic disjunction reveals his capacity to be an intellectual and the worker at the same time.

What the aesthetic disjunction entails is a coexistence which is not ordered according to structures of reflection following the form of time as it appears in the Kantian inner sense (whose internality has nothing to do with an individual subject but absorbs the realm of social experience as well). As such this coexistence becomes a generic space for thinking beings that are equal insofar as they dissociate themselves from the forms by which their milieu is differentiated through temporal coherence of collective reality. Rancière uses the Foucauldian term 'heterotopia' to name this generic and unqualified space of equal capacity to think, but the meaning he gives to it differs from Foucault's concept. For Foucault heterotopias bring together places which are 'in themselves incompatible'.[46] They are places of otherness where the normal order can be subverted or where the abnormal are placed. What most clearly distinguishes them from Rancière's heterotopia, however, is that they are historically constituted places which serve specific functions in the established social order, even though this may be one of transgressing elements of that order. For Rancière, in contrast, heterotopia is not a specific place but rather *any* place whatsoever insofar as it effectuates a dissociation of intelligence from social, historical or geographical determinations. It is a place of the other where the other is 'the effect of a reconfiguration of the distribution of places, identities, capacities'.[47] While for Foucault a heterotopia is 'not freely accessible like a public place', for Rancière it is 'the place of the indeterminate as the place of the whoever, the place that can be occupied by anyone at all'.[48] In contrast to particular places, Rancière's heterotopia is merely a manifestation of the principle that '[t]here is no specific territory of thought'.[49]

Now, if the heterotopic disjunctive relation 'neutralizes the division' between the terms in conjunction, this '*neutralization* is not at all tantamount to *pacification*'.[50] In other words, the disjunction introduces a specific clash between the classes, but this is not one where the class of sensibility would try to subject the intelligent class under its rule (which in Kantian terms would mean making the agreeable, that which pleases the senses, prevail over the moral good). Rather, the conflict is between the temporally undetermined space of infinite substitutability and the social division of labour based on an aim-oriented order. This conflict can be understood as a conflict between the two meanings of *partage*, in the sense of division or distribution on the one hand and in the sense of sharing on the other. It is clear that the social signification of classes is reduced here to an order of intellectual capacities which, for Rancière, conditions the division of social classes. However, to the extent that the blurring of this division takes place through a dismantling of aim-oriented temporality, it is difficult to see how the transition from intellectual equality to overcoming of the social order can take form. But Rancière is committed to remaining within this difficulty: 'Emancipated workers could not repudiate the hierarchical model governing the distribution of activities without taking distance from the capacity to act that subjected them to it, and from the action plans of the engineers of the future.'[51]

Schiller's metapolitics fails to capture this logic and reintroduces the unified time in terms of the humanity reflecting itself. '"Free appearance,"' as Rancière comments on Schiller, 'becomes the product of a human mind which seeks to transform the surface of the sensible appearances into a new sensorium that is the mirror of its own activity' (DS, 118; cf. PA, 27). This means precisely that the Schillerian educational project tends to rearticulate a unified temporality into the disjunctive rupture of the aesthetic, in order to turn humanity into a self where its activity is once again reflected upon its passivity. Hence, Schiller's project 'aims to overcome political dissensus' (AD, 33). An introduction of an aim-oriented process is aimed against emancipation, which for Rancière can exist only in the present.

If the conjunction is to be understood according to the structure which is in accordance with the experience of temporality while the disjunction dismantles such an experience, then the clash between the classes or between the two meaning of *partage* is seen as a conflict with temporal coherence of emancipation as opposed to its presence in space lacking uniform temporality. I claim that what is imposed against temporally determined reality is a certain kind of detemporalized spatial coexistence. While Rancière would not claim that space and time can exist in distinction from each other, the logic of his argument tends to play spatiality against a uniform time. As he describes this in relation to the history of art, when the 'non-relation of means and ends … destroys the representative paradigm of the intelligent form given to inert material [...w]hat collapses at the same time is the principle of correspondence between the poetic art of time and the pictorial art of space'.[52] This collapse of the correspondence between time and space comes with a form where spatiality disturbs its subjection to a temporal order. There is a certain sense in which Rancière seems to understand this in terms of overturning the order of primacy between time and space or, to speak in Kantian terms, of the inner and outer senses. I will now try to unwrap this claim.

The order of primacy between space and time

If time as a form of *inner* intuition has as its object always the self, space is the form of intuiting *outer* appearances. Given the inherent link between time and the self, time has a certain privilege over space in Kant. All our intuitions are in time but only some are in space; while non-spatial appearances are possible, non-temporal are not.[53] Moreover, the appearances which are structured in spatial relations can be related to solely through time and the internality of the self. Or, as Kant himself puts it, we 'deal with' (*befassen*) spatial representations only 'through the mediation' (*vermittelst*) of time.[54] Spatial relations are thus subjected to time, and they are impossible as such. Time cannot be thought on the basis of spatial externality and without structuring it according to the internalized hierarchy within the self. Rancière's project can be understood as an attempt to overturn this relation. This means that the relations within the sensible order do not witness to any internal temporal constitution.

A secondary status given to time can be illustrated by Rancière's discussion of Béla Tarr's films. In them, as Rancière explains, Tarr follows certain inventions of literature which came to being by

> discovering that, with the time of sentences and chapters, there were better things to do than to scan the stages [*étapes*] by which individuals achieve their ends. … It was possible to reconstruct … a little of that which made up the stuff of their lives: how the space in them made time for itself [*comment l'espace en eux se faisait temps*].[55]

This time is then simply the time of action approached spatially, with no scheme according to which it temporalizes itself. It is movement of time purely in the spatial present with no differential relations according to which it would be directed or predicted, projected into the past or future.

This spatial-external approach to time relates to an egalitarian and anonymous understanding of thought. Rancière has recently referred to a specific theme in Sartre, who criticizes the idea of consciousness as something which absorbs things into itself. Sartre describes consciousness as being '[o]utside, in the world, among others. It is not in some hiding-place that we will discover ourselves; it is on the road, in the town, in the midst of the crowd, a thing among things, a human among humans.'[56] Rancière acknowledges his debt to this theme where his 'Sartrean side' lies:

> For me thought is always something that is exposed, written and able to be shared with, and appropriated by, others. […T]he idea that what people have in their heads holds no interest. The only thing of interest is what they do with their thought, the way in which they conduct it materially.[57]

This is also one of the key features in the aesthetic regime of art. 'Thought, then, is no longer the interiority of the subject'; rather, it circulates in the outer space, between objects.[58] Such a scenographical thought includes a revocation of the self in favour of a certain anonymity formed through spatial externality. It deals with 'horizontal circulation of words and images, the way in which they become anonymous and lend themselves to multiple re-appropriations' in line of the literary logic through which I interpreted Rancière's Maoism in the previous chapter (OA, 215). Politics for Rancière has to be thought through such spatiality, which allows 'an identification with anonymity' as opposed to any social identities (MP, 73). Thought no longer unfolds in the combination of the self and time but in space. Unlike in Kant, space is not approached primarily through its mediation by time, but it is taken directly as spatial externality, and it is the spatial externality whose unfolding becomes time. I think that the 'Analytic of the Beautiful' speaks for Rancière of the paradigm of equality which is best understood in such an external spatial sense. The atemporality of the aesthetic experience is not for Rancière some kind of experience of atemporality as such but a spatiality which resists becoming synthesized through time. Before concluding this chapter, I want to briefly comment on one reader of Rancière in a way which allows to make an illuminating point in relation to this discussion.

The missing role of imagination

Joseph J. Tanke poses a question which tends to emerge from Rancière's discussions of Kant's aesthetics: 'in his readings of the aesthetic regime, Rancière discounts the significant role played by imagination.'[59] Tanke himself sets out to articulate a place for imagination that would fit Rancière's understanding of emancipatory politics, rereading Kant and early post-Kantians in light of Rancière. Tanke suggests that the reason for the virtual absence of imagination in Rancière's own work is that the concept is too traditional-philosophical and that it adjusts to reasoning according to models based on subjective faculties.[60] But there may be a more particular and theoretically significant explanation. At times when Rancière summarizes the stakes of the aesthetic judgement, he does follow Kant and puts it in terms of imagination and understanding (e.g. DS, 211). However, when he links it more substantially to his own thought, as in the texts discussed earlier, he prefers terms associated more clearly with passivity and activity. If in Rancière imagination does not have the role it has in the work of Kant himself, I would suggest that it is because imagination is what *mediates* the passive and active faculties whereas Rancière neutralizes them through *disjunction*. Imagination for Kant is after all not a passive capacity as such but an active aspect of otherwise passive sensibility mediating its relation with understanding.[61] Rather than establishing a non-relation between activity and passivity, imagination precisely merges them together.[62] Furthermore, imagination executes this mediation as a capacity of temporalization. As such its function is presented in the section on 'Schematism' of the first *Critique*. The notion of schema introduced there refers to 'the transcendental time-determination' which makes the 'application of the category to appearances … possible'.[63] Such time-determination is the product of imagination which Kant is careful to distinguish from a placeholder of mere images. While the latter are nothing but *spatial* figures, schemata offer the rules for their production, which amount to all possible forms of time-determination.[64] Imagination thus *categorizes* appearances by temporalizing them.

In Kant's third *Critique*, imagination is at work in an undetermined way, in a free play with understanding, obeying no pregiven rules. If Rancière is not fond of this notion, I would suggest that this is nevertheless because of its role as a function of temporal unification. Rancière is not after new forms of temporalization but, again, rupturous logic which does not forge a temporal coherence for collective reality. And it is precisely the failure to see this that risks rendering Tanke's collective imagination into a promise whose deliverer seems to be none other than time itself: 'We are long way from knowing what the imagination is capable of.'[65] This is not far from a gesture that Rancière would label as metapolitical in that it transforms the dissensual present into the promise of a future which comes to overcome this present. For Tanke, the collective imagination would be a capacity which allows 'unforeseeable discourses, gestures, and actions'.[66] But in my view the point for Rancière is not so much the arrival of the unforeseeable as such. What arrives may be unforeseeable but emancipation does not hinge on its arrival; rather, it hinges upon the absence of a need to wait for the arrival of anything. It is, however, such a collective futurity to which emancipation becomes to be linked when it is developed in terms of what is essentially a capacity for temporalization.

A reference to imagination by Rancière in *Mute Speech* (which Tanke does not discuss) is telling in this respect. Rancière refers to it in a discussion of the way the post-Kantians developed Schiller's conception of three ages of poetry, which was calling for a future where life and poetry would be one, overcoming their present separation. Imagination figures here as the capacity which allows this process of transformation to proceed: ' "Imagination" (*Einbildungskraft*) here is to be understood … as the power of *Bildung* that produces "images" which are the forms of life, the moments of a process of education of artistic humanity.'[67] As we saw earlier, while images as such are spatial configurations, their production is a matter of time-determination already in Kant. In imagination, it is then a question of spatial configurations being subjected to, and produced through, a primary function of temporalization. As such it does not allow rupturous or disjunctive relations to appear; it does not allow 'forms in space which are resistant to direction [*sens*]'.[68] Imagination thus signifies precisely the principle under which the equality present in Kant's theorization of beauty in the form of disjunctive relation – and in Gauny's experience of it – is suppressed through an introduction of a process of preparing a future.

* * *

I began this chapter by showing how Rancière thinks the revolution through the notion of the stage which puts emphasis on space as opposed to temporal schemes that would allow to predict or direct its course. Such temporal synthesis was operative in the concept of the self and the reflexivity it includes. I then developed this opposition of spatiality and the self through Kant to suggest a specific way in which the theme runs through Rancière's basic ideas concerning Kantian aesthetics. Rancière's reading of the aesthetic judgement could then be seen to lean on an idea of spatiality which rejects a synthesis that would situate it in time or temporalize it. Therefore, as I came to suggest, he is reluctant to develop his position in terms of imagination. In order to avoid mediating that takes place in space according to forms of time, he wants to dissociate space as a form of outer intuition from its synthesis in imagination.

But how should we understand such an emphasis on spatial externality? Is it just a movement of sensible presence as such, an externally perceived space-time with no account of its internal intelligibility?

Recently Rancière has associated the notion of the stage increasingly to the method of his thought. Staging, as he explains, concerns weaving together links in order to create both a certain sensible community and an 'intellectual community that makes such weaving thinkable' (A, xi). Now, our question concerns the way we should grasp this intellectual community whose existence consists in this activity of staging. What is the internal intelligibility of such an activity? To understand it, we need to go beyond the presence of a moving space-time. Another recent description of the method will clarify. 'The stage', Rancière now explains, belongs 'to what I call a method of equality because it ... destroys the hierarchies between the levels of reality'. What matters to us here is that these levels are also realities differentiated in historical time: a stage 'creates a transversal homogeneity in relation to ... historical contextualizations' (ME, 67/123, tm). Thus, as Rancière explains, the network of links it creates are not 'causal plots [*intrigues de causalité*] or even simply plots arranged in historical terms according to "before" and "after" [*intrigues d'avant et après en termes historiques*]' (ME, 29/59, tm). This means that the stage can be understood as a certain cross-historical sphere of egalitarian coexistence that exceeds the context of any specific space-time. Consequently, the primacy of space in Rancière should be extended to concern that which is spatio-temporally absent or inactual, by allowing it to construct the intelligibility of a cross-historical coexistence *as if* it was present at the moment of its historical construction. In the next chapter I will start tracing such a sphere setting out from Rancière's 1990s discussions of temporality in terms of anachronism.

4

Time and its discontents

In the previous chapter, we saw how space as a form of externality was emphasized in Rancière's notion of the stage and how his use of Kantian aesthetics could likewise be seen to be based on a certain emphasis of spatial externality over time. The question that was left hanging was how exactly we should understand the internal intelligibility of such an external-spatial emphasis, which in the end risked becoming a mere sensible reception of its unfolding as an empirical space-time. However, as we saw at the end of the chapter, the idea of stage also concerns its historical intelligibility in a way which avoids treating historical time according to 'before' and 'after', as Rancière put it. In this chapter I will set out to discuss the most important notion according to which Rancière thinks the temporality at work in history, namely 'anachronism' (or '*anachronie*', which Rancière sometimes prefers, or 'untimeliness', which he at times uses interchangeably with it).[1] I will argue that it should be understood not so much as a form of temporality but rather as a notion through which spatiality is extended to concern historical 'time', forming a kind of virtual cross-historical sphere for emancipation which brackets temporal differences. Insofar as this spatial understanding of history serves to think the principle of equality beyond temporal qualifications, it can be characterized as eternal. Abstract space hence serves as a certain eternity-function in Rancière's work.

In the second part of this chapter, I move to discuss the coexistence of multiple temporalities which Rancière conceptualizes with the notion of *anachronie*. Rancière links this question of coexistence of multiple times in one 'time' explicitly to his Althusserian background. Hence, I will address the question of cross-historical abstract space to assess Rancière's relation to Althusser's legacy on the question of multiplicity of times. Through a comparative discussion of Peter Osborne's notion of the contemporary, I will argue that Rancière's project should be seen to affirm Althusser's alleged 'failure' to think historical time in the singular in order to re-elaborate 'theory' as a generic intellectual capacity to break out from historical-temporal situatedness. I will then end this chapter by pointing out the symptomatic proximity of Rancière's notion of *anachronie* to that of *achronie* as another sign of its ultimate orientation towards an idea of thought and thinking beings as timeless.

Time, anachronism, eternity

The ambiguities of Rancière's approach to time become most evident in his discussions of anachronism. The topic has received some enthusiastic attention in the secondary literature where it has been hailed as a proof of 'the importance of time' in Rancière and used as a response to the critics who have pointed out allegedly ahistorical elements in his thought.[2] True, anyone who makes the claim of Rancière as a thinker who downplays time is obliged to work through his views on historical time developed to a large part through engagements with anachronism. These engagements continue the problematic of *The Names of History* and are developed in some shorter writings, most notably in 'The Concept of Anachronism and the Historian's Truth' (1996). I will not try to claim that time would be an unimportant question for Rancière. What I want to argue is that the question is posed only to approach it from a logic that aims not only to bracket any determining forms of temporality but also to avoid replacing them with new temporalizing forms.

As the subtitle of *The Names of History* indicates, the book provided a certain theory of 'the poetics of knowledge'. What lies under the poetics of the science of history is 'a knot of philosophical questions which ... concerns ... the relations of time, speech, and truth' (C, 22). These questions are not addressed as such, but they lie hidden in the poetic operations of the historian's writing through which a prohibition of anachronism is at work as 'a clandestine ontological argument' (C, 44). It can be claimed that Rancière's analysis of the poetics of historical knowledge and his search for alternative ways to write history do not state clearly what the philosophical implications of his own discourse are, concerning 'the relations of time, speech, and truth' (C, 22). I am interested in these implications.

The possible in time

Overall, Rancière's argument is a critique of a construction of the human being as a being whose forms of thought and action are tied to its time and a human coexistence which is likewise limited by temporal constraints. The most developed branch of the argument sets out from the claim Lucien Febvre makes in his book *The Problem of Unbelief in the Sixteenth Century: The Religion of Rabelais* according to which it is impossible for Rabelais to not have been a believer in Christian faith. The conditions of possibility for unbelieving were not available in his time which was thoroughly defined by Christianity. To claim the opposite would be to commit 'the worst of all sins, the sin that cannot be forgiven – anachronism'.[3] As another example of the same logic, Rancière refers to Paul Veyne's statements concerning Jesus and the Sermon of the Mountain, which according to Veyne could not express anything else than the Jewish mentality of the time. 'Jesus could only be a Jew of his time, Rabelais a Christian of his' (C, 36).

The broad polemic is thus against the idea that specific conditions of thought are tied to specific eras, that only certain utterances – and by extension actions – can be 'true' or intelligible in a given time. As Kristin Ross has pointed out, this argument could be targeted also to Foucault's concept of the episteme.[4] His distinction between different epistemes produced an idea of temporally distributed 'configurations within the space of knowledge' due to which '[t]he order on the basis of which we think today does not have the same mode of being as that of the classical thinkers'.[5] Foucault was criticized by not allowing to think 'change' or transition between different epistemes. He did not accept this critique as adequate, and Rancière has not criticized Foucault in these terms per se. Rancière has, however, distanced himself from Foucault's idea of temporally circumscribed, closed forms of thought, included within Foucault's historical epistemology.[6] Rancière's critique of Febvre's prohibition of anachronism can be understood along similar lines.

Rancière claims that what such stable forms of thought do is to eternalize time. He refers in this respect to the Platonic view of time as 'the mobile image of immobile eternity', claiming that this view is operative in the prohibition of anachronism upon which the historical science founds itself. In the face of such eternalization, Rancière's argument tends to *appear* as an ode to time and a determined rejection of that which is not time, that is, eternity, and the way eternity functions in historians' discourse to stabilize time. As he says, Febvre's goal, in accordance with the Platonic definition, 'is to abolish succession as such and to put in its place an image as similar as possible to the eternity of truth' (C, 25). To break out from this 'eternalized time' would be to allow it to move on, to think *time* properly speaking, that is, time in which a change of the course of things can occur (C, 46). The target of critique would thus seem clear enough: immobilization of time and rejection of change through a reference to eternity. Rancière's own position would thus seem to be: we are in time, everything changes and it is this liberating power of time that the historians have tried to neutralize; and their attempt is crystallized in the prohibition of anachronism. As Oliver Davis puts it, Rancière's primary motive is to attack reasonings which bar 'revolutionary *change*' where his own interest lies.[7] Although Davis is right to point out that in the background of Rancière's discussion of Febvre is the question of the French Revolution (which I will discuss in the next chapter), one cannot help noticing that the word 'change' is virtually absent not only in the article on anachronism but also in *The Names of History*. Although Rancière no doubt to some extent conceives his thought here to put importance to the dynamics of time, I want to show that there is also a tendency at work in it which resists such an emphasis, and that this tendency is more fundamental to his basic commitment to equality.

In an earlier article where the argument against the prohibition of anachronism starts to take shape, this prohibition is attached to a specific regime of history. This regime is compared to a different regime, characteristic to the classical social science where the becoming possible of the impossible is assigned to the movement of history. Following the Enlightenment conceptions of education, it is there a question of 'the temporalization of the truth'.[8] This means that new truths can emerge through a process of development of their conditions of possibility in history. Time was thus approached through what was developing in it. In contrast to this, the view represented by Febvre implies 'the impossibility of there ever beginning a time which would render possible a time of rupture with the time of impossibility [*l'impossibilité que commence jamais le temps qui rendrait possible le temps de la rupture avec le temps de l'impossibilité*].[9] Although Rancière might be more sympathetic to the idea of temporal development of the conditions of possibilities for historical novelty, which characterizes also the Marxist emancipatory project, than an idea of its straightforward impossibility, he is in no way aiming to restore the idea of temporal movement where new possibilities would develop.

Not satisfied with the idea of either stabilized periods or temporal becoming of the possible, Rancière comes to suggest that we should be able to think the event as an eruption of the impossible, or of the real:

> What in fact opposes the one and the other is a thought which ties truth to time without passing through the category of the possible, in leaning on the event as an im-possible [*im-possible*] act of singularity.[10]

In a footnote Rancière acknowledges the proximity of this idea with Alain Badiou's notion of the event.[11] However, in Badiou the event is conceptualized along with a scheme of temporalization which comes to realize the possibilities that it introduces through its vanishing punctuality that is retroactively constructed as a beginning of a truth-process. Already in 1989, reviewing Badiou's *Being and Event*, Rancière criticized the way Badiou frames the problem of politics according to a 'pure question of the construction of time'.[12] Badiou's event is an eruption of that which is not possible according to the situation which precedes it and where the event comes to open a temporal horizon of new possibilities which are realized in the process of drawing its consequences. The '*discipline* of time' amounts to a process faithful to the event as the beginning of the new.[13] Badiou is careful to relativize this beginning against any idea of 'a primal event, or a radical beginning'.[14] But for Rancière this is not enough. He goes further in insisting that, rather than figures of beginning and end properly speaking, there is 'the democratic banality of the experience of time which is that of birth [*génération*] and death'.[15] This naturalization of time should be understood as aiming to render it irrelevant for the formation of political and historical possibilities. Just like the idea of beginning here, Rancière has recently downplayed also the idea of qualitative novelty characterizing it as '*une fétichisation du nouveau*'.[16]

Thus, the extent to which Rancière's idea of the event could be developed in the Badiouian direction appears rather limited. It is no wonder that in the

1996 article on 'The Concept of Anachronism' where the discussion of Febvre's prohibition of anachronism is further advanced, Rancière no longer speaks about the event as the realization of that which is impossible. This is also more in line with Rancière's overall position which he has often described in terms of an attempt 'to think the conditions of possibility of such and such a form of statement or such and such an object's constitution', rather than locate sudden emergences of the impossible.[17]

Hence, when Rancière states that it is 'a matter of questioning the connection between time, the possible and truth', I would like to argue that it is not so much a question of time and truth without reference to the possible but rather thinking the possible without ordering it according to time, be it in terms of a punctual eruption, process of development or discontinuous stages (C, 46). 'The historian ... does not have to identify the conditions of possibility and impossibility *with the form of time*' (C, 45/66, tm, emphasis added). Thus, 'the path along which speakers devote themselves to the truth of their speech' or 'the way in which fabrics of speech create truth [*la manière dont des tissus de parole font vérité*]' in history is linked to a different logic of the possible (NH, 96/194; GF, 85). As we will shortly see, this different logic is sourced from spatiality which allows Rancière to follow the detemporalizing tendency present in his work.

Space allows to connect and combine what is held separate by temporal distance. And it is such combining where for Rancière lie the stakes in history and historical existence. The problem, I claim, is much less the beginning of something new, much less the question of change, than overcoming differentiations of modes of being and thought. When Rancière says that we need 'to undo ... the knot of time with the possible', we should not read this as an attempt to think time that allows to go beyond what is held possible but to think the possible in a way which is not temporally formed (C, 46). Rancière does not attack the prohibition of anachronism because it bars change but first of all because it bars egalitarian coexistence. The ultimate target of critique in Rancière's discussion of anachronism is the idea that historical actors

> lived in another temporal universe, that is, in another universe of thought, where one [– i.e. Rabelais according to Febvre –] didn't have time to be a

non-believer. The historian ... uses specific stylistic procedures which separate this time from ours and makes it coagulate with itself [*coaguler avec lui-même*].[18]

In other words, for the historian from whose position Rancière dissociates himself, there is resemblance and co-belonging between historical subjects only to the extent that they belong to the same time. Rather than each other, '[h]istorical subjects must "resemble" their time' (C, 34). The fundamental orientation of Rancière's argument draws towards a principle of coexistence which is not temporal, rather than towards time where change is possible.

This point becomes clearer in a recent article where Rancière revisits his earlier discussion of Febvre and anachronism. Rancière now argues that the meaning of Febvre's historiography lies in the way it suppresses the idea of modern fiction theorized and practiced by Virginia Woolf. At the core of Woolf's idea was a 'simultaneity' as 'the presence of several times', rather than change, novelty or temporal sequence. It is to such a simultaneous togetherness of different times that Febvre then contrasted a 'homogeneous time' circumscribed within the limits of a given era.[19] Hence, in Rancière's argument concerning anachronism, it is a question of the form of the possible which is the possibility of egalitarian coexistence. Rather than the possibility of difference, it is a question of the possibility of the same, or the equal, in terms of bypassing or ignoring temporal differentiations.

The possible in space

Rancière makes a certain use of space in his discussion of Febvre and anachronism. After pointing out the narrative continuity between Plato's *Timaeus* – where the famous principle of time as a moving image of eternity is stated – and his *Republic*, Rancière turns to one of his favourite themes in the Western philosophical canon. This concerns Plato's seemingly trivial statements concerning artisans' lack of time in the latter dialogue. Workers, Plato says, do not have time to be anywhere else than their workplace. Rancière's first engagement with this assertion is found in *The Philosopher and His Poor* (1983) and follows his major book on nineteenth-century French workers, *The Nights of Labour* (1981). This latter book describes the blurring of the workers' class position by turning the perspective to 'free time' that they acquire by staying up at night, instead of spending their nights for sleeping and getting rest, that is, for reproduction of the labour power that they are paid for.[20] *The Philosopher and His Poor*, published two years later, deals with the question of time from another perspective, setting out from the theme of the lack of time in *Republic*. The idea Rancière puts forward there is that the workers, or the poor, are those who have, at least from the times of Plato, been marked by an absence of time for anything else than work, which excludes them from the practice of a capacity of active reflection concerning the use of time.

This understanding of the time of workers is essentially topographical. In the discussion of Plato it is attached to a concrete question of the spatial order of *polis* interlinked with a symbolic topography of different occupations that matches with capacities and times to occupy them and with certain bodies marked with them. This topography divides the time of those who have leisure for philosophical questions and those who need to spend their time in manual labour. Plato's artisans 'have no time to be elsewhere than the place [they] are geared for occupying—which means that [they] have no time to chat on the agora, make decisions in the assembly, or look at shadows in theaters'.[21] It is this spatial-distributive understanding of time, where a symbolic topography mirrors the spatial order of the city, that we encounter again in 'The Concept of Anachronism':

> Time ... separates the different ways in which to take part in the task of the city, which is that of imitating the eternity of justice in the time of human affairs. On the one hand, there are those who have time to concern themselves with contemplation of the divine model and the forms of its temporal realisation. On the other hand, there are those who have not the time for this, and who, as a consequence, only imitate eternity passively, by the fact of not having the time to do anything but the work to which their nature predestines them. (C, 38–9/62–3, tm)

There is thus a division of times into free and determined time, which corresponds to active and passive relation with eternal principles. It is a division between a capacity to decide how eternity is modelled in time and how to act according to eternal justice on one hand and a necessity to submit to such decisions passively on the other. Rancière holds this analogous with the division that the historian produces in his discourse, transferring Plato's conceptualization of *polis* to the historical discourse and the differentiation of times it operates with:

> The scientific city of the modern human and social sciences is modelled on the Platonic philosophical city. In this city of the modern human and social sciences the relation of the temporal order to the order of eternity must be assured by specialists according to a strict distribution. (C, 39)

The Platonic spatial order which differentiates between free time reserved for the aristocratic class and determined time reserved for artisans thus also characterizes the historical rationality based on the prohibition of anachronism, that is, of confusion of historical times. The Platonic model allows Rancière to picture different times in the same sphere of actuality. Therefore, it allows picturing the transgression of the situatedness in a determined (historical) time as a displacement between times which are equally present in space:

> What threatens the Platonic philosophical city are the artisans who escape their condition, who want to occupy themselves with more than their 'own affairs', and engage with the affairs of the city, even the affairs of philosophy. Likewise, what threatens the scientific city of history are words and thoughts that leave behind the strict obedience to belief similar to time. (C, 39)

It is indeed striking how Rancière posits this spatial model directly against the historical rationality that he is criticizing. The threat for Plato is that artisans leave the occupations that the order of the city reserves for them and claim equal share on the affairs of the city, an equal say on eternal principles. Analogously, the threat for the historian is that historical actors 'leave' the forms of thought reserved to them ('belief similar to [their] time') by the historian.

According to the logic of Rancière's argument, the historical actor is then no longer subjected to forms of thought attached to a specific historical period. Instead, she appears as an agent possessing the same intelligence than the historian, capable of the same forms of thought. The historico-temporal differentiations concerning a given era are bracketed and a certain historical actor taken *as if* she belonged to the same present with the historian. Space as a dimension where, in Kant's words, '[a]ll things are next to one another' serves as a sphere of actuality, or quasi-actuality, that renders differences equally available in the same sphere.[22]

This spatial metaphor is crucial in Rancière's discussions of the relations of the possible and time in the 1990s. It paves way to his more recent use of spatial terms precisely to describe the ways he conceives the forming of the possible. Thus, Rancière speaks of a 'topography of the possible' or 'a landscape of the possible' that his writings aim to paint.[23] He takes as his task to always reframe a 'map of that which ... is possible' (GF, 577). We have seen in Chapter 2 that Rancière criticized the *nouveaux philosophes* for their cartographic thinking. If a certain idea of cartography returns in Rancière, the point is that it no longer concerns maps structured, like the Foucauldian epistemes, by 'grids of time' but in contrast frees them into a cross-historical coexistence of equal intelligence.[24] The poetics of historical knowledge that Rancière develops in the 1990s through his critique of historians like Febvre aims to simply bracket time in order to avoid limiting and differentiating conditions of possibilities of thought through their historicization. This relates directly to the logic of political emancipation in Rancière which Alain Badiou has described as follows: 'The virtual city of equal collectivity, separates itself suddenly, while at the same time remaining in contact with the "police", that is, with the established socio-historical order.[25] We can now see that this virtual city of equality is not temporally situated, but it opens a cross-historical coexistence into a specific historical situation, a specific historical time.

As the passages quoted earlier concerning the Platonic model of the city show, it is a question of a division of those who have an active relation to eternal principles and those who need to obey them passively. Rancière's use of this metaphor tends to render the status of eternity in his argument rather ambiguous. If the discussion of anachronism set out to criticize the idea of 'eternalized time' behind Febvre's prohibition of it, Rancière's use of Plato tends to picture a transgression of this eternalization not so much in terms of temporal change than as a certain claim to equal share of *eternal* principles. Indeed, the way Rancière models his discussion according to space renders the distinction between time and eternity difficult to sustain.

Eternity-function

Rancière has stated that historians' rejection of anachronism amounts to a fear of the speaking being and added that this fear stems from the fact that, with such a being, they are engaged with time (GF, 79). Thus, as I acknowledged already in the beginning of this chapter, Rancière's discussion of anachronism might indeed appear as an argument for time and against any eternalizing rationalizations. Yet, I have suggested that the relation between time and eternity tends to appear ambiguous due to the use of spatiality that Rancière leans on through his reference to Plato in his discussion of anachronism. Furthermore, if we accept my general claim that Rancière's dismantling of the prohibition of anachronism rejects any particularization or differentiation of the forms of thought by time, it seems to leave an ambiguous meaning to that which is not time, that is, the eternal. For, to dismantle time's capacity to impose differentiations seems to implicate a quasi-eternal status for the sphere of overcoming those differentiations, which, as I have shown, appears as a certain cross-temporal sphere of intelligibility modelled according to space.

This ambiguity in relation to temporality on one hand and eternity on the other can also be traced in the ways Rancière describes anachronistic use of words. On one hand, they are presented in terms where temporal horizons come to overlap: 'To affirm oneself as a speaking being ... implies that one renames oneself and requalifies one's situation with words borrowed from others and other times.'[26] This is why 'there are different times that overlap [*se télescopent*], ... there is ... future in the present, because there is also present that repeats the past, because there are different temporalities in the "same" time' (GF, 82). This temporal non-coincidence has been linked by Oliver Davis to the Heideggerian tradition and thus been read as a testimony of an essentially *temporal* form of the existence of historical actor.[27]

However, one can also find in Rancière references to the use of words in history which lean on the notion of eternity in a positive sense and aim less to its rejection than the rejection of its specific forming according to time. Thus, Rancière speaks of 'bodies seized by the eternity's externality to time [*hors-temps de l'éternité*]', as they are seized by words that belong to other times.[28] As he states, anachronistic words 'short-circuit the appropriate [*bon*] relation of time to eternity' (C, 39/63, tm). In other words, such a use of words makes relation with eternity in a way which bypasses the way this relation is formed in a specific time. Thus, as I want to insist, Rancière's point here is not to describe a form of differential temporality that would shape the relations of coexisting times and the being of the historical actor.[29] What Rancière is in the end interested in is not speaking the truth of or in time but speaking the truth tout court.[30] He is not interested in temporal conditions of historical action but a capacity of self-authorized action. This is why his argument retains a positive relation to 'eternity'. This relation is according to me absolutely vital for Rancière. For the ultimate intelligibility behind the idea of words borrowed from other times is to bracket time, to think *as if* temporal differences were not relevant and to think *as if* the realm of thought would be eternal. It serves to model a certain 'eternity-function' to be played out in time against time.

We should also read in this light Rancière's discussion in *The Names of History* of the heretical relation to the Scripture, which, as Rancière argues, the historian of mentalities turns into an expression of peasant culture. The historian approaches heretics by simply exchanging the determining role of the Church *of a given time* with the determining role of peasant culture *of a given time*. What Rancière wants to think about is the relation to the Scripture of the heretic as such – who is for Rancière the paradigm of historical actor – without a mediating role of institutions or established orders belonging to a given time (NH, 88–9; cf. GF, 70). This should remind us of the way Mao's texts were read during the Cultural Revolution, short-circuiting not only the leading role of the authorities but also the specific contextualizations that they would have been able to provide for instruction. Mao's writings which stemmed from specific historical contexts thus became de facto trans-historical scripts for revolution.[31] This describes then a certain eternity-function which is not mediated and limited by the temporally distributed regime of the possible. Words that are used anachronistically serve to model such a relation. Once again, the logic of Rancière's argument does not aim to think specific forms of temporality but is a way to think a sphere of the possible that exceeds given temporalizations, that is not subjected to temporal evolutions and can in this sense be understood as quasi-eternal. Spatiality, understood as a cross-historical sphere, serves to mobilize this eternity-function. It serves as a dimension where the eternal is available to time in ways which are not readily determined, in the very form of 'eternal' availability of different 'times' to each other.

Achronie

The positive idea of eternity which seems to be at work in Ranière's discussion of anachronism or '*anachronie*' can be further clarified with a reference to the notion of '*achronie*', or non-time. There seems to be a certain symptomatic link between the two terms, and by tracing this link, I want to argue against an understanding of anachronism in Rancière as a kind of strategic notion, which would imply a specific historical consciousness. In contrast, I claim that Rancière's use of anachronism is best captured as a notion which orients towards ideas of human intelligence as essentially non-temporal or timeless.

Despite the appearance of anachronism in a positive sense in Rancière and its enthusiastic reception in the secondary literature, it is not really an adequate concept for Rancière. This is partly clear in the very article on 'The Concept of Anachronism': 'There is no anachronism', as Rancière states there. He continues, however, saying that

> there are modes of connection that in a positive sense we can call anachronies: events, ideas, significations that are contrary to time [*prennent le temps à rebours*], that make meaning [*sens*] circulate in a way that escapes any contemporaneity, any identity of time with 'itself'. An anachronie is a word, an event, or a signifying sequence that has left 'its' time, and is thus endowed with the capacity to define new temporal switching points [*les aiguillages*], to carry out leaps from one temporal line to another. And it is because of these switching points, these jumps and these connections that there exists a power to 'make' history. The multiplicity of temporal lines, even of meanings [*sens*] of time, included in the 'same' time is the condition of historical activity. (C, 47–4/67–6, tm)

At the end of the day, anachronism, or untimeliness, is of course thinkable only if we acknowledge some kind of unity of time in relation to which anachronisms are understood, thus rendering anachronism into a specific form of temporality. Such a temporality could then mark a specific period or an existential or ontological structure.[32] My claim is, however, that when Rancière talks about anachronism it cannot be grasped as a form of temporality. The leaps between times, that 'we can call *anachronies*', should not be thought in temporal terms but rather as points of non-time within time, points which draw connections between elements that exist in different times while bracketing their very temporal existence.

As a matter of fact, in the literature that has mentioned Rancière's discourse on the question, one finds a reference to a term which better shows his fundamental intuition: *achronie*. In a text from 1993 entitled 'Éloge de l'anachronisme en histoire' Nicole Loraux is promoting a certain use of anachronism in historical discourse. Referring to the general view among the historians that anachronism is to be considered 'the principle sin' in their discipline, she says:

> Indeed, such censorship prohibits any consideration of 'another time' inside of the time of historians – this other time which Jacques Rancière named in a recent study '*achronie*' and of which I say for now that it is this time that one experiences when the time is, in a very Shakespearean manner 'out of joint', this other time that one has to in any case postulate if only to give a status to all that which, in a given epoch, thinks ahead of itself, in the mode of anticipation.[33]

Loraux is referring to an oral presentation given by Rancière in 1991–2.[34] It is thus reasonable to assume that before Rancière chose to use 'anachronism' and derivative terms, he considered '*achronie*' as a more suitable name for what he is after. It is curious that the form of 'other time' is given a name of 'non-time' or 'timelessness'.[35]

The word '*achronie*' is used by Gérard Genette in his analyses of different forms of anachronisms as a means of 'emancipation' from narrative temporality in Proust's *In Search of Lost Time* through transgression of the chronological order.[36] The concluding section of his essay is entitled 'Vers l'achronie'. There Genette concludes that Proust's work includes not only complicated structures consisting of overlappings of different forms of anachronism which 'tend to disrupt somewhat the reassuring notions of retrospection and anticipation' but also forms which invoke 'existence of temporally indefinite narrative segments'. In addition to these there are '*achronies*'. These are defined as events whose temporality remains fully indeterminate, events '*sans date et sans âge*'.[37]

In Rancière, who appears to have first used *achronie* to name what he later coined as *anachronie*, the two cannot be fully distinguished, and the non-time is at work in his discourse of anachronism. There are two perspectives at work, one that tries to demonstrate timeless equality between speaking and thinking beings and another which tries to situate its expressions in time. From the first perspective this situatedness appears as *achronie*, non-time, in the midst of time; from the second perspective, it appears as anachronism, as a temporal displacement. As he has stated in an interview, when explaining how old words can be used in new historical contexts and thus acquire transgressive power, '[i]t is by phrasing these ageless words that the proletarian starts to speak' (ME, 73/133, tm). The words used out of context are understood to be words '*sans âge*', a phrase used also by Genette to describe *achronie*. It is a question of what I have suggested to call eternity-function earlier. That is, words that are immanent to history – and in this sense have a history – are used in a way which brackets this history. What Rancière calls 'anachronie' aims to do justice to this bracketing, that is, to a capacity to act in time in a (quasi-)timeless way.

What Rancière is really getting at is the action of the speaking being which does not arise from its being in time and is not constrained by time but demonstrates its capacity to think independently of any historical context in which it thinks and acts. To draw philosophical conclusions from Rancière's discourse, we should thus reach beyond Genette's narrative category, to an earlier use of the Greek word for non-time. The philosophical implications of Rancière's critique of historians' discourse become more visible in reference, for example, to Plotinus's use of '*achronos*' in reference to thought. As he says, 'every act of intelligence is timeless [*achronos pasa noēsis*]'. In the site of intelligence, 'each and every thing is present [*estin hekaston paron*]', and 'there is no discursive thought or transition from one to the other [*oude diexodos oude metabasis aph' heterou ep' allo*]'.[38] The 'discursive thought', *diexodos*, means here an aim-oriented speech which moves in time towards a specific goal.[39]

Rancière's acknowledgement of anachronism or untimeliness is thus related to something more radical, that is, to a detachment of intellectual acts – as that which makes emancipatory practice possible – from temporality. His idea of untimeliness is less a temporal category which structures specific historical periods than an idea which describes equality of thought as unsuitable for temporalization.

Let us take, for example, Rancière's recent 'Postface' for a re-edition of *La Parole ouvrière*, a collection of workers' discourses that he edited with Alain Faure in 1976. At the time, the tendency to think equality as a radical dissociation of historical time had not yet taken form and Rancière's thought of workers' emancipation was more closely linked to the actualities of the social dimension.[40] After explaining, in the new postface, the sociopolitical context from which the research leading to the publication of the anthology had set out, Rancière admits that one can question its relevance in 2007. It would be easy, he explains, to point out that the workers' struggles of the nineteenth century bears very little interest from today's perspective. If they had some relevance in the immediate post-68 context, by now they have lost all actuality. He then states that if one pays attention to different aspects one could instead claim that the analogy with the situation in the organization of labour today could say something about the relations between the social order and the workers' struggles. 'But', Rancière then concludes,

> these forms of actuality and inactuality do not touch the core of the problem. To be sure, *La Parole ouvrière* was written in a time where workers' struggles and the hope for emancipation were more present than today. But at the same time, the choice to show thought at work there where one expected to find popular effervescence made this anthology inactual. This inactuality remains today just as strong as yesterday. Equality of intelligences remains the untimeliest [*la plus intempestive*] of the ideas which one can feed to the social order [*que l'on puisse nourrir sur l'ordre social*].[41]

What is crucial here is that equality of intelligences appears to bypass any questions of not only timeliness but also untimeliness in the sense where a *specific* image of the past would manage to resonate with a *specific* feature of the present. Such a feature would be the precarious conditions of the nineteenth-century workers, and they would resonate with the precarious working conditions of today. To bring the two together would then be a way to adjust the specific visions and practices of emancipation of the former time to their absence in the latter time. This would be a practice of anachronism that would be first of all 'about time, not outside it or beyond it', as Kristin Ross describes the Rancièrian untimeliness.[42] In it, as she argues, 'particular actions and points of view' must be 'resuscitated with care and attention'. Past times can 'be mobilized against dominant ideology. Provided of course that the right transversals are created.'[43]

This kind of carefully designed anachronism implies another temporal vision to counter a specific time. Furthermore, it assumes specific effects for bringing the two times together and thus necessarily some kind of temporal unification of the two which also marks the time of the untimely action itself as well as that of the actor. This kind of strategic untimeliness is absent in neither Rancière nor his readers.[44] In my view, however, it does not allow to see what is distinctive in the logic of Rancière's position. And, as we can see, Rancière shows a certain frustration to this kind of thinking: the questions of *specific* relations between different times, that would allow or not an effective anachronism 'do not touch the core of the problem', as he writes in the passage quoted earlier. They are too much linked to a *temporalizing* perspective, while equality of intelligences, on the basis of which Rancière thinks emancipatory practice, is, as I would claim, unsuitable to any time, unsuitable to temporal order as such, unsuitable to temporalizing reason. It is no longer untimely because it refers to another time. Rather, it is untimely because, while appearing in time, it belongs to no time.

Geneviève Fraisse, Rancière's colleague from *Les Révoltes logiques* collective, has linked this kind of timelessness to the radical Cartesianism of Poullain de la Barre. Poullain was an early feminist thinker who drew radical conclusions from the Cartesian *cogito* as dissociated from the bodily substance and argued that the mind 'has no sex. Considered independently, the mind is found to be equal and of the same nature in all men, and capable of all kinds of thought.'[45] Rancière has compared Poullain's radicalization of Cartesianism to that of Jacotot who

> draws from the Cartesian *bon sens* a fundamental idea: there are no several ways to be intelligent, no division between two forms of intelligence, that is, between two forms of humanity. Equality of intelligences is first of all equality of intelligence to itself [*égalité à soi de l'intelligence*] in all its operations. (GF, 412, cf. IS, 16).

In bracketing bodily differences, the imposition of equality as the basic logic of emancipation also bypasses historico-temporal differentiations which cannot touch human intelligence. This is why Fraisse has said of Poullain's feminism that it is 'from no time [*d'aucun temps*]'. While fascinated by Poullain's radicality, Fraisse notes that it implies a necessary 'abstraction of history'. And, '[f]or the one who seeks to historicize the question of the sexes, a logician of equality appears to be more enigmatic than one might have expected'.[46] Poullain's radicality is both welcome and problematic, for it does not allow to historicize itself, making it difficult to articulate it in relation to historically mediated, specific social relations with which the sex difference is always entangled.[47]

A similar enigma haunts Rancière's discourse which cannot be taken as a straightforwardly historicizing work or a work that gives unambiguous importance to time. To be sure, we are in time and the basic characteristics of time is that it differentiates or models things according to ordered differences. Anyone who puts primacy on time needs to subject being to a logic of differentiation. What Rancière does is best understood from the opposite angle. Thus, he emphasizes the same and the ways the same disturbs or bypasses temporal evolutions. This is also why his discourse on anachronism, while giving a certain positive sense to it, at the same time needs to state that there is no anachronism. In a word, his discourse on anachronism draws towards the idea of *achronie* which we should understand according to the timelessness of human intelligence.

Althusserian legacies

To counter critiques of anachronism amounts for Rancière to an attempt to acknowledge a certain kind of coexistence of different times within the same present. There is 'difference of temporalities in one and the same present', for 'every present is defined by anachronies'.[48] The approach to history through the idea of coexistence of different times is a theme through which Rancière is in broad continuity with Althusser's problematic whose notion of historical time, as we saw in Chapter 1, was based on such an idea. Recently Rancière has claimed to have 'been more faithful to that idea than Althusser was himself' (ME, 47–8). What I have tried to show in this chapter, however, is that the logic of Rancière's thought in this respect is driving towards a coexistence which tries to bracket temporality altogether. Thus, when he says that there are 'different temporalities in a "same" time [*dans un 'même' temps*]', the 'same' cannot be grasped as time (GF, 82).[49]

The present defined by multiple times is for Rancière one which has other times at its disposal but which is at the same time dissociated from any specific temporal form. As he puts it, the present 'is required to compensate for the lack of its own time'.[50] The act of this compensation is understood as producing a configuration of times without being limited by any temporal form as its pregiven horizon or 'without a prejudgment concerning the specific configuration ... which defines a time'.[51] Any such configuration which comes to define 'a time' thus appears to be thought against a background of activity which is not itself reflected on any form of time. That Rancière tends to utilize space to render intelligible this activity has been recently explicitly stated by him in a passage where he acknowledges his debt to Feuerbach on this question:

> What time classically denies is coexistence. Space is of course supposed to be the form coexistence takes, and this means that in order to think of time as coexistence, you have to in a way turn it into a metaphor, often through space. (ME, 58/108, tm)

To be sure, emancipatory action, that this coexistence of times serves to think, has to take place in time to the extent that it is in any way thought to occur in material reality. Rancière invokes spatiality, however, in order to avoid giving any temporal structure or form to this time which would posit a specific distribution of possibilities for such action and in so doing differentiate between the capacities of historical actors. The point in this avoidance is to shift the emphasis on the actor, to shift the emphasis from the time of this actor to its capacity. Consequently, Rancière's ideas of multiple times should not make us see him as a thinker interested in forms of time per se but as a thinker of a capacity which brackets any temporal framework for its practice.

In this section, and in light of what I have developed, I want to assess Rancière's statement according to which his notion of multiplicity of times bears affinity with Althusser. What is the relation of Rancière to the Althusserian legacy? I will start with a discussion of another post-Althusserian thinker whose primary concern remains to be historical *time*. This will clarify the extent to which there can be a positive influence of Althusser on Rancière despite the fact that, whereas the former was interested precisely in historical time, the latter is looking for a way out of it.

Contemporaneity of coeval times

Peter Osborne's post-Althusserian conceptualization of the coexistence of multiple times through the notion of the contemporary differs from Rancière crucially in that it retains time, in the singular, as an underlying field in which different temporalities coexist. His most extensive theorization of the coexistence of times can be found in the book *Anywhere or Not at All* which, as the subtitle indicates, sets out to formulate a *Philosophy of Contemporary Art*. A central notion that the book tackles is thus that of 'the contemporary' that contemporary art helps to articulate. The contemporary consists of 'a coming together of *different but equally "present"* temporalities or "times"'.[52] As Osborne knows well, to the extent that the times remain multiple, the disjunctive conjunction of times cannot be unproblematically articulated in a temporal unification. Osborne's key gesture is thus to present that the 'contemporary' means something like a togetherness of times rather than being in one time. The oneness of time is structured only problematically as a Kantian regulative idea according to which it is 'as if' we were living in one shared time, albeit such time is, for the moment at least, beyond possible experience.

Contemporary art is according to Osborne potentially able to offer an adequate articulation and reflection of a disjunctive unity of distinct temporalities and respond to the demands posed by its problematic pre-unification through the Kantian idea. If the conjunction of times is readily designed to be temporally unified, however, it is because the idea is mirrored against the reality of the 'essentially abstract' and wholly objective unifying function of the 'subject-structure of capital'.[53] The fiction of the contemporary thus seems to correspond to this time of capital by adding to it something like a 'lived' dimension in the form of collective human subjectivity which it is lacking: Contemporary art offers 'a stand-in for the missing political collectivity of the globally transnational, which is both posited [at the external or abstract level] and negated [at the lived or existential level] by capital itself'. There is thus a process of temporalization behind the conjunction of multiple times, and Osborne's work has to be seen as being concerned with forming a subjective experience of this objective time-determination of our lives by capital and 'the self-development of the value-form'.[54] Our '*will* to contemporaneity – a will to force the multiplicity of coeval social times together' then risks figuring merely as a will to find a subjective expression of a temporality pre-formed by capital.[55] The question that Osborne's theory readily raises is that, if there is real transgressive value in contemporary art, how radically is it able to push off from its ground within the form of time determined by the process of global capital?

As we saw in Chapter 1, Althusser's philosophy was characterized by an attempt to think discontinuous historical time understood as a coexistence of multiple times. This time appeared as essentially rupturous, without being able to be conceived under any form of continuity. Yet, Althusser's overall project was conceived as *aimed towards* a political effectuation of a historical rupture. The impossibility to think the rupturous temporality in relation to such an aim-oriented movement, capable of recognizing the present of revolutionary action, marks the impasse of the Althusserian project. Osborne can be seen to set out from Althusser's failure, which he criticizes in an earlier book, *The Politics of Time*. There he explains how Althusser was unable to think the unity of historical time, that is, to conceive a 'common *time* within which to think the articulated co-existence of [the] various constitutive temporalities' of the whole.[56] Hence the failure to fulfil the task of historical materialism, that is, to think the transition of one mode of production to another. By the same token, the present of politics became impossible to situate in time, in any real historical 'now'. The coexistence of times could only appear in the form of a whole that consisted in relational analyses of times and their absences from the standpoint of localized presents but did not allow to think these relations in any unified developmental movement of time. In the end, this meant that the Althusserian coexistence of times was not temporal, but it figured as a spatial abstraction. As Osborne explains well, it was formed solely on the connections produced as an 'abstractly relational coexistence [which] takes it out of time altogether into the purely analytical space of synchrony'.[57] In the end, it is 'a-temporality' characteristic to structuralist topography, 'a purely analytical space in which the temporality immanent to the objects of inquiry is repressed'.[58]

As the reader might guess, in my opinion it is such a detemporalized, and hence 'abstract', spatiality that Rancière will pursue, rather than try to 'correct' Althusser's failure. Before developing this claim, I will briefly refer to the early Rancière, however, who seems to have held a similar view to Osborne.

Osborne refers to Johannes Fabian's notion of 'coevalness' and argues that multiple temporalities must be understood as coeval so that they would coexist 'in a way which is determined by the social dimension of their spatial relations'.[59] The spatial relations refer here to the actuality of simultaneously existing social relations that allow the standpoint of a specific historical present. Such a standpoint would guarantee that the relationality shared by multiple temporalities arise from an actual spatio-temporal development of the social reality. Historical time articulated to the social space is thus the opposite of the atemporal space 'of a disembodied "theory"' that we find in Althusser's topographical coexistence of multiple times.[60] Coevalness is thus a necessary, albeit as such insufficient, condition for a 'restitution of a totalizing conception of historical time within which to move'.[61]

In his critique of Althusserianism in the early 1970s, Rancière argues in a rather similar way that the Althusserian abstract theory suppressed 'the dimension at work there where the relation of a discourse to its object involves a relation to its social function'.[62] Against such an abstraction Rancière wanted to link Marx's writings to the social space-time of class struggle. The point was thus precisely to argue how practices that can be conceived as distinct and thus develop in their own temporal rhythms must arise from the evolutions of the same social process. What Althusser distinguished as separate practices with their own temporalities were nothing but 'forms (political, economic, ideological) through which the class struggle is fought' (AL, 189 n.10). The early Rancière thus wanted to dive into the social space-time and the way the classes were positioned in struggle in it. His critique was based on the conflict between what 'science' (Marx) was saying and what 'ideology' (workers) was saying, tracing the relation within the social between the two *positions*, thus presenting workers' discourses as 'localized, territorialized counter-discourses' (GF, 119). What he thus encountered in the early stages of his studies in working-class history was a 'constant re-balancing of power above by power from below'.[63] The task was to retrace the logics according to which this rebalancing forms itself and the coeval coordinations of the social space-time that resulted.

However, the view based on the struggle with such determinate positions in the social order quickly started to appear suspicious to Rancière from the viewpoint of emancipation. He saw it to lead to just another version of historical necessity, tracing the power relations between different social positions. As the editorial of a 1977 volume of *Les Révoltes logiques* describes such a viewpoint:

> Does it not substitute, for the old determinism of 'the development of productive forces' or the fatalism of the repressive State, the visions of a social balance reproduced in the form of conflict: a ... conflictually self-managed

universal harmony [*une harmonie universelle conflictuellement autogérée*], which returns to the theoretician the role of stating what is necessary?[64]

Such a scheme lost sight of the most important question:

> How to see in the act of dissidence or of refusal, in its setbacks or in its recoveries, something else than the passage of necessity or the play of balancing the social machine: [how] to see there ... an emergence of freedom [*l'émergence d'une liberté*]?[65]

Osborne notices in his own way a similar problem in Fabian's notion of coevalness: It has allowed to approach 'the more directly political form of a questioning of the social functions of ... representational practices'. But rather than solving it, 'it has thus charted the ground of its *insolubility*, as the space of an ongoing negotiation and struggle'.[66] One must envision a way out of the historical space-time in its present stage, and for Osborne this happens through a re-elaboration of historico-temporal orientation taking account of the multiple times in which the present consists. Rancière, however, wants to abandon any 'unifying form which used to be called simply *history*'.[67] He does not go about theorizing historical time as a way out of the functioning of 'the social machine' and the balance of forces that inhabit it. Rather, as I want to argue, he approaches it through a virtual or abstract space of connections that is supposed to shatter its coeval unity and allow to impose an egalitarian space upon the determined social relations and their historical mediation. This is best seen as a kind of heretical Althusserianism which affirms Althusser's 'failure' to account for a unity of historical time.

Theory in revolt

If Rancière's early critique of Althusser bears something of what Osborne after Fabian calls coevalness, his subsequent relation to Althusser goes the opposite way and is best understood from the side of an abstract space where distinct times resonate in each other without deriving from the actual social structures of a specific temporally evolving present. Rather, they arise from the intellectual 'power of making links' as such.[68] The problem is then no longer the abstraction from the social context of class struggle as such but the way the access to the 'theoretical', that is, abstract and disembodied, perspective to the whole is barred from some people. In other words, the problem is

> the logic of the inequality of intelligence, separating those who can understand the connections of the whole from those who are entrapped in the universe of the particular and all the more separated from their own experience, which has been entirely captured in the nets of science.[69]

In Althusser's terms, those incapable of articulating the links remain in the *'necessarily closed* space' of ideology, where any attempt to upheaval remains futile (RC, 54).[70] This closed space of ideology is first of all closed from 'theory', that is, a capacity to articulate the whole of the social order. As we saw in Chapter 1, this whole showed any localized present from a point of view of a rupturous temporality that dislocated it. Thus, it allowed a breakout from the ideological enclosure which safeguarded the functional unity of the social structure through ideological continuity of time. In doing so, however, it risked rendering any articulation of a unified temporality on it impossible. Now, I claim that it is precisely this impossibility that Rancière's thought leans on. It makes the capacity to articulate a whole in a way which shatters the temporal unity of this whole a capacity of emancipation as such, that is, a capacity of self-authorized conceptualization of one's practice and the context of this practice which is no longer mirrored against any unity of historical time. In this way, the Althusserian disembodied sphere of theory becomes a space of egalitarian relationality which leans on the Jacototian principle 'everything is in everything' (IS, 41). Any localized present is now understood as a point from which opens an access to the 'decentred' abstract space where the relations that make up the 'whole' are articulated, that is, where the conditions for emancipation (from spatio-temporal determinations) can be present anywhere at any time by making any place and any 'time' resonate in any other place or 'time'. Such a whole does not mirror the real functioning of the social order but becomes a creative sphere that renders possible a certain self-sufficiency for emancipatory action by allowing any network of relations with absent 'times' to be constructed to serve as an empowering context for this action.

If Rancière's early way of approaching the workers' emancipation was intimately linked to the coordinates of the social order, *The Nights of Labor* marks a turning point in his trajectory. The workers' discourses 'were no longer the fragments of a whole that had to be explained; instead, they were making a whole themselves, reconstructing' a network of links that made the framework of intelligibility of their action and emancipated it from the social order in place.[71] By the same token, Rancière's own discourse

> could no longer be a discourse explaining those writings by locating them in the whole of the connections that made them *possible*. Instead, it had to start from the reality of their intellectual operations, reconfiguring a whole world of experience.[72]

In other words, the workers' discourse was no longer related to the social dimension which would provide the perspective of the whole from which it would arise, but it was approached as a space where the whole itself is articulated or created. Just like the Althusserian space of theory, it cannot be seen to be situated in the space-time of social reality. In contrast, it forms a cross-historical space where Rancière's own thought moved in an atemporal togetherness with that of his object. 'The whole is everywhere', as Rancière puts it.[73] This is reflected in his

> mode of writing in which the intellectual exercises of the researcher, those of his 'objects', those of antique philosophers, and those of modern sociologists are assigned the same mode of existence, the same status as performances of speaking beings relating their intellectual adventures.[74]

For Rancière this kind of textual space is not separate from the question of transgressive political action. For, it provides precisely the non-localized sphere which allows to approach the social order by shattering its functional unity and its location within the order of this unity. It serves to 'extend the community of equal speaking beings and open new paths for the circulation of thought'. But these paths provide the egalitarian space of intelligibility for 'other forms of disruption of the dominant temporality … when unexpected crowds of anonymous persons … affirm their refusal of the way in which the spaces and times of our lives are managed'.[75]

The space of 'theory' thus offers the sphere of intelligibility for a rupturous practice in the social reality. This space is multitemporal in that it is formed of anachronistic use of words and ideas. Yet, as I argued before, this 'anachronism' or untimeliness cannot be grasped as temporal in any real sense. Rather, like the Althusserian topography of multiple times, it is a semiological space that represses the temporality of its elements.[76] Hence, Rancière understands it simply as consisting of 'signifying sequences' which make a 'history of what the words put in order among the bodies' in a space of 'travelers weaving their path in the forest of things and signs'.[77] It is certainly symptomatic of Rancière's atemporal approach to time that he tends to refer to 'times' as elements similar to signs. Rendering intelligible one's historical position amounts to a 'rearticulation [of] the connections between signs and images, images and times'.[78] Time features as an element that can be put into relation with any other element. The important point to notice is that *it is not itself a medium of such a relation* or a form of production of such a relation. In Rancière's discourse, 'times' need to be reduced to elements that are separate from empirical time and not seen as orienting or ordering forms within it. They simply form combinations whose elements do not have any common basis on the social space-time other than the dislocated location of their articulation. To approach the question of temporality in this manner speaks less of any attempt to think time than to think a capacity to use the 'times' of history for rendering one's practice intelligible in a way which brackets its *temporal* existence properly speaking.

This kind of coexistence of times which goes beyond, rather than derives from, the actual social order is supposed to allow a maximal degree of freedom for a (re)articulation of this social order and one's place in it. However, it is clear that the very meaning of the social becomes problematic here, to the extent that this perspective brackets its historically and geographically mediated existence. The broad idea of this model follows the Althusserian atemporal sphere of the relationality of times, where '[w]hat is ... grasped as absences in a localized presence is precisely the non-localization of the structure of the whole' (RC, 252). It is this non-localization articulated only through interrelations with other times, which renders it impossible to conceive it from any properly historico-socio-temporal standpoint. In this sense emancipation comes to figure as a togetherness understood through an abstract and detemporalized relational space. The specifically emancipatory logic, as it is at work in Rancière's thought, comes then to be articulated through a radical dissociation from time and dissolves any idea of historical-temporal present. It can thus be read as a radicalization of the Althusserian 'disembodied "theory"', understood through cross-resonances between times in an abstract atemporal space, whose transgressive power is in the refusal to model one's practice according to any given form of temporalization. Emmanuel Renault has hinted towards this link between Rancière's specific understanding of egalitarian practice and Althusserian 'theory'. As he says, in Rancière 'a philosophy of political freedom grounded in the communist principle of equality' is 'rearticulated in the epistemological (that is, Althusserian?) and Maoist terms of the "equal competence of everybody"'.[79]

To recap, Rancière's relation to Althusser includes two moments. First there is a forcing of science into the social dimension, into the localized, historically specific realities of class struggle from which its objects are extracted and onto which they are rearticulated. This tendency dominates his critique of Althusser analysed in Chapter 1. It then becomes to be supplemented by an opposite movement, as it were, where any localized present is brought into an abstract and disembodied sphere of 'theory', understood no longer as an exclusive realm in contrast to ideology but as the sphere of equality of intelligences. Emancipatory practice comes then to be rethought via a detour of this abstract space – a 'detour of theory', one is tempted to say – which attempt is informed by the semiological revolt of the Cultural Revolution, as analysed in Chapter 2. Accordingly, if Rancière first started to study discourses that reflect specific ideology of workers, in *The Nights of Labor* the workers were seen as becoming intellectuals, through 'a symbolic rupture which is constituted by the entry into writing, that is, into the domain of the literate'.[80] The working class was no longer 'claiming its place'.[81] Rather, it rendered this place into an undetermined sphere of equality from which to construct the space of one's emancipation without rooting this space in the social space-time of one's situation or in any temporal logic concerning its evolutions. The access to this atemporal sphere of equality of intelligences was emancipation as such.

As Rancière has noted, Althusserianism represented for him an 'adventure in theory' on one hand and a 'dogmatism of theory' on the other (GF, 327). His own project can be seen to deconstruct the dogmatic side in order to keep the adventure, which he reconstructs according to the Jacototian idea of equality. For this reason, Rancière tends to see Althusser's 'Marxist aristocracy' *also* as a liberating moment, first of all because it allowed a radical politicization outside the Party authority.[82] Yet, there is no doubt that the concrete historical experiment of the Chinese Cultural Revolution serves as the bridge leading from Althusser to Jacotot and allowing Rancière to see Althusserian 'theoreticism', itself strongly influenced by Mao, in a framework of an immediate realization of radical equality. When Rancière says that Althusserianism 'sort of' meant that Marx could be read free from authorities, we should of course be thinking about the Cultural-Revolutionary Maoism which reduced the whole of Marx's work to the phrase 'it is right to revolt'.[83] It is in the light of this maxim that theory can appear as a sphere of self-authorized articulation of practice against the social order.

5

The Jacobin anachronism

In the previous chapter we saw that anachronism is a central concept for Rancière to think history and historical time. After associating it with the logic of abstract space, I suggested that, although a way to approach temporality, it bears a certain relation with an idea of non-time and eternity. Such an idea is nevertheless to be understood in a dialectical or interventional relation to temporal evolutions, rather than as a distinct hypostasized sphere with its own independent existence. This chapter will draw on this association of anachronism with eternity in order develop a specific reading of the political logic at work in the historical context from which Rancière's discussions of anachronism ultimately stem, that is, the French Revolution. For, the question of anachronism does not concern only the narrative principles of historiography. It also concerns the revolutionary practice that the prohibition of anachronism serves to delegitimize. Hence, Rancière's notion of anachronism constitutes a, largely indirect, defence of this practice and enables us to distinguish a specific intelligibility in it.

Certain radial aspects of the French Revolution have been dismissed as anachronistic at least since Benjamin Constant's liberal interpretation of the Revolution.[1] Many of the revolutionaries' writings and speeches refer constantly to figures of antiquity as examples.[2] At times, the revolutionary project itself is understood as a return of 'the beautiful days of Athens and Rome', as Marat writes.[3] The same 'freedom has overwhelmed [*ébloui*] both the Romans and the French'.[4] Or, as Saint-Just says, '[t]he revolutionaries must be Romans'.[5] Marx and Engels famously quote this phrase by Saint-Just in their critical remarks on the Jacobins based, precisely, on anachronism. In their eyes 'Robespierre, Saint-Just and their party fell because they confused the ancient' world with the contemporary society.[6] Hence, it is especially, if not exclusively, the radical, Jacobin current which is known for their references to antiquity. Summarizing Marx and Engels's view, François Furet makes this aspect into a defining feature of Jacobinism: 'anachronism is another name for Jacobin ideology.'[7] Furet emphasizes the affinity of the young Marx's reading of the Revolution with the traditions of its liberal interpreters, especially that of Benjamin Constant, arguably the originator of the argument concerning anachronism.[8] Furet does not refer to Marx's later notes on the anachronism in the French Revolution, in *The Eighteenth Brumaire of Louis Bonaparte*, where they are repeated in a slightly more defensive and less critical tone.[9] Furet's reading of Marx is related to his own historiographical project which runs from the 1960s through the bicentennial of the Revolution in 1989 and revolves around an argument of the revolutionary culture as unsuitable for the late twentieth century – and hence, as we might add, anachronistic.[10]

When Rancière argues, in *The Names of History* (1992), that the modern social sciences are unable to cope with the mode of historicity constitutive of the French Revolution, a central aim behind his endeavour is to revoke the revisionist historiography of François Furet. Such a historiography is haunted by the 'original ghost of social science', that is, 'the revolution in the clothing and discourse of antiquity', as Rancière says, in a phrase which is effectively a quotation from Marx although not marked as such.[11] With his positive understanding of anachronism Rancière then sets out to provide the political logic rejected by revisionist historians with a historiographical intelligibility, which can be interpreted as an implicit rehabilitation and defence of the Jacobin practice.[12] Rancière is mostly silent about the French Revolution itself, and although the political context from which the arguments on anachronism arise is clear, the logic is displaced and generalized in Rancière's own work. His own ways to render intelligible the historicity of emancipatory practice nevertheless mirror the revolutionary discourse in that it 'makes the voice of Antiquity resonate in the present' (NH, 30). Consider, for example, his frequent references to Pierre-Simon Ballanche's retake of the story of the plebeian secession from the city of Rome in 494 BCE, originally related by Livy.[13] It is a story of the plebeians' negotiations with the patricians on the conditions of their return to the city. Ballanche rewrites the story in the context of the nineteenth-century workers' struggles. He offers Rancière an example of an anachronistic coexistence of times which is not based on any actual historical space-time but is rather a resonance of an absent time in the present, where it offers a framework of intelligibility for transgressive practice:

> One apparently needed this detour via a reinvented Roman antiquity in order to meet the living experience [*le vif de l'expérience*] of the common people of 1830. One needed this radical inactuality [*inactualité*] in order to meet the inactuality which is at the core of any refusal of the 'natural' order of things, that is the natural order of domination.[14]

According to Rancière, the plebeians' 'expressions enter into an immediate resonance with the thoughts and preoccupations of these emancipated people [*hommes*]' of the nineteenth century.[15] The time of the ancient Rome 'communicates directly with the present of those who have together decided to shatter [*bouleverser*] again the order of times'.[16] In 2016 when Rancière is writing a preface to a republication of Ballanche's text, he hears the same resonance in 'Nuit Debout'. The protest movement which unfolded in France in 2016 itself 'echoes in the attempt of the workers who, at the time of Ballanche, were seeking to shatter the normal cycle of days and nights'.[17]

Thus, Rancière understands emancipatory actors through a certain cross-historical coexistence which resembles the revolutionaries' references to the antiquity. Just like the radical revolutionaries at the end of the eighteenth century referred to the ancients as their contemporaries, the logic of Rancière's discourse on emancipation leans on an idea of a certain virtual contemporariness, rendering irrelevant historico-temporal differentiations when it comes to emancipatory practice. As he says in relation to one of his nineteenth-century heroes: 'How could I be nostalgic about Jacotot when I continue to be his contemporary?' (GF, 438).[18] The apparent affinity that Rancière bears with the radical current of the French Revolution, on one of the questions it has been most notably criticized for, begs some discussion of Rancière in light of the broader intelligibility behind the 'anachronistic' practice of that current. What I have in mind concerns the idea of 'eternal rights' as principles which level temporal differences. From the very beginning the French Revolution drew on such principles, affirmed in the Declaration of the Rights of Man and the Citizen. As we will see, Rancière defends the logic of the Declaration, although his own thought in no way follows through the French revolutionary discourse as such. I will now spend some time discussing this logic, which will help understand the stakes in the questions of temporality in Rancière and clarify his relations with the revolutionary project, and especially the radical Jacobin current, regarding the question of time, anachronism and eternity.

Abstract principles and social mediations

It would be too hasty to refer the 'anachronistic' practice of the French Revolution to the lack of historical consciousness, which was nothing like today. True, we are talking about a pre-Marxist revolutionary practice, and the theorizations of historical development of the socio-economic relations as the essential framework of any political practice were not available. One should nevertheless not emphasize this aspect at the cost of a more positive understanding of what, following Furet, can be called the Jacobin ideology, whatever the faults of the latter might have been. Namely, already then the argument against this ideology was calling for a necessary consideration for historical mediation of social relations, as opposed to the 'abstract' approach of the Jacobins. The latter was blamed for not taking into account the structures of the established order and the different material interests interlinked with it.[19] Thus, a version of the idea of something like a materialist understanding of history which emphasized the importance of the social relations in place was there, albeit not in any elaborated form. As the debates concerning the colonies show well, between the more radical reasoning and the one which tried to contain its effects, the dispute was not at the level of the questions of justice and equality per se. Rather, at stake was the order of primacy between the moral principles and temporal-historical mediation aimed at their realization. Thus, instead of a moral support for slavery, the ones in support of the colonial status quo insisted simply that the established social order cannot be changed just like that. The colonial 'regime is absurd, but it is in place [*établi*]', as Barnave puts it.[20] Malouet states that 'no human being who is not lacking in sense [*sens*] and morality can assert this doctrine'. The question for him was whether it was *possible* to abolish slavery in colonies in the light of the current state of affairs. 'And Malouet considers that for the time being it is not possible.' It is simply not the moment for it, although the situation could, as he argues, change 'in the long run'.[21] In a similar vein, Maury argues that the efforts to achieve active citizenship for the people of colour are 'praiseworthy but premature': 'That people of colour become, after a certain amount of time, after a certain number of generations, active citizens, I see that and I desire that.'[22] Likewise, Goupil states that 'it would be just that the free men of colour would obtain their political rights, but the circumstances do not allow this'.[23]

We can see that the argumentative logic followed by the apologists of slavery in this debate did not concern its moral justification. Rather, the established state was justified through an allegedly objective reference point provided by time. The social reality needed to submit to the order of time, no matter how unfortunate this was. According to this logic one needed to set out from a given historical reality and approach the question of reaching a more just state of affairs on the basis of the possible and probable evolutions of this reality. The Declaration of the Rights of Man and the Citizen, and the idea of eternal natural rights behind it, was the main vehicle of justification and intelligibility of the revolutionary event. But according to the argument of the side that aimed to restrain its application, it was a question of the extent to which a given 'way to exist can reconcile with the principles posited by this declaration'.[24] Florence Gauthier notes the affinity that this argumentative logic has with some aspects of Marxism and historical materialism. She quotes Jean-Pierre Faye who has argued that Barnave, who supports the containment of the effectivity of universal rights, appears as a historical materialist *avant la lettre*: 'It is not metaphysical ideas that lead the masses in the course of the revolutions, but the real interests.'[25] 'The premises from which we begin are not arbitrary ones', as Marx and Engels famously wrote in their polemic against Feuerbachian materialism: 'They are the real individuals, their activity and the material conditions of their life, both those which they find already existing and those produced by their activity.'[26] Marx's theory of history no doubt becomes more elaborated, but the question of reconciliation between material circumstances and emancipation remains the pivotal point of his thought while the dimension of this reconciliation is the temporally structured reality of history. It could be suggested – if only tentatively – that in the background of Marx's endeavour there is a lost argument for an intelligibility of a more immediate revolutionary project and a concession made to a reaction against it. While allowing to bring a revolutionary project down to earth from utopian heights, it is at the same time a testimony to a lost argument for a more immediate realization of such a project.

For those who resisted drawing the full consequences of the principles, the latter were to be subjected to social conditions, rather than vice versa. The argument that any claim for rights is secondary to the time of their applicability, determined by the mode of historicity of a given state of things, was a strategy to grant power to private property and the circulation of goods without any hasty human intervention. The prevailing of the reactionary tendency within the Revolution is marked by the 1795 Constitution, which, as Gauthier argues, builds on a theory of 'the rights of man in society', rather than the theory of 'natural rights'. It thus consolidates the logic based on the primacy of the more or less undisturbed unfolding of the socio-economic tendencies.[27] The new constitution opens the door for effectively cancelling the revolutionary project. As Dupuy formulated the urgent task of the reactionaries in 1802: 'to substitute for seductive theories a reparatory system whose combinations are attached to the circumstances and change with them'.[28]

The crucial point was that the *eternal* nature of the rights – or their independence of any specific time or place – was replaced by 'the society' which subjected them to the existing state of affairs and its socio-historical evolutions. This was then the point where the conception of rights as 'invariable and … always … the same in all times and all places' was given up.[29] As Mirabeau, one of the composers of the 1789 declaration, put it, the declaration was directly 'applicable to all times, all places and all climes'. Commenting on this statement Mike Haynes and Jim Wolfreys write that its 'claims … stretched across the known world and beyond it. They stretched into the past and they stretched into the future.'[30] While the idea of transhistorical rights is foundational for the French Revolution in general, one of the distinctive features of the Jacobins consists in taking this idea as seriously as possible, with the aim of drawing full practical consequences from equality and justice traversing time and space. Consider, for example, Robespierre: 'What kind of a system is it where a person, who is a citizen at a given point of the French territory, either partly or completely stops being one if he passes to another point? What kind of a system is it where the one who is a citizen today is no longer a citizen tomorrow?'[31] The message of his interventions often amounts to a determined rejection of any tendency to 'take local institutions for eternal principles'.[32]

There was a gap between institutions and the principles because the nature of the latter did not allow to fix them to any spatio-temporal particularity. The rights could not refer to any specific state of affairs but simply justified and rendered intelligible the revolutionary practice as it went along in its attempt to transform the existing order into a more egalitarian one. In direct opposition to the reactionary tendency, the rights was a way to hold on to the revolutionary project as a direct implementation of equality and justice in varying circumstances and despite them. In this sense the dynamics of the application of the rights was paradoxically fuelled by the insistence on their invariant nature which put them at odds with the idea of time as unfolding difference. Thus, the consistency of Robespierre's principles corresponded to a necessary fluidity of the ways different situations appeared in their light.

> His conception of politics was characterised both by fixed principles and striking inconsistencies and changes of tactical position. In many cases the inconsistencies themselves stemmed from the very rigidity of his principles as he sought to adapt general theoretical principles to the tortuous complexities of revolutionary politics.[33]

This describes a logic of action which cannot be reflected on a uniform duration. The principle of equality resists temporalization of concepts or, if you like, their schematization in the Kantian sense.[34] It does not adapt itself harmoniously with the sensed reality but rather intervenes in such a reality from a distance.

The course of the events is thus perhaps not so well understood through a temporal evolution but as a shattered time of revolutionary turmoil whose consistency, based on practical principles, is other than spatio-temporal consistency. It is not a question of times that are changing but of eternity's intervention in time. It was perhaps this discrepancy which the revolutionaries tried to repair by developing novel ways to represent time.[35] However, that the principles on which revolutionary *practice* drew could not easily accommodate to a specific spatio-temporal form may follow from the very logic of natural rights, whose function consisted in allowing emancipatory effectivity on the historical reality by being subtracted from its evolutions. If we understand the rights and their relation to temporal reality like this, it becomes impossible to positively represent the egalitarian human nature or think an *established* society on the basis of these principles. This is what Rancière is getting at in his reading of the rights in terms of a gap.

The gap in the rights

There was thus a *gap* between the eternal rights and the social order in which they were to be applied. While the latter was a result of historical evolution oriented by different class interests, the former was thought to be based on human nature. By nature, human being was free and equal, and the rights allowed to play this freedom against inequalities in the social relations. Conversely, those who were occupied in retaining these inequalities held that 'one must entirely erase the word "nature", because there is a contradiction between the natural rights and social rights'.[36] According to them, the invocation to an eternal nature amounted to an abstract and metaphysical confusion which did not pay attention to the varying factors of the social order and the ways they develop. While the practice of the radical current had played out *between* these two, the 1795 Constitution aimed to consolidate the order based on private property and thus watered down the force of natural freedom against social position.

Rancière's reading of the rights is best understood as an operation which displaces the 'eternity' or the atemporality of the rights from the positive definition of either 'man' or the 'citizen' to the *gap* between them. He thus displaces them from any substantial idea of human nature as much as from the material circumstances of a social creature. Lacking a positive content, the rights become merely an instance of the 'logic' at work in them. Thus, when Rancière refers to the Declaration of the Rights of Man and the Citizen, it is precisely the gap (*écart*) in the very title that he finds crucial, because the gap allows their effectivity through a dissociation of the revolutionary practice from the determinants of the existing order. This is why he frames his discussion as a rejection of different critics of the rights, from Burke to Marx to Arendt to Agamben: 'The basic argument of all these authors ... is that two subjects are simply one too many.' In other words, 'these rights had something wrong with them, namely their duplicity' (DS, 55). The duplicity – which, as he says, is neutralized in today's 'Human Rights' – is for Rancière what allowed to make the rights effective, however, precisely because it allows to posit one term against the other:

> Citizenship means, on the one hand the rule of equality among people who are inferior or superior as men that is as private individuals subordinate to the power of ownership and social domination. On the other, by contrast to all the restrictions to citizenship – from whose scope many categories of people are excluded and which limits citizens by placing certain problems out of their reach 'man' entails an affirmation of the equal capacity of everyone and anyone. (DS, 56)

Rancière does not understand human 'nature' as more fundamental than 'society', but he sees one term as a vehicle for an imposition of equality as opposed to the order represented by the other term. The logic of the rights remains, that is, the contradiction within them, which allows their emancipatory effectivity by offering a position that stands opposed to the order in place.

Despite avoiding a reference to eternity as such, the logic of the gap effectively has a similar *function* than the idea of eternal rights, in opposing a historically constituted state of affairs. The gap is thus the mode of *performing* the eternity of rights. Or, it provides the rights with an 'eternity-function', the idea of which I developed in the previous chapter. This is how the invariability of Rancière's 'maxim of equality' guides his conceptualization of the use of rights (ME, 90). Moreover, the logic within the rights belongs to the more general logic of literarity discussed in Chapter 2. Thus, it links the declaration of rights to the practice I analysed through the Cultural Revolution where those in revolt were empowered by the authority of the Little Red Book. It is a capacity to rearrange the relations between words and reality and by the same token the historical coordinates based on them. As Rancière explains, 'Reference texts – the Rights of Man or the Old Testament – … permit the articulation of an experience' of those in revolt. They offer

> phrases and arrangements of phrases that transform, into something visible and utterable, what had no place to be distinguished and was heard only as inarticulate noise, moving into common space new subjects, new legitimacies, and forms in which the former can argue from the latter. (NH, 93)

This 'common space' is made of displacements of socio-historical coordinates that make up the identity of each of us and circumscribe the possibilities of our thought and action. Hence, the rights enable a practice of those who are 'elsewhere than in their place' forming a dislocated space within 'the very gap' that they enable (AD, 118). They operate with 'inappropriate' combinations of 'places' and 'times' which form the common between-space where emancipatory action (un)situates itself. This between-space is the very quasi-eternal cross-historical sphere discussed earlier which the 'anachronistic' use of words mobilizes.[37] In this sense, Rancière articulates the eternity of the rights through the interventional logic that their use puts in action.

The logic of the rights is thus directly related to that of anachronism and the spatial logic which grounds its intelligibility in Rancière. 'The rights of man *and* of the citizen' belong to the same logic which forms the 'monstrous conjunction[s]' of 'properties that are not contemporaneous with each other' (NH, 34). It draws on a cross-historical contiguity able to draw direct connections, to form direct coexistences short-circuiting temporal differentiations and to fuel emancipatory action through these connections and coexistences. Rancière is thus contemporary with Jacotot, just like the activists of the 'Nuit Debout' are contemporary with the nineteenth-century French strikers and the Roman plebeians at the Aventine Hill or the Jacobins with the Romans. For all of them revolt against time as an order which establishes borders and polices historical states of affairs.

The radical French revolutionaries were not merely affirming such a transhistorical coexistence, however, but emulating past examples in wanting to bring forth a just state of affairs which went beyond anything that had existed before. Their project was thus intimately linked to the idea of making progress and thus presupposed temporality as an ordering principle. In a certain sense, Rancière paradoxically insists on the idea of eternal or transhistorical principles in a purer form, precisely by not allowing them to align with any ordered process of temporalization or specific states of affairs as stages of such a process. By the same token, this translation of the eternal or transhistorical into a temporally dispersed or cross-historical spatiality risks paralysing any revolutionary *project(ion)*. In taking the revolution completely 'outside the assurances of subordination, into the uncertainties of conjunction', this logic prevents the revolution from orienting itself towards any specific state of affairs, that is, from forming any representation of a desirable future and moving towards it (NH, 94). The eternity is purified through a paratactic intelligibility which links together times without conceiving itself as temporally mediated. For Rancière the practice of rights simply opens a *space* for cross-historical intelligibility of revolutionary practice while radically weathering the capacity to orient such a practice in time.

Dissolving the logic of periodization

The influence of antiquity which erupted in the revolutionary practice during the French Revolution was anticipated in Thomas Hobbes's *Leviathan*.[38] Rancière's discussion of anachronism in *The Names* partly sets out from Hobbes's fear that the stories of the ancients cause people to revolt against their legitimate sovereign ruler.[39] 'The anachronistic and homonymic confusion' of words might thus realize an 'inappropriate superimposition of times' and cause the contractual state to collapse (NH, 34, 30/66, tm). Rancière reads later historians as being motivated by the same fear, which is both theoretical and political. A contract is by definition historical and historically established; better, it is a constitution of the time of history as such, leaving behind the state of nature. I would argue that what is at stake for Rancière in the Hobbesian fear as well as in the French Revolutionary practice is precisely nothing else than a collapse of the time of history conceivable as a succession of periods. This can be seen in the passage where Rancière distinguishes Hobbes's view on the dissolution of the body politic from previous theorizations of political unrest:

> It is henceforth no longer a matter of the classification of regimes, and of the causes that *transform one regime into another*. It is a matter of the life or death of the body politic as such. The question no longer pertains to the laws of conservation of each single regime and to the causes of its ruin, but to the laws that conserve the body politic, whatever it may be, and to those that also prompt its dissolution. (NH, 19/42–3, tm, emphasis added)

What Rancière is saying here is that there is a dissolution of ordering of history according to temporal succession. At stake is a logical break between the succession of historical time and its dissolution. Another way to put it is that the question of the revolution is no longer that of transition but a dissolution of the form of time that makes the question of transition intelligible.[40] The body politic is an order which is recognizably in a specific time. It is in such an order where it makes sense to talk about periods or eras and which secures the functioning of temporal operators at the social level.

The stakes should now be clear: Rancière's defence of anachronism is about dissolution of ordering of history temporally, not a reflection of its temporal form. Rancière does not see emancipatory action as a movement between different states of things or a transition between historical regimes, understood as both social and discursive conditions for realizing justice and equality. While we can read Rancière's defence of 'anachronistic' intelligibility of revolutionary action to include a certain affinity with the radical current of the French Revolution, taking only one aspect from it, he risks rendering the revolution as a *process* unintelligible. It is well known that this process included self-destructive elements, and in a sense the Rancièrian reading could be seen as an attempt to clear the logic of the revolution of these elements while remaining faithful to the 'eternal' ideas which drove it. I will look at these elements by looking at the logic of the Terror.

Chronophobia and the Terror

Robespierre describes the Terror as justice realized in full, as quickly as possible, without mediations: 'Terror is nothing else but prompt, severe, inflexible justice.'[41] 'The exercise of Terror was ... a race against time', as Sophie Wahnich puts it, and she quotes Georges Couthon: 'The time taken to punish the enemies of the *patrie* cannot be more than that needed to recognize them; it is not so much a question of punishing as of annihilating them.'[42] There was a fundamental discontent with time which appears almost as a mirror image of the demand to let time pass, made by the defenders of the colonial order discussed earlier. For Robespierre and others, the passing of time was seen as a danger that risked taking the process out of the control of the revolutionary actors. The extreme fear of conspiracies or *intrigues* linked to the Terror can also be read as a fear of an underlying temporal plot – an *intrigue* – that was leading the events in secret from the actors.[43] The passing of time was thus in some sense experienced as a threat as such, and it fuelled attempts to constitute a new temporal order according to an 'ideal of a uniform "transparent" time'.[44] The chronophobic tone had been imposed on Robespierre by the course of the events already a few years before the Terror was launched: 'If one gives to despotism time to recognize itself, the calls of good citizens are denounced as acts of insurrection, freedom disappears and servitude remains.'[45] It was a question of speed but can also be seen more radically as a battle against time as such, through an attempt to establish eternal justice on earth once and for all. Indeed, Robespierre's view did not lack messianic undertones.[46] In this sense, it was also a question of 'reconciliation' of timeless natural justice and historical temporality, the natural law and society.[47] It was this tendency that took hold of things in the Terror. The revolution then gave up the risky realm where things were able to proceed by retaining some kind of gap between the principles on one hand and the differentiations of the social order on the other, while at the same time mediating this gap and disciplining the bouncing rhythm of the revolutionary process in order to bring the social order closer to what was announced by the principles. This is a point at which the revolution moves from being a logic of intervention and conflict to being a principle of establishment.

Now, Rancière's position figures as an attempt to avoid fusing the principle of equality immediately into the social order. Rather, he posits the non-temporalizable principle of equality against any historico-temporal order, by playing one time against another, a text against a reality, a fact against a law and so on. We could say that if the Terror was a struggle against time on time's terms, so to speak, Rancière is doing nothing else than attempting to take a certain sovereign position against time. If Robespierre characterized the Terror as 'speedy justice' for Rancière equality bypasses questions of time and timing. The move here is similar to the one in relation to the Cultural Revolution. If in China equality was thought to be realized 'as quickly as possible', Rancière would later theorize equality as a point of departure and not an aim, in order to free emancipation from being a race against time – which, he thinks, cannot be won.[48] The perspective of the immediate in the sense of 'as soon as possible' is replaced by a certain irrelevance of the questions of temporalization in relation to equality. Equality is an eternal point of departure. The time of realizing it is not a time that would *proceed* towards a specific state of things. It is not a unified, structured time at all.

In the radical French revolutionary logic, however, it was still a question of realizing an aim by realizing the principle in an order of time. And, in the face of an actual project, what else could it be about? Indeed, the whole intelligibility of the revolution from the perspective of its most uncompromised actors leaned on holding together the course of the events towards an aim. One had to 'mark clearly the aim [*but*] of the revolution, and the point [*terme*] where we want to arrive'.[49] As Robespierre puts it, the aim was 'the reign of eternal justice'.[50] Yet, it was interlinked with the temporality of its realization, and this process was considered by Robespierre to be permanent.[51] The reigning of justice should thus be understood as a form of practice and the collective actor organized around and by it. This practice was to secure equality as far as possible while establishing some institutional structures enabling control over the socio-economic order. 'We want an order of things where the distinctions only emerge from equality itself; where the citizen is subjected to the magistrate, the magistrate to the people, and the people to justice'.[52] The crucial things were the mechanisms of popular control over those who practiced governance.[53] Thus, if any social order necessarily includes a certain distribution of roles and functions, the popular capacity to intervene in the injustices of such an order was to be held primary. 'As Marat puts it, [t]he citizens' right to assemble where they want and when they want, in order to engage with *la chose publique*, is inherent to every free people.'[54]

Any moment is acknowledged as a potential moment for popular insurrection which was based less on any order of time than on the capacity of the people and their right to practice this capacity, which was a capacity to interrupt any temporal course. In my view, Rancière, too, is committed to such a capacity. This capacity allows that '[a]t certain moments, an authority called "the people" appears as a subject of power that is no longer the usual one' (ME, 135/236, tm). Now, Rancière is not willing to give a temporal measure to the occurrence of such 'moments'. True, according to one of the principles he is best known for, politics is rare (D, 17, 39).[55] Many of his commentators have focused on the principle of rarity.[56] However, the idea which expresses a temporal modality applicable to the emergence of politics is anything but an adequate characterization of Rancière's understanding of emancipatory logic. Rather, the point about rarity of politics should be seen as an indication of the difficulty that Rancière, too, has when trying to pin down the *temporal* structure of politics. It comes as no surprise, then, that he has since regretted this 'sorry business of rarity' and emphasized the availability of any time to popular insurrection and the capacity on which it is based.[57] 'The essential element *in every present* is to know what, in that present, manages to revive the idea of a common capacity in the form of practical action' (ME, 135/237, tm, emphasis added). The logic of emancipation amounts to the principle that acknowledges a capacity of equality which is prior to any order of times and places. Politics might be rare in the universe that is temporally determined. But Rancière's whole philosophy of emancipation is marked by a rejection to submit to such a universe. There is no temporal order that it would adjust to, but, following Marat, Rancière holds that the people can manifest its authority at any time and in any place.

We find a similar spatio-temporal indetermination in the notion of *patrie*. 'In Robespierre, the *patrie* is not a geographical site, a territory, or a country. The *patrie* is where the natural rights are [*se trouvent*]', and they were wherever they were successfully practiced.[58] *Patrie* is then an eventual and a practical concept which goes against the idea of *establishing* any kind of reign, be it one of eternal justice. Rancière agrees that the core of the revolutionary concepts lies in practice. The rights belong to 'those who make them a reality'.[59] The problem in his conception, however, is that it tends to see this practice in terms of a configuration of a community which is not spatio-temporally situated at all but which rather leans on an abstract space of contiguity as the sphere of intelligibility of the revolution. This sphere then brings nothing but indetermination as such to the social order of times and places. It is a 'community without contours and without a centre, where displaced speakers multiply and create events of words that are never given in person: people or nation; *patrie*, revolution, proletariat [*communauté sans contours et sans centre où se multiplient les parleurs déplacés qui font événement des noms dont les corps n'est jamais donné en propre: peuple ou nation; patrie, révolution, prolétariat*]'.[60] Such a community is not found in 'designatable localities' but refers to a logic of action that 'creates the unlimited space of new paths ... making subjects of speech and history travel in the hazardous intervals between material places and symbolic places, between names and bodies, conditions and knowledges' (NH, 92, 93/187–8, tm).

In this way, he aims to radically dissociate any determined coordinates of the socio-historical space-time from the sphere of revolutionary practice which he conceives as a non-situated space of cross-historical contiguity. However, this comes at the price of losing grip of the course of events which was vital for the revolutionary project. Namely, if for Robespierre *patrie* was not a designated territory but the site of applying the natural rights, there were specific conditions that needed to apply in an actual social order for the principles to have any reality.[61] The practice based on rights was to be in a processual unity safeguarding those conditions in specific time and place. On one hand, there was the right to form an expression of popular sovereignty wherever and whenever. On the other hand, there was a distribution of roles that tried to build the institutions to allow such a right a reality. All this required collective discipline, calculation and a temporal unity of the process. It is characteristic of Rancière that he pays virtually no attention to such disciplinary conditions or refuses to acknowledge them as a necessary aspect of revolutionary practice. Whereas such conditions always tie this practice to specificities of a given historical situation, for better or worse, Rancière sees the core of the revolutionary logic in a verification of non-locality of the practice in the coordinates of a social space-time.[62] However, here he only follows the logic of his position, which is oriented according to an idea of revolt against (spatio-)temporal ordering of reality.

End of politics

This logic of revolt stems partly from the way Rancière identifies the purposeful aspect of politics with an idea of putting an end to politics, that is to say, an end to the practice of equality. This identification cancels in advance all attempts to arrange the relations between the two logics included in the rights by insisting on the spatio-temporal indeterminacy of the sovereignty of the people, while simultaneously recognizing the discipline of time required for making such a sovereignty effective in the social order. Rather than a task for the revolutionary process to tackle, Rancière considers this a fatal paradox.

> The paradox of politics is this inclusion of its 'end' ['*fin*'; to be understood as both 'end' and 'aim'], which means also justice [*le droit*] done to the appearance of the people, the procedures and the systems [*dispositifs*] of visibility which maintains and neutralizes the people.[63]

According to Rancière, any change in the social order is conceived as putting an end to emancipation, precisely by *establishing* a determined process of transformation in it. Whatever the claims of emancipatory politics, the moment they have a determined effect in the social order and change the ways in which roles, functions, times, and places are organized in it, emancipatory logic is itself neutralized or 'wronged' (*tordu*). Any claim for justice is conceived only negatively as expressing 'the wrong' (*le tort*) in the social order which can be responded to at best by a new form of 'wronging' (*tordre*) the principle of equality. This paradox only becomes sharper when Rancière divides it into two terms, separating the logic of emancipation from the logic of 'the police'.[64] Its model form is the Platonic *polis* – what Rancière calls an 'archi-politics' and equates it with an 'archi-police' (D, 68/103, tm). Though Plato's model is the most radical of the police orders, any police order shares its logic and differs essentially from the logic of emancipation. All the police orders amount to putting an end to the egalitarian contiguity where all place, times, roles and so on are available to anyone at all.

Rancière seems to associate too quickly any temporal reflection linked to aim-oriented action with a *telos* as an operator of objective determination of historical time which takes free agency away from historical actors (cf. D, 75). Consequently, all aim-oriented politics is turned into the police. Through such a gesture we risk losing all tools to think properly subjective time-determination where the course of time would be adjusted to political principles. But this means that there is no revolutionary project as a process able to keep together the claim for equality and the control of a socio-economic order. Or rather – because Rancière is careful to never straightforwardly deny the existence of such processes – they remain an 'enigma', as Antonia Birnbaum has recently put it.[65] The Rancièrian emancipation resembles much more the anarchic reality of the early Cultural-Revolutionary revolt than the French Revolution. In the former the dynamic of the revolt appears precisely as its dissociation from any direction through common temporalization. Yet, what he shares with the most radical current of the French Revolution is the uncompromising primacy of a practical principle and the conviction that it must remain sovereign in relation to historical conditions. It must be the point of departure, and the attempt to realize it should not be limited by any principled discourse on its applicability. This may be the most valuable lesson of Rancière's work, and one which it is worth articulating into our own political axioms, however different a direction we may otherwise take.

Conclusion

In this book I have tried to demonstrate that the way Rancière thinks emancipation and equality draws on spatiality in a way which is incompatible with organized temporalities. The logic of equality insists on spatial contiguity, and its dynamics refuses to submit to ordered time. Therefore, the thinking of any ongoing or enduring political *process*, to say nothing about a political *project*, is deeply problematized within his framework. To conclude, I would like to anticipate the main point on which my argument might be challenged.

One might object that I have concentrated overly on the logic of equality and emancipation *as such*. I have thus neglected, as one might argue, that it is in a substantial relation with the social order, or 'the police', that emancipation is able to 'process' the 'wrongs' of such an order and where it can align with some consequential trajectories. After all, as Rancière has himself stated, politics and the police are always 'interwoven' with each other.[1] The police is a structure which determines the parts, places and roles for each in the social order. It articulates the 'matching of functions, places and ways of being' (DS, 36). It guarantees that the social order is a coherent unidirectional whole where functions and roles match with each other and allows the predictability of the function of the social to continue. It can be argued that, engaging with the police, emancipation can be aimed at redirecting or twisting the directions of the police logic. In relation to the social order, structured by the police, equality could then arguably even make some *progress*. A quick look at two distinctive interpretations of the relations between politics and the police in Rancière should allow me, however, to point out the problems included in the attempts to mediate the relations between equality and the police.

Jean-Philippe Deranty has argued that 'the political' (*le politique*) serves for Rancière as a place of mediation between these two dimensions. It allows to think ways in which equality is not only verified as such but in which aspects of the social order can be 'redressed', although at the same time Deranty is careful to separate Rancière's model from any teleological movement towards a reconciliation.² His characterization of Rancière's 'paradoxical dialectic' as both 'decidedly nondialectical' and formally 'dialectical' is telling of the problematic nature of the question of mediation between equality and the unequal social order in Rancière.³ The difficulty is real and present in Rancière's own writings, which make Deranty's interpretation legitimate as such.

However, as Samuel Chambers has convincingly argued, despite some explicit appearances in Rancière's texts, 'the political', as the realm of mediation on which Deranty's argument is based, does not really fit Rancière's conception of emancipatory politics and its relation with the police.⁴ Chambers himself emphasizes politics and the police as radical opposites whose conjunction cannot point to any realm of dialectical or quasi-dialectical mediation. Two logics 'blend', as Chambers argues, and yet at the same time politics paradoxically remains a radically disruptive 'other' to the police. While politics cannot be substantially 'uncoupled' from the police, their confrontation cannot be understood through a mediating term.⁵ Although it offers a persuasive critique of Deranty's attempt to think the two through a mediating principle, Chambers's own solution becomes in my eyes even less satisfying than that of Deranty. Namely, in lack of any mediating term, Chambers ends up thinking the paradoxical contact of the two logics simply from the viewpoint of the police order. Thus, he ends up with 'a commitment to ... the politics of the police in the quite elemental sense of changing, transforming, and improving our police orders'.⁶ This is a striking conclusion, and it is hard to see how a practice based on absolute equality of anyone with anyone could be harnessed to cultivate reformed police orders which are by definition premised on 'the denial of equality' (D, 35).

Yet, Rancière's texts open towards both Deranty and Chambers's interpretations and both of them are attentive readers of Rancière. If they are haunted by questions concerning the *consequentiality* of the Rancièrian practice of radical equality in the social order, it is because Rancière, too, is at times haunted by such questions. As Chambers puts it, politics 'requires ... direction'.⁷ However, in Rancière, as I have tried to argue in this book, the logic of emancipation as such does not offer it, and cannot offer it, without contradicting its most fundamental commitments. This is why Chambers needs to look for a direction or orientation from the police logic. He also shows why Todd May, another distinctive reader of Rancière's political thought, does not manage to produce a plausible interpretation of Rancière. While my sympathies lie more with May's motives that those of Chambers, I agree with the latter's rejection of May's insistence on 'pure politics' insofar as this would mean that emancipatory politics is seen as pointing to a state of things *'after'* the police order.[8] For Rancière, equality is self-sufficient in the present, and emancipation is not differentiated from the order of domination *in time*. This is finally what it means that emancipation takes place *within* police orders or is interwoven with them. The logic of emancipation affirms equality *now* – or if you like, 'now and forever', insofar as every egalitarian now shares in one and the same subtraction from its temporal qualification. Strictly speaking, the only thing that can *develop* and be *directed* is the police order. This is the reason why Chambers invests in it.

Chambers's reading is particularly helpful precisely because it allows us to see that in order to make Rancière's notion of emancipation a manageable project it must align with the police. Chambers thus allows us to clearly see the choice: when it comes to organized directed projects, Rancière either stands as a reformist or falls as a radical. Either one accepts that a claim to radical equality is not really that radical but readily channelled towards 'better' forms of its denial; or one acknowledges Rancière as a radical thinker of revolt along the lines I have drawn in this book. In the latter case, however, we may need to accept that his account of radical politics is marked with serious problems and limitations. For me, it is more useful to appreciate his attempt to insist on full, uncompromising and immediate principle of equality. As such it can offer elements and emphases that can be borrowed for renewed attempts to think more organized processes of emancipation. Here it is possible to point towards such attempts only very tentatively.

The way Rancière's work privileges a human *capacity* of emancipation, rather than historical circumstances of political action, is well worth taking seriously. It is a valuable reminder that the order of primacy between the two is not set in stone but a question of which we decide to emphasize and build on. Rancière takes the independence and the radical sameness of this capacity too far, however, in not allowing historically determined conditions to put any significant constraints on it. One reason for this, I think, is the background from which he comes to develop his position. Rather than from any positive accounts of a practical capacity, it stems, as we know, from Althusser's radical rejection to reflect action on the givenness of the continuity of time. This opened the way to a quite specific appreciation of the Cultural Revolutionary revolt, boosted by the way the events of May 1968 came as a *surprise* for the young Althusserians. These factors encouraged Althusser's most original and uncompromising students to think politics in the most radical forms of rupture not only in time but also, so to speak, *from* time. Lardreau's self-cancelling notion of revolt showed the stakes in the most extreme form. Rancière no doubt manages to engage with the actualities of revolt better than Lardreau, but the negative approach with which he begins drives him to think human capacity through a certain independence from temporally structured operators rather than through positive engagements with objective forms of temporal constraints. It is due to the lack of a more positive and substantial account of a subjective capacity that Rancière needs to lean so extensively on yet another form of objective determination, that is, a certain abstract spatiality which for him allows more egalitarian modelling of things, more indifference to differences. Abstract spatiality also allows him to rethink Althusserian *theory* directly as an egalitarian capacity, as we have seen.

However, we should recall the practical aim-orientedness in relation to which Althusser originally tried to rethink history while leaving this practical side almost completely undeveloped. That is perhaps the point where we should re-enter the Althusserian project and put it in dialogue with practices articulated in clearly strategic terms. As we have seen, the French Revolution might offer one example for such a practice. As for Rancière's Maoist post-Althusserianism, it might offer ways to allow more freedom for articulating and justifying the historical intelligibility of revolutionary action. The cross-historical contiguity that figures in Rancière can be helpful in reconsidering the nature of 'eternal' principles and capacities, that is, principles that cannot be reduced to the factuality of historical circumstances.

Notes

Introduction: Spatiality, equality, intelligence

1. Benjamin, *The Arcades Project*, 912.
2. Bensaïd, *Marx for Our Times*, 82. Peter Osborne's ongoing project forms one of the most elaborate attempts to re-conceptualize historical temporalization within the Marxist tradition (see e.g. his *The Politics of Time* as well as the more recent *Anywhere or Not at All*). Alain Badiou can be given as an example of a thinker who is less interested in thinking historical time per se but who acknowledges the great importance of temporal ordering for political organization. I will later discuss both Osborne and Badiou in relation to Rancière on these questions.
3. Cf. Ross, 'Historicizing Untimeliness'.
4. Robson, 'Jacques Rancière and Time', 309.
5. Rancière, 'In What Time Do We Live?', 11.
6. Ibid., 12. As Christian Fajardo argues in an interesting recent article, 'Upon a closer look, it becomes evident that, for Rancière, there are no forms of prohibition that are not crossed "by the idea that 'it is not the moment yet', 'it is no longer the moment' or even 'it has never been the time'"' ('Jacques Rancière: Aesthetics, Time, Politics', 4, quoting Rancière in *La Méthode de l'égalité*, 108). Fajardo also mentions that multiple times coexist 'in the same space' in Rancière (as well as in Walter Benjamin) but he does not thematize this spatiality (see 'Jacques Rancière: Aesthetics, Time, Politics', 6).
7. Kant, *Critique of Practical Reason*, 5:94, 5:99.
8. Rancière, 'Un-What?', 593.
9. Rancière, 'Art Is Going Elsewhere', 72; IS, 16.
10. Feuerbach, *The Fiery Brook*, 54.
11. Ibid., 54/17, tm.
12. Wartofsky, *Feuerbach*, 174.
13. Feuerbach, *The Fiery Brook*, 54.
14. Ibid., 235/327, tm.
15. Ibid., 234.
16. Ibid., 235.
17. PP, xxv; cf. ME, 148; Rancière, 'Work, Identity, Subject', 207; 'Only in the Form of Rupture', 270–1; 'Interview with Jacques Rancière' (by Nina Power), 80.

18 Rancière, *The Edges of Fiction*, 115; Rancière, 'Anachronism and the Conflict of Times', 14; Rancière, *The Edges of Fiction*, 115, tm; for explicit references to Feuerbach's concept of space, see AL, 5–6; PP, 6; ME, 148.
19 Feuerbach, *The Fiery Brook*, 54.
20 Rancière, *The Edges of Fiction*, 115.
21 Rancière, *Modern Times*, 23.
22 Ibid., 25, 48.
23 Feuerbach, *The Fiery Brook*, 235, tm.
24 Mustafa Dikeç, who has done the most substantial work on Rancière from the perspective of spatiality, has referred to this meaning of the Greek *dēmos* while discussing Rancière. However, it is strange that Dikeç does so only through Benveniste's etymological studies, while disregarding the passages where Rancière himself invokes the spatiality of *dēmos*. José Luis Moreno Pestaña touches on this theme briefly in 'Castoriadis, Rancière: Quels apports pour une philosophie du tirage au sort en politique?'.
25 On Cleisthenes's reform, see de Ste. Croix, *Athenian Democratic Origins*, 136–79; Cartledge, *Democracy*, 65–75; on the spatial meaning of demos specifically, see Elden, 'Another Sense of Demos: Kleisthenes and the Greek Division of the Polis'. See also Laura Quintana's brief discussion of Cleisthenes's reform in relation to Rancière in her *The Politics of Bodies*, 172; notice, however, that the translation of this passage of the book, which first appeared in Spanish, is incorrect and as a result misrepresents the logic of Cleisthenes's reform as Rancière understands it; the original, Spanish formulation can be found also in Quintana, 'Institución y acción política 149–50.
26 Rancière, 'Entretien avec Julia Christ et Bertrand Ogilvie', 170; 'Dissenting Words' (interview by Davide Panagia), 124.
27 See e.g. Rancière, 'Entretien avec Jacques Rancière' (interview by Nicolas Poirier), 30.
28 Rancière, 'The Thinking of Dissensus', 6.
29 As Christian Fajardo shows very well, the police order is held together precisely by a certain *temporal* homogenization (Fajardo, 'Jacques Rancière, Aesthetics, Time, Politics').
30 Rancière, 'The Thinking of Dissensus', 6; GF, 242.
31 FW, 104; Rancière, 'Work, Identity, Subject', 213.
32 Rancière, 'The Thinking of Dissensus', 6.
33 Ibid.
34 Rancière, 'The Aesthetic Dimension', 10.
35 Rancière, 'Discovering New Worlds', 35.

36 Rancière, 'The Divorce of the Eye and the Hand' (interview by Sezgin Boynik), 5.
37 Kant, *Critique of the Power of Judgment*, 5:294.
38 Kant, *Groundwork of the Metaphysics of Morals*, 4:438. On the relation of *sensus communis* to the Categorical Imperative, see Onora O'Neill, *Constructions of Reason*, 24–7.
39 Todd May has compared Rancière with Kantian ethics and suggested that Rancière's idea of democratic community could be interpreted along the lines of Kant's kingdom of ends consisting of fully equal subjects. May adds, however, that Rancière's model could not be reduced to the idea of obligation and Kant's overemphasis on the rational. While I agree that Rancière is much less interested in theorizing the obligatory nature of equality than Kant, I don't think that this needs to imply any downplaying of reason as such in favour of 'sympathy' or 'sensitivity' (*The Political Theory of Jacques Rancière*, 114–15). More recently, May has defended a stronger connection between Rancière and Kant's ethics without reference to such language of emotions. I agree with the broad line of his reading (see Todd May, 'Kant via Rancière: From Ethics to Anarchism').
40 Kant, *Critique of Practical Reason*, 5:34; IS, 138.
41 My English translation of the relevant chapter of the thesis is published in Rancière, *Marx in the Woods*.
42 Rancière, *Marx in the Woods*, 12.
43 Ibid., 13–14.
44 Ibid., 18.
45 Rancière, 'La Méthode de l'égalité', 509.
46 Rancière, *Dissenting Words*, 318, 248, emphasis added; cf., Kant, *Groundwork of the Metaphysics of Morals*, 4:438; see also Kant's analogous remarks on the idea of perpetual peace in *The Metaphysics of Morals*, 6:354.
47 Rancière, *Marx in the Woods*, 24–5; Rancière explains that the difference between Kant and the young Marx is, however, that while for the former it is the a priori legislative faculty which exceeds its limits, for the latter it is the empirical reality of private interest which drives the antinomic dialectic.
48 Kant, *Prolegomena*, 4:362.
49 Kant, *Critique of Practical Reason*, 5:95.
50 As we shall see in Chapter 1, it is Guy Lardreau, Rancière's fellow Maoist activist, who follows this logic through in his later work.
51 Cf. Marx and Engels, *The German Ideology*, 193–6; *The Communist Manifesto*, 40.
52 Kant, *Critique of Pure Reason*, A811/B839.
53 'The reflection that Kant makes use of in his critical philosophy has to reflect itself' in order to internalize everything into the processes of the genesis of the Concept (Hyppolite, *Genèse et structure de la Phénoménologie de l'esprit de*

Hegel, vol. 1, 123). As Hegel famously puts it, time is 'the Concept in its very existence [*der daseiende Begriff selbst*]' (Hegel, *Phenomenology of Spirit*, 27, tm); cf. Stanguennec, *Hegel. Critique de Kant*, 46, 52.

54 For some of the most notorious examples in Marx himself, see *Capital*, vol. 1, 929; 'Preface to *A Critique of Political Economy*', 426.

55 Louis Gabriel Gauny, Letter to Retouret, dated 2 February 1834, in Gauny, *Le Philosophe plébéien*, 165; see also ME, 109, and Rancière's short writing entitled 'I no longer have faith in time'.

56 Proust, *Kant*.

57 Birnbaum, *Égalité radicale*, 93.

58 Shapiro, 'Radicalising Democratic Theory', 203–4; see also Shapiro, 'The Presence of War'.

59 In his discussion of Deleuze's work on cinema Rancière criticizes precisely the way it is based on an epochal differentiation, which for Rancière includes a hidden teleology and approaches the history of cinema as a 'history of redemption' (*Film Fables*, 111, cf. 114). According to Rancière, this history is actually based on a contiguity of two logics (Deleuze's 'time-image' and 'movement image') which cannot be temporally distinguished, and as such Rancière embraces it (112–13). This means, as I would argue, that for Rancière emancipation is always already at work through non-temporalizable gaps and displacements between the two logics.

60 Dikeç, *Space, Politics and Aesthetics*, 95.

61 Dikeç, 'Space as a Mode of Political Thinking', 670.

62 Ibid., 669.

1 Can rupture be thought?

1 Balibar, 'Althusser et Mao', para. 11.

2 The best study of Althusser's thought in the context of political history is Gregory Elliott's *Althusser* (1987, 2nd edn, 2006).

3 In his posthumously published autobiography, Althusser himself claims that the theoretical autonomy was itself a strategy which enabled him to make this political move as a member of the French Communist Party (*The Future Lasts Forever*, 196). Étienne Balibar is sceptical of this apology of 'theoreticism' ('Avant-propos pour la réédition de 1996', xiii–xiv).

4 In 1956 Mao describes Stalin's early 'struggle to defend the legacy of Leninism against its enemies', saying that 'Stalin expressed the will and wishes of the people' ('Stalin's Place in History' (1956), in *Works of Mao Zedong by Date* (online)). He

was, however, harshly critical of the late Stalin's economism which 'says nothing about the superstructure. It is not concerned with people; it considers things, not people.' Stalin's perspective is, Mao states, 'almost completely wrong' ('Critique of Stalin's *Economic Problems of Socialism in the USSR*' (1958), in Mao, *On Practice and Contradiction*, 117).

5   Mao, *On Practice and Contradiction*, 69.
6   Claudia Pozzana has recently suggested that Mao may have been aware of Althusser's anti-Hegelian reading of his article and influenced by it. This is based on Mao's 'Talk on Problems of Philosophy' (1964) where he discusses the same issues regarding the relation between Marxian and Hegelian philosophies which Althusser had raised while referencing Mao ('Althusser and Mao').
7   Althusser, for example, calls Husserl, Heidegger and Bergson 'spiritualists', throwing extremely hostile and dismissive remarks on Bergson specifically (*The Humanist Controversy and Other Texts*, 7, 5).
8   Rancière, 'La Conception pseudo-marxiste de l'aliénation', n.p. For Rancière's later self-critique of this article, see AL, 42.
9   Later Althusser wanted to save Hegel as a thinker of 'a process without subject', blaming an ideological reading of him on the Young Hegelians' anthropological interpretation. 'Thanks to Lenin, we can begin' to understand Hegel correctly (*Lenin and Philosophy and Other Texts*, 124).
10 Balibar, 'Althusser et Mao', para. 10.
11 Mao, 'On Contradiction' (1937), in *On Practice and Contradiction*, 76–7.
12 Balibar, 'Structural Causality, Overdetermination, and Antagonism', 115.
13 As Balibar puts it: 'Structuring a set [*ensemble*] of practices is *nothing else than making intelligible* the way they affect each other' ('Avant-propos', viii, my emphasis). Stefano Pippa has suggested that the very idea of structural causality in Althusser in the end stands for contingency (Pippa, 'Althusser and Contingency', 58–60). As I will suggest in Chapter 4, in Rancière this form of intelligibility is transformed into a generic intellectual capacity to articulate a context for one's action independently of its spatio-temporal position.
14 To be more precise, in Marx the epistemological break emerges as a double theoretical revolution, or as an invention of historical *and* dialectical materialism; see, e.g., FM, 32–4, 39.
15 Cf. PSPS, 14:

> *In an existing science, the theoretical work that produced it is no longer visible to the naked eye; it has completely passed into the science as constituted.* There is a hidden danger here, because we may be tempted to treat constituted Marxist science as a given or as a set of finished truths. ... We may consider it as an absolute, finished knowledge, which poses no

problem of development or research. ... We may also – in so far as it gives us a knowledge of the real – believe that Marxist science *directly and naturally reflects the real*, that it sufficed for Marx to *see* clearly, to *read* clearly – in short, to *reflect* in his abstract theory the essence of things given in things – without taking into account the enormous work of theoretical production necessary to arrive at knowledge; and we shall then be treating it in an *empiricist* fashion.

16 Rancière, 'Only in the Form of Rupture' (interview by Peter Hallward), 259.
17 Rancière, 'The Concept of Critique and the Critique of Political Economy: From the *1844 Manuscripts* to *Capital*', in Althusser et al., *Reading Capital*, 81–199.
18 Rancière, 'La Conception pseudo-marxiste de l'aliénation'; 'Le Concept marxiste de rapport de production'; cf., ME, 13. I will not discuss these articles or Rancière's contribution to *Reading Capital* in this study.
19 For a relatively detailed account of this context with particular attention to *Cahiers pour l'Analyse*, see Peter Hallward, 'Theoretical Training'.
20 Miller, 'Action of the Structure' (1968).
21 Bourg, 'The Red Guards of Paris', 483.
22 Duroux and Balibar, 'A Philosophical Conjuncture', 178.
23 'Une Catastrophe pour révisionnisme français; une grande victoire du marxisme-léninisme' (author not given), *Garde rouge*, no. 2 (December 1966), reprinted in Kessel (ed.), *Le Mouvement 'maoïste' en France*, vol. 1, 200. 'Through its resolution, the Central Committee [of the PCF] has ruined the granite base of the Party: theory' ('Le Marxisme 'n' est pas un humanisme' (a text stating the political line of the Althusserian Maoists after the PCF's ban on theoretical anti-humanism), quoted in Kessel (ed.), *Le Mouvement 'maoïste' en France*, vol. 1, 148).
24 It is worth noticing, however, that anonymity was a general policy of CML after the foundation of the UJC-ml and does not need to have a particular bearing in Althusser's case. On *Cahiers Marxistes-Léninistes*, see Chateigner, 'From Althusser to Mao'.
25 See, e.g., Mesner, *Mao's China and After*, 300–1.
26 'Decision of the Central Committee of the Chinese Communist Party Concerning the Great Proletarian Cultural Revolution' (1966), in *Important Documents on the Great Proletarian Cultural Revolution*, 130.
27 Althusser, 'On the Cultural Revolution', 6.
28 Ibid., 10.
29 In Althusser's reading, as Claudia Pozzana says, 'the specific novelty of the events was described by means so symmetrical that it was unable to grasp its stormy and unpredictable character' ('Althusser and Mao').

30 Karol, *The Second Chinese Revolution*, 47; cf. Mao, 'Reading Notes on the Soviet Text *Political Economy*' (1960–1), in *Works of Mao Zedong by Date*. The question of political and historical agency of peasants was one of the dividing factors between the leftist and rightist tendencies in Chinese communism. Ever since 1949, the CCP had been preoccupied with the problem of organizing peasants politically, and the Great Leap Forward marked a new and more radical phase in experimenting with 'an original political role for the peasants' (see Russo, *Cultural Revolution and Revolutionary Culture*, Chapter 2, quotation from page 35).
31 See Karl, *Mao Zedong and China in the Twentieth Century World*, 58–9.
32 'In the Great Proletarian Cultural Revolution, the only method is for the masses to liberate themselves, and any method of doing things in their stead must not be used' ('Decision of the Central Committee', in *Important Documents*, 137–8).
33 Karol, *The Second Chinese Revolution*, 12.
34 Karl, *Mao Zedong and China in the Twentieth Century World*, 125.
35 Mao, 'Directives Regarding Cultural Revolution' (1966–9); 'Talk at a Meeting of the Central Cultural Revolution Group' (9 January 1967), in *Works of Mao Zedong by Date*.
36 Mao, 'Talk at the Enlarged Meeting of the Political Bureau', March 20, 1966, in *Works of Mao Zedong by Date*.
37 'Circular of the Central Committee of the Chinese Communist Party' (1966), in *Important Documents*, 112–13, 118.
38 Mao, 'Talk at the Enlarged Meeting of the Political Bureau' (20 March 1966); 'Talk at a Meeting of the Central Cultural Revolution Group' (9 January 1967), in *Works of Mao Zedong by Date*.
39 'Decision of the Central Committee', in *Important Documents*, 146; cf. Badiou, *The Communist Hypothesis*, 123–5. For Badiou, the Cultural Revolution failed precisely because it insisted on the party form.
40 Mao, 'Directives Regarding Cultural Revolution', in *Works of Mao Zedong by Date*.
41 For a description of the revolts of the youth, see, e.g., Gao Yuan's *Born Red*. I will return to this aspect of the Cultural Revolution in the next chapter.
42 UJC-ml, 'Résolution politique de la Ire session du Ier congrès de la U.J.C. (m.-l.)' (January–February 1967), extract reprinted in Kessel (ed.), *Le Mouvement 'maoïste' en France*, vol. 1, 205.
43 See Kessel (ed.), *Le Mouvement 'maoïste' en France*, vol. 1, 270–7; see also Bourseiller, *Les Maoïstes*, 82–3. Cf. Mao on investigations: 'Everyone engaged in practical work must investigate conditions at the lower levels. Such investigation is especially necessary for those who know theory but do not know the actual conditions, for otherwise they will not be able to link theory with practice'

(*Quotations from Chairman Mao Tse-Tung*, 230). For the significance of this idea for French Maoism, especially in relation to the group Union des Communistes de France Marxiste-Léniniste and Alain Badiou, see Bosteels, *Badiou and Politics*, 112–15.
44 UJC-ml, 'Rapport de la cellule de voyage Albanie', quoted in Kessel (ed.), *Le Mouvement 'maoïste' en France*, vol. 1, 273.
45 UJC-ml (untitled text by a subcell in Bretagne), quoted in Kessel (ed.), *Le Mouvement 'maoïste' en France*, vol. 1, 274.
46 UJC-ml, 'La Situation actuelle et nos tâches' (December 1967), reprinted in Kessel (ed.), *Le Mouvement 'maoïste' en France*, vol. 1, 285, 286.
47 Both ideas come from French translations of Mao's texts where *enquête* and *établissement* refer to varying lengths of engagement with the masses, from a few months (*enquête*) to a few years (*s'établir*) (Smith, 'From Etablissement to Lip', n.p.).
48 UJC-ml, 'Sur les groupes d'établissement' (March 1968), in Kessel (ed.), *Le Mouvement 'maoïste' en France*, vol. 1, 279.
49 Ibid.
50 UJC-ml, 'A propos des perspectives d'organisation d'un détachement du prolétariat' (December 1967), in Kessel (ed.), *Le Mouvement 'maoïste' en France*, vol. 1, 299–300; cf. Bourg, 'The Red Guards of Paris', 488.
51 UJC-ml, 'Sur nos tâches d'organisation. Rapport du Groupe Nord' (December 1967), in Kessel (ed.), *Le Mouvement 'maoïste' en France*, vol. 1, 304, cf. 307.
52 Smith, 'From Etablissement to Lip'.
53 See, e.g., Bourseiller, *Les Maoïstes*, 106–7.
54 Pierre Victor (alias Benny Lévy, the leader of the GP), interviewed in Manceaux, *Les Maos en France*, 193.
55 Ibid.
56 Ibid., 216.
57 Ibid.
58 Lenin, *Collected Works*, vol. 19, 21.
59 SO, 107 n.1; cf. Le Dantec, *Les Dangers du soleil*, 146.
60 In Althusser's words, we can read in Lenin a 'specific theoretical form of the Marxist dialectic in its directly political existence' (RC, 31). This reading has to be 'symptomal', though, that is to say, it has to produce the questions to which Lenin answers without knowing it. The same procedure is to be at work in our reading of Marx, following Marx's own method of dealing with classical economists (see RC, 29–34).
61 Althusser, 'On the Cultural Revolution', 2.
62 Ibid., 2, 3.

63 Foucault is not, however, looking to construct a general paradigm of discontinuous temporality which would underlie changes of epistemes:

> My problem was not at all to say, 'Voila, long live discontinuity, we are in the discontinuous and a good thing too', but to pose the question, 'How is it that at certain moments and in certain orders of knowledge, there are these sudden take-offs, these hastenings of evolution, these transformations which fail to correspond to the calm, continuist image that is normally accredited?' But the important thing here is not that such changes can be rapid and extensive, or rather it is that this extent and rapidity are only the sign of something else. (*Power/Knowledge*, 112)

64 Miguel de Beistegui explains it well: 'Beneath the "system" of the true and the false, the principle of veridiction and the *desire* to find and speak the truth, which we consider to be part of human nature, and with which philosophy itself identifies, there is a "phenomenon" of an entirely different kind, namely, a struggle, a will (*volonté*) to appropriate, dominate and subjugate' ('The Subject of Truth', 84–5).
65 de Beistegui, 'The Subject of Truth', 85.
66 Cf. Lardreau, *Dialogues avec Georges Duby*, 14–15.
67 The course list of the philosophy department of the University of Vincennes from the academic year 1969/70 is telling of the particular interest in the notion of 'stage'. When Judith Miller was lecturing on 'The 3rd stage of Marxism-Leninism: Maoism', Rancière taught a course entitled 'Theory of the 2nd Stage of Marxism-Leninism: The Concept of Stalinism' (Driver, *The Exploding University*, 171).
68 Cf. Lardreau, 'Science est-elle policière ?' (interview by Bernard-Henri Lévi), 59; SO, xx.
69 'Marxism does not have a history. The only continuity which can be read in it, is the desire of the oppressed to get rid of oppression' (SO, 104 n.1; cf. During, *Exit Capitalism*, 141).
70 Lardreau, 'Science est-elle policière ?', 59.
71 Hallward, 'Reason and Revolt', 16.
72 In Chapter 2, I will discuss the idea of 'establishment', relating it to the practice of the *établis*.
73 In principle the agent of this mediation is the Party. However, Lardreau states that it can also be done by the masses themselves, and the status of the Party is not further elaborated in the book. This relates to the general ambivalence relating to the question of the Party in the philosophy of the Cultural Revolution and the way it was adopted in the post-68 France. On one hand, the existence of the Party did not seem to be fully compatible with the absolute authority of the masses; on the other hand, its status was not questioned.

74 This is why, as we shall see in Chapter 4, Rancière affirms anachronism whereas Lardreau fully rejects it.
75 Lardreau, *La Véracité*, 150.
76 As Alberto Toscano sums up Lardreau and Jambet's position in *L'Ange*, '[t]he key is to render oneself useless to mastery' ('Mao and Manichaeism', 55).
77 Lardreau and Jambet, *L'Ange*, 10.
78 Lardreau and Jambet, 'Entretien avec Gilles Hertzog', 55.
79 For a critical reading of Lardreau and Jambet's position in *L'Ange*, and its comparison with Alain Badiou's Maoism, see Bruno Bosteels, *Badiou and Politics*, 144–8.
80 Lardreau and Jambet, *Le Monde*, 280.
81 Lardreau, *La Véracité*, 230.
82 Ibid., 211.
83 Ibid., 250.
84 Ibid.
85 The text was composed for publication in Latin America and came out in French only in 1973, in the journal *L'Homme et la société*. At the time of writing it, as Rancière explains in the foreword of the 1973 version, the self-sufficiency of the on-going revolt would have made the publication of a theoretical intervention 'laughable' in the French context ('Sur la théorie de l'idéologie. Politique d'Althusser', 31). On the background of the text and the political tensions within the context of university, see the 'Introductory note' from 2010 in AL, 127–8.
86 Tanke, *Jacques Rancière*, 17.
87 See ibid., 8, cf. 3.
88 Kant, *Critique of Pure Reason*, A687/B715.
89 Cf. Althusser, 'Student Problems', 11: 'Marx has shown that the division of labour has *two forms* [i.e., technical and social] which are sometimes distinct and sometimes confused.' However, later Althusser would himself argue, much like Rancière here, that 'every "technical" division, every "technical" organisation of labour is the form and mask of the *social* (= class) division and organisation of labour' (*Lenin and Philosophy and Other Texts*, 183–4). This statement appears in a postscript, added in 1970 to the canonical essay 'Ideology and Ideological State Apparatuses' (1969). The essay can be seen as a response to the leftist critique manifest in Rancière's essay where Althusser tries to integrate it to his own discourse. In fact, Rancière thinks that his essay on Althusser from 1969 where he talks about "ideological apparatuses" might have affected Althusser's theory of Ideological State Apparatuses. As Rancière sees it, Althusser's adoption of the concept of ideological apparatus nevertheless repeats the failure to include

an adequate understanding of class division in his discourse: 'The notion of ideological state apparatuses offers – it is true – a certain representation of bourgeois domination. But there is something missing from the picture it paints: the class that is dominated' (AL, 76). As Grahame Lock explains Althusser's essay on the ideological state apparatuses 'caused anxiety in some circles' around the Party ('Introduction', in ES-C, 2).

90 Althusser, 'Student Problems', 14–15, quoted in AL, 138.
91 As Rancière has later described the procedure:

> We need to return to Marx's own thought if we are to get communist practice out of its impasse. But Marx's own thought is not to be found in Marx's texts, it is only to be found in a practical state in Leninist political action. However, at this point the displacement appears to constitute a vicious circle. Lenin *practiced* the Marxist science of historical materialism. But he did not formulate the principle of scientificity. So, the theoretical principle of Leninist action must be sought once again from the Marxist texts. ('Althusser', 531)

92 AL, 55; cf. the section 'Theory for militants' earlier in the text.
93 Elliott, *Althusser*, 179.
94 AL, 52. This is the reason why Rancière has later noted that this first phase of the distinctively Althusserian philosophy – despite the machinery of indefinite deferral that it generated – 'has inappropriately been called "theoreticism"', thus implying that it had in fact serious political effects ('Althusser', 532).
95 ES-C, 73, quoted in in AL, 105.
96 Rancière, 'La Nouvelle orthodoxie de Louis Althusser', *Le Monde*, September 12, 1973.
97 Lardreau, *La Véracité*, 241.
98 Ibid., 271.
99 'Directives Regarding Cultural Revolution' (1966–9), in *Works of Mao Zedong by Date*.
100 Stage or scene becomes a central notion for Rancière (see Chapter 3).
101 Rancière, 'Utopistes, bourgeois et prolétaires' (1975).
102 This is the core of Rancière's critique of Marxism which he will make repeatedly in his subsequent work: Historical actors are entrapped between the past that is already gone and the future that is not yet here. This entrapment in time renders their actions futile and illegitimate (see SR, 70; PP, 94; NH, 31).
103 Rancière, 'Utopistes, bourgeois et prolétaires', 88.
104 Ibid., 88.
105 Ibid., 96.

106 Rancière, 'Introduction', in Rancière and Faure (eds.), *La Parole ouvrière*, 18.

107 Rancière, 'Utopistes, bourgeois et prolétaires', 94. At this point Rancière acknowledges the Marx of the 'Theses' who poses the famous question of the education of the educators:

> The question whether concrete [*gegenständliche*] truth can be attributed to human thinking is not a question of theory but is a *practical question*. Man must prove the truth, i.e. the reality [*Wirklichkeit*] and power [*Macht*], the this-sidedness of his thinking in practice. ... The materialist doctrine concerning the changing of circumstances and upbringing forgets that circumstances are changed by men and that it is essential to educate the educator himself. This doctrine must, therefore, divide society into two parts, one of which is superior to society. (Marx, 'Theses on Feuerbach' (1845), 3–4, tm)

108 Along these lines, the editorial of the volume 5 of *Les Révoltes logiques* – a journal of a research collective Rancière founded in 1975 – states that the guiding question of the collective's historical studies 'is not concerned with what we have to do, but ... with what we will [*ce que nous voulons*]' (3–4). We can readily make the critical remark, however, that this is not a useful distinction to the extent that it gives up any attempt to think a dialectical relation between the two. Rancière starts moving early on away from such a mediated relation between the 'objective' and the 'subjective'.

109 Rancière, 'Utopistes, bourgeois et prolétaires', 92

110 Ibid., 93, 89.

111 Drevet, *Le Socialisme pratique*, Paris, 1850, 224, quoted in Rancière, 'Utopistes, bourgeois et prolétaires', 89.

112 Rancière, 'Utopistes, bourgeois et prolétaires', 90.

113 Marx and Engels, *The German Ideology*, 47.

114 Rancière, 'Utopistes, bourgeois et prolétaires', 88.

115 Rancière, 'Autonomie et historicisme', 59.

2 Rancière's literary Maoism

1 Rancière, 'Democracy, Dissensus and the Aesthetics of Class Struggle' (interview by Max Blechman et al.), 294, my emphasis; cf., e.g., Rancière, *The Emancipated Spectator*, 19, 43; *Hatred of Democracy*, 97; see also Davis, 'Editor's Introduction', in *Rancière Now*.

2 Lardreau was never an *établi*. Together with Christian Jambet – who did become one – Lardreau worked at *lycées* to support revolts and to encourage students to choose the path of *établissement* instead of an academic career (see Linhart, *Volontaires pour l'usine*, 46–7, 168–9; see also Hamon and Rotman, *Génération*, vol. 2, 44–5). Overall, thousands of young people became *établis*, and it is obvious that different subjective motivations behind this practice were multiple. My discussion here concerns the broad ideology of *gauchisme* whose organizational framework was largely, although not solely, that of UJC-ml and GP.

3 GF, 663. A discussion of *établissement* could also be contextualized differently by linking it back to Simone Weil's experience as a factory worker in the 1930s (see her *La Condition ouvrière*). Indeed, as Donald Reid relates, her figure 'was haunting journalists' accounts of the *établis*' at the time. However, he adds that, despite Weil and a few other possible points of comparison, 'there was no real precedent' for the *établis* in French history. '[T]he real model was Chinese communism', albeit an 'imaginary' one (Reid, 'La Grand Récit des établis', 35). While not pursued further in the present book, a comparison between the *établis* and Simone Weil is nevertheless a worthy endeavour, especially in the context of Rancière. Rancière refers to her in his *Short Voyages to the Land of the People*. The book includes an introduction which frames its topic explicitly in terms of Maoism (for Weil, see pages 124–5; for Maoism, page 2). Edward J. Hughes has discussed Simone Weil's account of her factory work from the perspective of Rancière's thinking. He shows well that Weil shares (the later) Rancière's emphasis on 'social disaggregation' as well as an aspiration to escape one's 'self' (*Egalitarian Strangeness*, 135, 137). Gilles Hanus has defined the practice of *établissement* in similar terms, as 'putting the Self in crisis' (Hanus, 'Renverser l'ordre des choses', 58).

4 Gilles, 'La Cause du Peuple: marxisme ou anarchisme ?', 2. Lardreau touches upon the problems included in the restricted spatial perspective to revolt: 'If the living conditions of the masses are the very source of their knowledge, of all knowledge, it is also true that they impose limits to this knowledge. Even if attachment to the factory allows grouping together, as attachment, it also means dispersion' (SO, 122). This quotation is from the same passage where Lardreau acknowledges the role of the Party as a function of mediation of revolt. The whole passage occupies a symptomatic place in *Le Singe d'or* bringing up themes whose relation to the general position of the book remains underdeveloped.

5 Serge Guillemin, interviewed in Linhart, *Volontaires pour l'usine*, 187.

6 'La Science est-elle policière ?', 60.

7   As we saw in Chapter 1, the incapacity to not presuppose historical orientation for the realization of emancipatory revolt would eventually make Lardreau give up any hope for such a realization.
8   GF, 663. It is such a pregiven force which allowed Rancière to first go to the archives 'with the idea at the time that I would find the "real" [*vrai*] working class, the "real" workers' discourse, the "real" labour movement, the "true" [*veritable*] workers' socialism, all that you could imagine and hope for as true' (ME, 21; see also 22–5). Rancière's 'Introduction' to *La Parole ouvrière* (1976), an edited collection of workers' texts, is still ambiguous in this respect. His emphatic rejection of any idea of origins risks being contradicted by his discourse on *a class* claiming *its* place, developing *its* identity (Rancière and Faure (eds), *La Parole ouvrière*, 8–9). In the 'Postface' of a re-edition from 2007, Rancière notices this himself, saying that there was still an idea of a unified 'working class voice' and thus *one* working class whose unity he would question in *The Nights of Labour* (1981) (ibid., 340–1; cf. Rancière, 'The Myth of the Artisan' (1983), 9).
9   Sartre, 'Avant-propos', in Manceaux, *Les Maos en France*, 14, my emphasis.
10 Rancière, 'Citoyenneté, culture et politique', 58.
11 Linhart, *The Assembly Line*, 59–60/60–1, tm.
12 See, e.g., Rancière, 'What Does It Mean to Be *Un*?', 565; ME, 28; 'On Ignorant Schoolmasters', 4.
13 This topic has been rarely mentioned in the literature on Rancière and in my knowledge never discussed in any detail. A passing reference can be found in Jean-Philippe Deranty:

> The year 1968 and those that immediately followed had a profound impact on Rancière on a theoretical, but also, judging from rare biographical indications, on an existential level. Throughout his writings, we hear the reverberation of the appeal made to intellectuals to 'get off their horses' … as a famous Mao aphorism put it: that is, to overcome class boundaries in real life as much as in thought, an injunction that led many *gauchiste* intellectuals to 'establish' themselves in factories ('A Journey in Equality', 3)

14 'Getting down from the horseback' was a phrase favoured in the Maoist circles. For the use of this metaphor in Mao, see 'Some Experiences in Our Party's History' (1956), 328; 'Speech at the Chinese Communist Party's National Conference on Propaganda Work' (1957), 426; 'Criticize Han Chauvinism' (1953), 87, in Mao's *Selected Works*, vol. 5; cf. Rancière, *Les Mots et les torts*, 33.
15 SV, 2, 32; cf. Rancière's recent references to Wordsworth's voyage in his *Le Temps du paysage*, 91, 95.

16 'Cartography' is of course used to describe Foucault's work at the time, by himself as well as by Deleuze (see Foucault, *Dits et écrits*, vol. 2, 725; Deleuze, *Foucault*, 23–44). Rancière has later stated that he 'was not so excited ... about this theme' in Deleuze and Foucault (ME, 259). He did not attack them directly, however, as he did Glucksmann who according to him was misusing Foucault (Rancière, 'Joan of Arc in the Gulag' (1975), in *The Intellectual and His Double*, 109–10).
17 Rancière and Rancière, 'The Philosophers' Tale' (1978), 81, 87.
18 Ibid., 79.
19 Ibid., 79/11, tm. In the expression '*grilles du temps*' we can hear an echo of Foucault's statements concerning the episteme of the Classical age in *The Order of Things*:

> The entire system of grids [*grilles*] which analysed the sequence of representations (a thin temporal series unfolding in men's minds), arresting its movement, fragmenting it, spreading it out and distributing it in a permanent table, all these distinctions created by words and discourse, characters and classification, equivalences and exchange, have been so completely abolished that it is difficult today to rediscover how that structure was able to function. (303–4)

The expression hence signifies a consolidation of a temporal order through space.
  Georges Didi-Huberman has recently discussed the metaphor of seismograph in Aby Warburg, who uses it to describe Burckhardt and Nietzsche's thinking. For Warburg, Didi-Huberman relates, 'The historian-seismograph registers in a tactile fashion the symptoms of the age ...; then he transmits these ... for others to look at' (*The Surviving Image*, 72). The description accords with the point about the hierarchy of knowledge which Rancière wants to make with the metaphor of seismology. However, Didi-Huberman's argument links seismography to an idea of '*confusion of times*' and hence to 'anachronism' (ibid., 83). With reference to Didi-Huberman's discussion of Aby Warburg in another book, Rancière has criticized Didi-Huberman's understanding of anachronism in terms of a symptom. For Rancière, such an interpretation serves to articulate the concept of anachronism back into an underlying temporal coherence (see 'Anachronism and the Conflict of Times', 119).
20 Rancière and Rancière, 'The Philosophers' Tale', 94.
21 NH, 60; Michelet, *Introduction à l'histoire universelle*, 4.
22 For a reading of these, see Nikulin, '*The Names in History*'. Nikulin explains well Rancière's own favouring of 'paratactical' writing which according to me should be seen in light of the broader principle of spatiality at work in Rancière's thought (81–3; cf. Davis, *Jacques Rancière*, ix).

23 This means that discourse is not an external element commenting on a narrative, but it is integrated into the movement of the latter (NH, 56). For Rancière's understanding of the difference between document and monument, see his *Figures de l'histoire*, 26.
24 The English edition translates *sens* consistently into 'meaning' and thus loses the important aspect following from the double meaning of the word. To bring this aspect visible, I have here translated *sens* into 'meaning/orientation'.
25 NH, 65; Michelet, *Œuvres complètes*, 3:610, quoted in NH, 57.
26 Rancière is here making the same claim in relation to history that Foucault had made on political theory: we still haven't 'cut off the king's head' (Foucault, *The Foucault Reader*, 63).
27 Ross, 'Historicizing Untimeliness'.
28 Rancière: 'The Method of Equality', 282.
29 Christian Ruby makes a similar observation than Ross about spatialization, while noticing also the positive dynamic use that Rancière makes of spatial terms (Ruby, *L'Interruption*, 42–3, 45–6).
30 See also Mustafa Dikeç's critique of Ross's dismissal of the role of spatiality in Rancière (*Space, Politics and Aesthetics*, 84–9). Notice, however, that Dikeç does not refer to *The Names of History* from which Ross's discussion as well as my own here set out. This is not a surprise insofar as the conflictual relation between space and time that I am tracing questions Dikeç's reading of the role of space in Rancière which he understands according to a unity of space-time.
31 Ralph Freedman describes Rilke's relationship with Marthe Hennebert as follows: Rilke

> befriended her out of pity and from a profound compulsion to remake her, perhaps because her visible misery struck a responsive chord in his own mind. Rilke referred to her as a worker with a horrendous history of exploitation, a young girl, '*ouvrière*, with an infinitely long past that almost destroyed her'. ... [...H]e was eager to offer her a new life, help her become someone, learn something. (Freedman, *Life of a Poet*, 313)

32 Rancière is quoting a letter from Rilke to Magda von Hattingberg (Benvenuta), in *Rilke and Benvenuta*, 12.
33 Bruno Bosteels has shown the role of 'nonplace' in recent French philosophy in an article where Rancière, too, is discussed. Although his analysis shows in a very helpful way that Rancière's notion of the nonplace is linked to a broader problematic in recent French philosophy, I would nevertheless insist on slightly different view when it comes to Rancière's use of it. Bosteels appears to read Rancière broadly in terms of a dialectical *process* based on the 'interplay between the nonplace and the new place', thus subjecting the spatial functions to a

temporality through which emancipatory politics *proceeds* in order 'to move beyond' to a qualitatively new situation (Bosteels, 'Nonplaces', 132; Bosteels refers here to Rancière's *The Disagreement* where the phrase '*un nouveau lieu*' appears once). I will have later a chance to show the problematic status of processuality (Chapter 3) as well as temporal qualities such as 'the new' in Rancière's work (Chapter 4). These are not at all absent in it, but they are all the same obscured and sometimes explicitly downplayed by the writer himself. Bosteels is a devoted reader of Badiou, and his reading of Rancière here tends to produce a misleading proximity between the two French thinkers. Whereas Badiou remains a thinker of organized processes, in respect to Rancière, ideas of processuality, or proceeding, remain problematic. As this book argues, spatiality in Rancière should not be understood as a function of dialectics which comes to temporalize it but as an intervention of a logic that clashes with temporal determinations as such. For Rancière nonplace is that which disturbs the temporal consistency of the established historical situation by imposing a disoriented and undirected sphere upon it. The logic of emancipation consists in 'a pure inscription of a place without a place [*d'un lieu sans lieu*], of a place which disturbs the natural order of the places and functions' (Rancière, 'Sens et usages de l'utopie', 69). Its effectiveness is not so much a 'new place', i.e., a place differentiated from the 'old' through temporal operators, but it marks a malfunctioning of a temporally unified situation as such and introduces a self-sufficient egalitarian coexistence to it.

34 Rilke to Countess M., September 26, 1919, quoted in SV, 101.
35 Rancière, 'After What', 251
36 Rancière, 'La Représentation de l'ouvrier ou la classe impossible' (1983), 102–3.
37 Badiou, *Theory of the Subject* (1982), 248–58; cf. Lacan, *Écrits*, 161–75.
38 Rancière, 'Discovering New Worlds', 35.
39 There are some confusions in discussions concerning the emergence of the concept of *littérarité* in Rancière. In a chapter entitled 'Literarity' of his *The Lessons of Rancière*, Samuel A. Chambers makes strange distinctions around it: 'To summarize, the term *literariness* [in *The Names of History*] appears earliest; it is then followed by a very particular use of the word *literary* (in the sense of the political animal as a "literary animal"); and this is followed in turn by the coinage of the word *literarity* (at the end of *Flesh of Words*)' (Chambers, *The Lessons of Rancière*, 190 n.24; this note summarizes the genealogy Chambers develops in the body of the text as well as in an earlier article 'The Politics of Literarity'). In Rancière's French there is no distinction between 'literarity' and 'literariness', however, but these are simply different ways to translate the word *littérarité*. In addition to the noun *littérarité*, Rancière uses, to be sure, the adjective *littéraire*. The use of the adjective is not followed by the use of the noun, however, but the terms '*littérarité*' ('literariness') and '*animal littéraire*' ('literary

animal') are both introduced in *The Names of History* (NH, 52/108, 76/153). Brian Whitener likewise misses the term '*littérarité*' in *The Names*, claiming that it is introduced 'later' ('Nonrelation and Untimeliness in Jacques Rancière's *The Names of History*'). Allison Ross is also wrong to claim that 'the concept of "literarity" first appears in the 1995 book – *La mésentente*'; not, however, because the term would not be used in this book, as Chambers claims – it is indeed used in it – but because it had already been introduced in *The Names of History* (Ross, 'Expressivity, Literarity, Mute Speech', 136; Chambers, *The Lessons of Rancière*, 190 n.24; the term '*littérarité*' appears on page 61 of *La Mésentente*). The person who gets it right is Gabriel Rockhill who correctly refers to *The Names of History* in the 'Glossary of Technical Terms' added to his translation of *Le Partage du sensible* (PA, 87). The fact that Chambers refers to this glossary as a confirmation of his own statements no doubt adds to the confusion of his discussion (*The Lessons of Rancière*, 190 n.24).

40 Rancière has linked the principle of 'literarity' to 'literature' in his many accounts of the latter. However, literarity is not reduced to the art of literature and does not stem from it. It is a 'transhistorical' form which describes the emancipatory capacity of human beings (ME, 56). 'Literarity is one thing and literature is another thing', as Rancière puts it (GF, 431). When literature is born, the principle of literarity is incorporated into it in ways that are multiple and contradictory (see, e.g., FW, 110–11; Rancière, *The Politics of Literature*, 3–30). I will not focus on these here, for I am more interested in how 'literarity' relates to Rancière's (implicit) rethinking of Maoism.

41 Rancière, 'La Représentation de l'ouvrier ou la classe impossible', 103.
42 Rancière, 'In What Time Do We Live', 11.
43 Rancière 'La Poétique du savoir', 6.
44 Ibid.
45 Le Dantec, *Les Dangers du soleil*, 163.
46 Interviewed in Linhart, *Volontaires*, 173.
47 Le Dantec, *Les Dangers du soleil*, 163.
48 Rivenc, 'Quelques reflexions sur l'établissement en usine', 27; cf. Jenny Chomienne: 'The "true life" must be elsewhere', interviewed in Linhart, *Volontaires*, 102; Danièle Léon: 'The rallies at universities did not seem to me to correspond to reality. I was looking for a way out' (ibid., 122); Jean-Pierre Marchant: 'The truly revolutionary life was elsewhere' ('L'Épreuve du réel', 6).
49 Cf. SO, 127. While there was fascination in GP with the theme of burning books, Rancière has described the sentiment in the Maoist circles around him somewhat differently: 'When I was a Maoist, I remember that there was this saying that we liked a lot: "we must not burn the books of reactionaries, for if we burn them, we won't be able to criticize them"' (Rancière, 'Sur l'interruption'

(interview by 'Groupe Interruption'), n.p.). Hence, the Gauche Prolétarienne was not ideologically unified, and the anti-bookish attitude, characteristic of its leadership, was not shared in the same way across the organization.

50 Lévy, 'Introduction aux Cercles Socratiques' (1978), n.p.
51 Rancière, 'Discovering New Worlds', 28.
52 Robert Linhart, a letter to Nicole Linhart dated 14 August 1967, quoted in Linhart, *Le Jour où mon père s'est tu*, 31.
53 It has been often pointed out that the visits to China by French Maoists at the time where carefully orchestrated by the Chinese authorities to reassert the idealized view of the Cultural Revolution among the French Maoists. For a recent reference, see Jones and Smith, *Strategy of Maoism in the West*, 38.
54 Linhart, *Lénine, les paysans, Taylor*, 59–60; meanwhile Linhart had had his own experience as an *établi* which challenged the presumptions concerning a unified working class (see earlier in the text). Badiou has stated that many of the former activists of the GP later abandoned the Maoist cause exactly because they had mistakenly believed that the revolution was taking place in the immediate actuality, as opposed to seeing the movement as 'the start of a long journey' ('Roads to Renegacy', 126). In a certain sense, as I want to argue, Rancière's analysis goes the opposite way insofar as for him the problem was that the 'here and now' remained too much attached to a temporalized project.
55 Lévy, 'Introduction aux Cercles Socratiques'.
56 FW, 137; the phrase 'plain of history' is borrowed from Althusser himself (see FM, 180). For Althusser's own discussion on the idea of 'the imaginary Debt [the intellectuals] thought they had contracted *by not being proletarians*', see FM, 27.
57 Rancière's idea of literarity and space between words and things bears certain affinity with Derrida. The most important difference, however, concerns the latter's emphasis on 'deferral' and 'temporalization-temporization' as the space of *différance* (Derrida, *Margins of Philosophy*, 10). This allowed Derrida later to articulate his notion of 'democracy to come' in terms of messianic wait, albeit the Messiah – or democracy – would never arrive (Derrida, *The Politics of Friendship*, 104, 306; Derrida, *Rogues*, 86). Rancière sympathizes with Derrida's notion of democracy but rejects what he calls 'an infinite wait for the Event or the Messiah' (DS, 61). The Other is for Rancière not an unreachable horizon of wait but amounts to factual 'inventions of subjects and objects' in 'the broken time' of emancipation (DS, 60). For Rancière, 'the to-come' in Derrida's notion of democracy means that it is 'non-present' (Rancière, 'La Démocratie est-elle à venir?', 167; consider also how Rancière rejects the idea of a 'promise of an equality-to-come' insisting on 'the reality of a basic equality' (Rancière, 'On Ignorant Schoolmasters', 5)). Mark Robson misses this crucial difference in

his otherwise useful comparison between Rancière and Derrida (Robson, '"A Literary Animal"').

58 Gramsci, *Pre-Prison Writings*, 39.
59 Ibid., 40.
60 Ibid., 41.
61 FW, 103. 'It can get into the hands not only of those who understand it, but equally of those who have no business with it; it doesn't know how to address the right people and not the wrong people' (Plato, *Phaedrus*, 275e, quoted in PP, 40). A great interest in this theme in Plato is another point that Rancière shares with Derrida (see Derrida, *Dissemination*, 76–84; cf. GF, 353).
62 Bell, 'Writing, Movement/Space, Democracy', 135.
63 'Althusserianism's true legacy, the revisionist sign on the forehead of authoritarian leftism, is precisely the kinship between repression-by-science and repression-by-the-proletariat, a kinship that finds expression in the mission, entrusted to a group of intellectuals (representatives of science or of the proletariat), to drag the petite bourgeoisie away from its illusions and into the place of its *theoretical formation*, or its proletarization' (AL, 53).
64 Linhart, *Volontaires*, 55; cf. Philippe Gavi: 'Every time I read *La Cause du Peuple* I get the impression that for you everything that a worker says is right' (Gavi et al., *On a raison de se révolter*, 44–5).
65 Kristin Ross explains this aspect well in her 'Translator's Introduction' in the English edition of *The Ignorant Schoolmaster*.
66 See, e.g., Rancière, GF, 409–10; 'On Ignorant Schoolmasters', 10–11; Ross, 'Translator's Introduction'.
67 The only other person in my knowledge who has recognized this is Andrea Cavazzini, the Italian translator of *Le Maître ignorant*; see Cavazzini, *Le Sujet et l'étude. Idéologie et savoir dans le discours maoïste*, 79 n.12, 80 n.13, 115; cf. Cavazzini, 'Le Maître impossible. Pour un bon usage du *Maître ignorant*', 96.
68 Leese, *Mao Cult*, 92, cf. 105.
69 Ibid., 94; cf. Leese, 'A Single Spark', 31–2. It should be mentioned that repetition and mechanical copying had a central role in Chinese primary school education. Such method was not seen to contradict creative use of language but, as Jonathan Unger relates, 'the view ... was that primary school memorization *led* to a more proper and more creative use of language' (*Education Under Mao*, 68). In reference to Jacotot's discussion of Racine, Rancière writes: 'The secret of genius is that of universal teaching: learning, repeating, imitating, translating, taking apart, putting back together' (IS, 68).

70 On the editorial history of the Little Red Book, see Lei Han, 'Sources and Early Printing History of Chairman Mao's *Quotations*'.
71 As an example of such an 'absurd' application of principles one can cite the story of Peking Red Guards who changed the traffic from right hand to left hand, judging the old system *rightist*. By the same grounds, they interchanged the meanings of the traffic lights, reckoning that it was obviously counter-revolutionary to stop at red (Yan and Gao, *Turbulent Decade*, 75; see also Gao, *Born Red*, 119).
72 Cook, 'Preface', in *Mao's Little Red Book*, xiii.
73 Recall the way Rancière has later described his own way of working: 'As to my method, it will be that of children's guessing games, where the question is how two things resemble or differ from each other' (*The Future of the Image*, 91–2).
74 Rancière, 'On Ignorant Schoolmasters', 4.
75 Ibid.
76 Ibid.

> The method of inequality supposes that you must start from *this* point and try to reach *that* point by following one step after the other. The method of equality supposes that you can start from any point and that there are multiple paths that can be constructed to get to another point and still another one that is not predictable. There is a multiplicity of paths, a multiplicity of ways of constructing one's intellectual adventure, but a prior decision has to be made beforehand: the decision that one can do it because one participates in an intelligence that is the intelligence of anybody. (Rancière and Honneth, *Recognition or Disagreement*, 139–40)

77 Leese, *Mao Cult*, 105, my emphasis. 'The most dangerous aspect of the working style proposed by Lin Biao … remained the repetition of catchphrases without the ability to relate them to the spirit of Marxism-Leninism or Mao Zedong Thought' (ibid.).
78 Jacotot, *Enseignement universel. Droit et philosophie panécastique*, Paris, 1838, quoted in IS, 63/107, tm; cf. 131.
79 IS, 20. Rancière claims to have followed the 'Jacotot Method' in his archival research before knowing about its explicit existence: 'I just threw myself into it, starting with a heap of fairly scattered leads that came at me from all sides' (ME, 26, cf. 67). Rancière's intuitive application of Jacotot's principles before discovering him is perhaps another indication that we should recognize in them the radical Maoist political context once close to Rancière.
80 Leese, 'A Single Spark', 34.
81 Rancière, 'Aesthetics against Incarnation', 190.
82 Lin, 'Foreword to the Second Edition of *Quotations from the Chairman Mao Tse-tung*' (1966), n.p.

83　Karl, *Mao Zedong and China in the Twentieth-Century World*, 125.
84　Jones, 'Quotations Songs', 46. In Chapter 4 I will argue what is hinted at here, namely that anachronism and untimeliness in Rancière are best understood as applications of spatial logic to historical time so that history turns into a kind of cross-temporal space where spatial logic features as a method to transgress historical differentiations.
85　Lin, 'Foreword to the Second Edition of *Quotations from the Chairman Mao Tse-tung*' (1966).
86　Leese, *Mao Cult*, 105; cf. Birnbaum, *Les Maoccidents*, 43.
87　Rancière, 'Aesthetics against Incarnation', 174.
88　'The dominated do not remain in subordination because they misunderstand the existing state of affairs but because they lack confidence in their capacity to transform it' (AD, 45).
89　Interviewed in Myrdal and Kessle, *China* (1970), 128–9.
90　Rae, *Spider Eaters*, 98, 115.
91　Ibid., 115.
92　Leese, 'A Single Spark', 37.
93　In Rancière 'mute speech' or 'mute discourse' describes errant words characteristic of the paradigm of writing and the possibility to link whatever meanings to them. This is why the Platonic critique sees the mute discourse paradoxically as 'too loquacious' addressing itself to anyone at all with no better knowledge (PP, 39–40). The idea of 'mute speech' gave a title to a book published in 1998 where Rancière studies the paradoxical relations of this structure to Western literature and literary theory (see Rancière, *Mute Speech*).
94　D, x. A better translation of *mésentente* might be a 'missed understanding', as Davide Panagia has suggested (*Rancière's Sentiments*, 82).
95　At the analytical level, then, Rancière appears to affirm the factional divisions which for many made the experiment of the Cultural Revolution so problematic and marked its impasse. As Badiou says, '[t]he mobilization of the masses, among the youth and the workers, was huge. But it destroyed itself through divisions, factions and anarchic violence' ('Beyond Formalization' (interview by Bruno Bosteels and Peter Hallward), 352; cf. Badiou, *The Communist Hypothesis*, 145). According to the Rancièrian interpretation, the egalitarian core of the movement lies in the logic which is nevertheless not immune to such violence or in any way guarantee that the intellectual equality, on which it is based *in principle*, is maintained (regarding this problem, cf. Birnbaum, *Égalité radicale*, 55). That Rancière has explicitly dissociated his position from the historical experiment of the Cultural Revolution does not for me justify his silence on the relations that his discourse nevertheless appears to bear with it (AL, xvii).
96　Lin, quoted from a Chinese source in Leese, *Mao Cult*, 109, my emphasis.

97 Leese, 'A Single Spark', 37.
98 'Mao's faith in the people derived in part from his belief in the historical teleology of Marxism, but it was also grounded in practical experience' (Cook, 'The Spiritual Atom Bomb and its Global Fallout', 9). For a good account of Mao's philosophical-historical conceptions, see Starr, *Continuing the Revolution*, chapters 8 and 9.
99 Yaung, 'Mao Quotations in Factional Battles and Their Afterlives', 70; cf. Leese, *Mao Cult*, 88.
100 Leese, *Mao Cult*, 21, my emphasis. Leese borrows the notion of 'directed public sphere' from Cheek, 'Introduction', 7; cf. Leese, 'The Mao Cult as Communicative Space', 625. Cheek has since made a more extensive use of this notion in his *The Intellectual in Modern Chinese History*.
101 Leese, *Die Chinesische Kulturrevolution 1966–1976*, 48; cf. Friedman et al., *Revolution, Resistance and Reform in Village China*, 92; Badiou, *The Communist Hypothesis*, 127.
102 Guo et al., *Historical Dictionary of the Chinese Cultural Revolution*, 181.
103 Mao, a letter to Jiang Qing dated 8 July 1966, quoted in Li, *The Private Life of Chairman Mao*, 461; Zhisui writes, 'Mao never really had a plan for the Cultural Revolution. But the letter to his wife revealed what he thought about it then' (ibid.).
104 Cavazzini, *Le Sujet et l'étude*, 79–80, 114–15.
105 Rancière, 'Un-What?', 593.
106 Karol, *The Second Chinese Revolution*, 12.

3 Politics of staging and the primacy of space

1 Henceforth, when I use the word 'stage' without giving the original French, it translates the word '*scène*'.
2 As Peter Hallward has shown, Rancière's notion of equality is fundamentally linked to theatre 'in both the literal and metaphorical senses of the term' ('Staging Equality', 111).
3 Rancière mentions both the Marxist vision of history and the revisionist historiography as examples of frameworks that aim in this way to processualize the revolution and to suppress the revolutionary stage (SR, 51). The procedure corresponds broadly to what Rancière would later call 'metapolitics'. In *The Disagreement* where the term plays a central role, it is attached first of all to Marx. Metapolitics, as Rancière writes, 'becomes the scientific accompaniment of politics, in which the reduction of political forms to the forces of the class

struggle is initially equivalent to the truth of the lie or the truth of illusion. But it also becomes a "political" accompaniment of all forms of subjectification, which posits as its hidden "political" truth the class struggle it underestimates and cannot not underestimate' (D, 85). It is noteworthy that Rancière first coins the term '*méta-politique*' to describe Alain Badiou's philosophy (Rancière, (untitled discussion of Badiou's *Being and Event*) (1989), 217). Badiou later published a book entitled *Metapolitics* where he makes positive use of the notion and includes two highly critical chapters on Rancière (Badiou, *Metapolitics* (1998)). Alongside metapolitics, in *The Disagreement* Rancière introduces 'para-politics' and 'archi-politics', associating the first to Aristotle and Hobbes and the second to Plato (D, 65–93). For a short critical introduction of these notions, see Bosteels, 'Archipolitics, Parapolitics, Metapolitics'.

4 Rancière, *The Lost Thread*, 121.
5 Heath, 'Introduction', in Aristotle, *Poetics*, xix.
6 Alessandro Russo has suggested that the political logic of the Chinese Cultural Revolution can be captured precisely through theatrical staging which is dissociated from underlying 'objective' explanations of the events. Having translated into Italian Mao's conversation with leading Red Guard figures on 28 July 1968, he was involved in a subsequent staging of the text. Consider the way he describes the project:

> It was most remarkable that the questions [addressed to Russo by the director and the actors] primarily concerned the subjective essence of the situation, what was happening solely on the stage. The director and the actors were mostly indifferent to the 'backstage' – not only in the sense of the vulgar version of the Cultural Revolution as an effect of plots and intrigues, but also from the perspective of a more classical socio-historical scholarly wisdom. ... [I]t was precisely their lack of attention to an allegedly objective backstage that allowed them to look at the text as deeply subjective, that is, as intrinsically political. (Russo, 'One Step, an Encounter', 5)

7 Rancière, *The Lost Thread*, 141/138, tm.
8 Rancière, 'Politics, Identification, Subjectivization', 59. 'A political subject is not a group that "becomes aware" of itself, finds its voice, imposes its weight on society' (D, 40; see also, e.g., DS, 53, 'The Cause of the Other', 29).
9 The relation of an emancipated individual to him- or herself is a pertinent theme in Rancière's work on workers' emancipation. See Edward J. Hughes's perceptive discussion centred around 'self-belonging' in *Egalitarian Strangeness*, 91–107.

10 For example, *The Nights of Labor*, Rancière's great study in workers' history, which consists in interlinking individual trajectories rather than any clear idea of a 'collective subject'.
11 'I no longer have faith in Time', 77; cf. Foucault, *The Hermeneutics of the Subject*, 448: 'One lives with the relationship to one's self as the fundamental project of existence.'
12 Foucault, *Power/Knowledge*, 69–70.
13 Kant, *Critique of Pure Reason*, A33/B50.
14 Ibid., B152.
15 Ibid., B152–3.
16 Ibid., B153–4.
17 Rancière, 'The Aesthetic Dimension', 1.
18 See Kant, *Lectures on Anthropology*, 25:15.
19 Schiller, *On the Aesthetic Education of Man*, 74.
20 Ibid., 81.
21 AD, 30; A, 44; cf. DS, 117; *The Emancipated Spectator*, 69.
22 'What is striking in the events of 1968 is that they were like a general strike that concerned the whole of the society. 1968 was not an insurrectional movement, but a subversive movement where everything stops, nothing functions anymore, and that which did function did so without hierarchies' (Rancière, 'Sur l'interruption', n.p.).
23 AD, 99; cf. the footnote 3.
24 PP, 198; cf. Rancière, *Staging the People*, 166; the key passage in Kant's *Critique of the Power of Judgment* in this respect is § 60.
25 PP, 199. This metapolitical line leads from Kant and Schiller, through Hegel, Hölderlin and Schelling's 'The Oldest System Program of German Idealism', to the young Marx. All of them aim to draw schemes for a futural movement in order to render correct the supposed 'failure' of the French Revolution (Rancière, 'A Few Remarks on the Method of Jacques Rancière', 122; cf. 'Esthétique de la politique et poétique du savoir', 84–5).
26 Deranty and Ross, 'Jacques Rancière and the Contemporary Scene', 13.
27 Davis, *Jacques Rancière*, 125.
28 AD, 33; cf. *Mallarmé*, 33. Mallarmé's metapolitics shakes hands with the Platonic archi-politics and its will for of the 'guidance of the community' (AD, 31; cf. *Politics of Literature*, 84). What characterizes this confusion in some modernist artists is, as Gabriel Rockhill argues, an 'attempt to invent tangible forms and material figures for a *life to come*' (Rockhill, *Radical History and the Politics of Art*, 153, my emphasis).
29 Rancière, *The Emancipated Spectator*, 57; cf. Rancière, *Ist Kunst widerständig?*, 9–11.

30 Rancière, 'Aesthetic Separation, Aesthetic Community', 5.
31 Cf., e.g., NL, 83.
32 Rancière, *En quel temps vivons-nous?*, 32.
33 Ibid., 60.
34 The idea that there cannot be the sensible as such captures Rancière's critique of Alain Badiou's inaesthetics (Rancière, DS, 211; cf. Badiou, *Circonstances*, 2, 98).
35 Rancière, 'The Aesthetic Dimension', 2.
36 Ibid.
37 Gauny, 'Le Travail à la tâche', in Rancière (ed.), *Le Philosophe plébéien*, 45–6, quoted in NL, 81/91, tm.
38 PP, 199. As Gabriel Rockhill observes, while in *The Night of Labor* Gauny's experience is part of a wider context of workers' emancipatory struggles, later Rancière tends to use it as an example of emancipation as such (*Radical History and Politics of Art*, 175). Unlike Rockhill, I don't think that the isolation of this passage from the historical context implies that Rancière's position has changed. Gauny's example simply captures the logic of emancipation at work in that context.
39 Edward J. Hughes links Rancière's work on Gauny's emancipatory practice to the context of the *établis* and Robert Linhart's narrative in *The Assembly Line*; see *Egalitarian Strangeness*, 97–8; cf. Chapter 2 of this book.
40 Rancière, 'The Aesthetic Heterotopia', 19.
41 Ibid., 20.
42 Ibid., 19.
43 Kant, *Lectures on Anthropology*, 25:15.
44 Cf. Kant, *Critique of the Power of Judgment*, §4.
45 Rancière, 'The Aesthetic Heterotopia', 20; on the 'finality without end' in Kant, see *Critique of the Power of Judgment*, §15.
46 Foucault, 'Of Other Spaces', 25.
47 Rancière, 'The Aesthetic Heterotopia', 20.
48 Foucault, 'Of Other Spaces', 26; Rancière, 'The Aesthetic Heterotopia', 23.
49 Rancière, 'The Aesthetic Heterotopia', 24.
50 Rancière, 'The Aesthetic Dimension', 3.
51 A, xv–xvi; cf. Rancière, *Modern Times*, 24; see also my discussion of the book in 'Transgressing Temporal Hierarchies'.
52 Rancière, 'Metamorphosis of the Muses', 24.
53 Kant, *Critique of Pure Reason*, A34/B50
54 Ibid., A34/B51, tm.
55 Rancière, *Béla Tarr*, 65/71, tm. The lack of particular focus on Rancière's engagement with cinema in the present book is not to be taken as a statement

concerning its significance for his thinking. Indeed, Geneviève Fraisse has stated that '[t]wentieth-century cinema afforded him the exceptional opportunity to discard entirely all hierarchies of place between individuals' ('Emancipation versus Domination', 50).

56 Sartre, 'Intentionality', 5.
57 OA, 215; cf. Rancière, 'La Paraphrase', 38.
58 A, 117; chapter 7 of *Aisthesis*, from which this quotation is taken, plays with the relations between interiority and exteriority; it develops an idea of interiority presented through external objects, as opposed to the classical Aristotelian drama, where external objects are presented through 'thought'. The paradigm for thought in respect to the latter is a prime mode of time-determination, that is, a causal plot (121–31).
59 Tanke, *Jacques Rancière*, 148.
60 Ibid., 149.
61 Kant, *Critique of Pure Reason*, A124.
62 See also Davide Panagia's different but very interesting discussion in *Rancière's Sentiments* where he dissociates Rancière's thinking from any 'politics of imagination' based on a particular idea of reverie (91). 'Such reverie ... is not the reverie of an imagination with a purpose but refers to activities without necessary or planned effects' (92).
63 Ibid., A139/B178.
64 'The schemata are therefore nothing but *a priori* time-determinations in accordance with rules, and these concern, according to the order of the categories, the time-series, the content of time, the order of time, and finally the sum total of time in regard to all possible objects' (ibid., A145/B184–5). In an underappreciated study, Andrew Gibson has suggested that Rancière belongs to a recent and contemporary tradition in French philosophy which tries to think 'an anti-schematics of historical reason'. For Gibson the key notion of this tradition is intermittency. It accounts for historical eventfulness which interrupts historical time as the form of existence of the concept. It constitutes a philosophy of history opposed to that of Hegel who, in Kojève's reading, historicized Kant's schematism. According to my argument, too, Rancière thinks against schematism, although for me the key idea is a certain un-schematized spatiality rather than intermittent events. See Gibson, *Intermittency*, 5–14, and Chapter 5 on Rancière.
65 Tanke, *Jacques Rancière*, 159.
66 Ibid., 161.
67 Rancière, *Mute Speech*, 76/58, tm.
68 Ibid., 138/133, tm.

4 Time and its discontents

1 Rancière points towards the difference between 'anachronism' and 'untimeliness' in a recent article, 'Anachronism and the Conflict of Times', 117–18.
2 Whitener, 'Nonrelation and Untimeliness in Jacques Rancière's *The Names of History*', n.p. Whitener refers to Gabriel Rockhill's and Peter Hallward's claims that Rancière's notion of politics is ahistorical (Rockhill) or that it might not help us think organization in the context of specific situations (Hallward). Whitener points out that these critiques lean too heavily on Rancière's seemingly structuralist presentation of his notion of politics in *The Disagreement*. By turning to the question of anachronism, Whitener aims to show the profound investment in historical *temporality* as a crucial element in Rancière's work. I aim to show that the detemporalizing tendencies in Rancière can be made clear precisely based on his discussions of anachronism.

   A pivotal text insisting on the importance of time in Rancière is Kristin Ross's oft-cited 'Historicizing Untimeliness', which informs strongly Whitener's analysis. In it Ross states that 'Rancière's battle … was and, I believe, continues to be a battle with strategies whose aim is the suppression of time' (22). However, Ross appears to confuse different figures of 'the end', such as the 'end of history' which Rancière has often analysed in his work, with the idea of suppressing time itself. But 'the end' is a temporal qualification par excellence. As Rancière describes its rationality (of which Rancière is critical) 'We are now in the end or the after. … Time we call the time of loss is still a time of continuity, archaeology, and heritage' ('After What', 246/191, tm). In other words, 'endism', as Ross calls it, is a strong figure of temporality, anything but a suppression of time.
3 Febvre, *Le problème de l'incroyance au XVIe siècle. La religion de Rabelais*, 15, quoted in C, 21.
4 Ross, 'Historicizing Untimeliness', 26–7.
5 Foucault, *The Order of Things*, xxii.
6 Rancière has acknowledged that his own conceptualization of different regimes of art is comparable to Foucault's archaeology. The difference is, however, that for Rancière these regimes can exist at the same time, and he is careful to remind his readers that they are not to be understood as eras (PA, 50; Rancière, 'A Politic of Aesthetic Indetermination' (interview by Frank Ruda and Jan Voelker), 21; cf. GF, 353). They are simply different forms of thought and perception that can in principle exist at any time (and in any subject). A certain ambiguity remains in this rejection of periodizing reasoning, however, insofar as Rancière also stresses that what we know as 'art' – that is, the aesthetic regime – has only existed for two centuries (*Aisthesis*, ix; for a good comparison between Foucault and Rancière

on this question, see Rockhill, *Radical History and the Politics of Art*, 145–50). Rancière nevertheless states that, as opposed to Foucault, his fundamental interest lies on a 'polemical arena rather than an archaeological one' ('Literature, Politics, Aesthetics' (interview by Solange Guénoun et al.), 13). Such a polemical arena should be understood as an egalitarian sphere where thought is able to transgress any temporally circumscribed conditions of possibility for its specific forms. Anachronism, as I will argue here, should be taken as a notion through which such a sphere is made operative in history.

7   Davis, *Jacques Rancière*, 68, my emphasis.
8   Rancière, 'Les Énoncés de la fin et du rien' (1993), 87; cf. Foucault's remarks on the Enlightenment as 'an enterprise for linking the progress of truth and the history of liberty in a bond of direct relation' (What Is Enlightenment', *A Foucault Reader*, 42–3).
9   Ibid., 85.
10 Ibid., 91.
11 Ibid., 91 n.1.
12 Rancière (untitled discussion of Badiou's *Being and Event*), 218.
13 Badiou, *Being and Event*, 211.
14 Ibid., 210.
15 Rancière (untitled discussion of Badiou's *Being and Event*), 224.
16 Rancière, 'Entretien avec Julia Christ et Bertrand Ogilvie, 200. It must be admitted, however, that Rancière often values and pays interest in different forms of novelty. This is obvious to anyone familiar with his writings on art, for example. What interests me here is a tendency in his work which cannot be captured by the idea of the new and even in some sense goes against it.
17 Rancière, 'Politics and Aesthetics' (interview by Peter Hallward), 209; cf. PA, 50; ME, 48–9.
18 Rancière, 'De la vérité des récits aux partages des âmes' (2011), 478.
19 Rancière, 'Anachronism and the Conflict of Times', 116.
20 NL, viii; cf. Marx: 'In capitalist society, free time is produced for one class by the conversion of the whole lifetime of the masses into labour-time' (Marx, *Capital*, vol. 1, 667). Consider also how Rancière's idea resonates in Olivier Rolin's fictive account of French Maoism: 'Back then, night didn't exist; the night for sleeping was a bourgeois invention' (Rolin, *Paper Tiger*, 7). The 'aesthetic experience' of Gauny discussed in the previous chapter also appears in *The Nights of Labor*, and it shows that the transgression of the temporal order did not concern only the time outside work but made its way also to the time and space of work (see Chapter 3).
21 Rancière and Honneth, *Recognition and Disagreement*, 136.
22 Kant, *Critique of Pure Reason*, A27/B43.

23 Rancière, *The Emancipated Spectator*, 48; Rancière, 'A Few Remarks on the Method of Jacques Rancière', 117.
24 Rancière and Rancière, 'The Philosophers' Tale' [1978], 79/11, tm; cf. Foucault, *The Order of Things*, 303–4.
25 Badiou, 'The Lessons of Jacques Rancière', 36.
26 Rancière, 'L'Histoire aujourd'hui', 60.
27 Davis, *Jacques Rancière*, 174 n.100.
28 Rancière, 'L'Histoire aujourd'hui', 61.
29 Rather than to any Heideggerian investment in the temporally finite nature of human being, Rancière's idea of anachronistic use of words should be linked to the Feuerbachian understanding of the quasi-divine capacity in human beings. Hence, we should hear an echo in Rancière of Feuerbach's description of the god-like power of words which can make 'present the past and the future' [*Entfernte*, literally 'that which is remote'] (*The Essence of Christianity*, 43). Rancière should be read here in the Feuerbachian framework to the extent that it is a question of human capacity before any structure of historical or existential temporality.
30 'There is thinking when one authorizes oneself to think … what [a] particular time considered illegitimate to thinking' (Rancière, 'Dissenting Words' (interview by Davide Panagia), 122).
31 See 'Education à la Lin Biao' in Chapter 2.
32 For a reading that makes anachronism in Rancière a form of temporality belonging to a particular era, see Gibson, 'A New Mode of the Existence of Truth', 113–14. For Giorgio Agamben, untimeliness means precisely to 'truly belong to [one's] time', that is, to respond to its 'exigency' (*What Is an Apparatus? And Other Essays*, 40, 39). He can thus understand his work in terms of doing what it has become the time to do (see, e.g., *Homo Sacer*, 14; *The Use of Bodies*, xix). Ultimately, for Agamben, the (un)timely task of our time is to grasp the structure of historical time itself (cf. *The Time That Remains*, 3). Rancière does not discuss Agamben in this context, but he has distinguished his own use of anachronism from Georges Didi-Huberman and Walter Benjamin. His critique is based precisely on the claim that these thinkers articulate the idea of discordance of times back into an overarching temporal coherence ('Anachronism and the Conflict of Times', 118–22). This argument relates to Rancière's earlier discussion of modernism in terms of a conflict between two principles of meaning. One presents it in an 'anachronistic and anarchic' disorder while the other seals it in a prehistory that structures its 'lateness' and 'anticipation' ('The Archaeomodern Turn', 26).
33 Loraux, 'Éloge de l'anachronisme en histoire', 23–4.
34 Ibid., 38 n.1.

35 Drawing perhaps on Loraux's article, Sophie Wahnich likewise links the word 'achronie' to Rancière (see 'Archives, objet empirique et intuition du rapport passé/présent de l'historien', 219; *La Longue patience du peuple*, 42).
36 Genette, *Figures III*, 121.
37 Ibid., 119.
38 Plotinus, *Enneads*, 136–7 (4.4.1).
39 See Sini, *Ethics of Writing*, 10.
40 Giovanni Campailla wants to re-elaborate Rancière's conception of emancipation by re-establishing its link with the social. *La Parole ouvrière* (1976) is thus probably the single most important source for his reading of Rancière (Campailla, *L'intervento critico di Rancière*).
41 Rancière, 'Postface', in Rancière and Faure (eds), *La Parole ouvrière*, 341–2.
42 Ross, 'Historicizing Untimeliness', 18.
43 Ibid., 25.
44 The prime example of Rancière's untimely intervention apt to a specific moment is well explained by Kristin Ross herself in the 'Translator's Introduction' of *The Ignorant Schoolmaster*. Following Ross, Goele Cornelisson situates *The Ignorant Schoolmaster* in the French situation of the 1980s and measures its relevance and irrelevance for the situation in 2011 ('The Public Role of Teaching', 16; cf. Schaap, 'Hannah Arendt and the Philosophical Repression of Politics', 156; Simons and Masschelein, 'Introduction', 3).
45 Poullain, *On the Equality of the Two Sexes* (1673), 82. For an overview of the relation between Rancière and the radical Cartesian tradition, see Zane Shaw, 'Cartesian Egalitarianism'.
46 Fraisse, *La Sexuation du monde*, 28.
47 This point can be linked also to Fraisse's direct critique of Rancière (who is not mentioned in her discussion of Poullain de la Barre). She has criticized Rancière's outright rejection of the need for a theory of domination by evoking the relation of domination between the sexes. The latter domination, she holds, is largely invisible and needs to be made visible through analysis. Thus, she contrasts her own project of 'reading [the] historical dynamic' of the discourses of inequality and emancipation to what she sees as Rancière's failure to properly do so (Fraisse, 'Emancipation versus Domination', 56).
48 Rancière, *Chronicles of Consensual Times*, 77; GF, 108. 'There is a multiplicity of lines of temporality present in any "one" time' (C, 46). 'There exists several modes of present, several kinds of sensible presentation at one and the same time' (ME, 148/259, tm).
49 This is also how we should understand Rancière's limited affinity with Walter Benjamin in respect to the question of coexistence of multiple times. While Rancière embraces Benjamin's notion of coexistence of times, he rejects the

way Benjamin sees this coexistence to crystallize into a form of temporal unity through an idea of 'now-time' (Rancière, 'A Politics of Aesthetic Indetermination' (interview by Frank Ruda and Jan Voelker), 28; cf. GF, 211; FW, 31; cf. Benjamin, *Illuminations*, 261–4).
50 Rancière, 'After What?', 249.
51 Rancière, *Les Scènes du peuple*, 7.
52 Osborne, *Anywhere or Not at All*, 17.
53 Ibid., 34, 35.
54 Ibid., 35.
55 Ibid., 27.
56 Osborne, *The Politics of Time*, 24, my emphasis.
57 Ibid., 28.
58 Ibid., 27–8.
59 Ibid., 28
60 Ibid., 29.
61 Ibid.
62 Rancière, 'How to Use *Lire le Capital*', 378/792–3, tm.
63 Rancière, 'Joan of Arc in the Gulag' [1975], in *The Intellectual and His Double*, 118.
64 Editorial, *Les Révoltes logiques*, vol. 5/1977, 6.
65 Ibid.
66 Osborne, *The Politics of Time*, 18.
67 Rancière, 'Autonomie et historicisme', 59.
68 Rancière, 'Un-What?', 591; cf. 'The Aesthetic Dimension', 4.
69 Ibid., 594.
70 'In Althusserianism and in the text that I had written for *Reading Capital*, there was this great theme of the agents of production who, by their very belonging to a certain practice, are necessarily unable to understand the system because of the place that they occupy in it' (GF, 639).
71 Rancière, 'Un-What?', 600.
72 Ibid.
73 Ibid., 593.
74 Ibid., 602.
75 Ibid., 604.
76 Osborne, *The Politics of Time*, 27.
77 GF, 83; Rancière, 'Un-What?', 593.
78 Rancière, 'Contemporary Art and Politics of Aesthetics', 49.
79 Renault, 'The Many Marx of Jacques Rancière', 186.
80 Rancière, 'The Myth of the Artisan', 13. Henceforth, 'everyone is an intellectual' for Rancière (GF, 119).

81 Rancière, 'Introduction', in Rancière and Faure (eds), *La Parole ouvrière*, 9.
82 Rancière, *Politik und Ästhetik. Im Gespräch mit Peter Engelmann*, 13.
83 ME, 12; cf. Palmusaari, 'Mao for Now' (review of Rancière, *The Method of Equality*).

5 The Jacobin anachronism

1 Furet, *The French Revolution 1770–1814*, 171.
2 For a particularly symptomatic example, see Billaud-Varenne's 'Rapport fait à la Convention nationale, au nom du Comité de salut public' [1794]. Billaud-Varenne goes through a series of heroic ancient figures associating them directly with the contemporary revolutionary drama. See also Robespierre, *Pour le bonheur et pour la liberté*, 49–50, 148, 294, 304–5.
3 Marat, *L'Ami du peuple*, 96, 13 January 1790, 2.
4 Marat, *L'Ami du peuple*, 518, 14 July 1791, 4.518.
5 Saint-Just, *Œuvres complètes*, 764.
6 Marx and Engels, *The Holy Family*, 122.
7 Furet, *Marx and the French Revolution*, 22.
8 Ibid., 11.
9 Marx, *The Eighteenth Brumaire of Louis Bonaparte*, 16–17. For Marx's multifaceted relation with the French Revolution, see Michael Löwy, 'The Poetry of the Past' (1989).
10 See, e.g., Furet, *Penser la Révolution française*; and Furet et al., *La République du centre*.
11 NH, 31/66, cf. Marx, *The Eighteenth Brumaire of Louis Bonaparte*, 16.
12 Rancière very rarely refers to the Jacobins. He has, however, rejected the discourse of Jacobinism as a form of dictatorship and associated it with popular democracy: 'As if "Jacobinism" was not initially a scarecrow created by the bourgeoisie to represent its hatred of the people as a hatred of dictatorship' (SP2, 113, see also footnote 8 on the same page).
13 See, e.g., IS, 96–9; D, 23–4, 50–1; *Figures de l'histoire*, 34–5. For Rancière the crucial point in this history is the way the plebeians demonstrate themselves as speaking beings, equal to the patricians.
14 Rancière, 'Préface', in Ballanche, *Première Sécession de la plèbe*, 22.
15 Ibid., 21.
16 Ibid., 23.
17 Ibid., 22.

18 This questions Andrew Gibson's interpretation of Rancière as a thinker whose work is characterized by a melancholy for passing moments of emancipatory politics (see his *Intermittency*, 202–45).
19 This is very well brought to light in Florence Gauthier's *Triomphe et mort de la revolution des droits de l'homme et du citoyen (1789-1795-1802)*. My presentation of the way in which the Jacobin logic clashed with the reactionary current leans heavily on the material quoted by her and follows the broad line of her reading of the Revolution.
20 *Le Moniteur*, no. 268, séance du 23 septembre 1791, 758, quoted in Gauthier, *Triomphe et mort*, 236.
21 Quoted in Gauthier, *Triomphe et mort*, 211. Gauthier quotes here volumes 128–36 of *Le Moniteur universel* without specifying the volume for each quotation.
22 Quoted in Gauthier, *Triomphe et mort*, 219.
23 Quoted in Gauthier, *Triomphe et mort*, 215; on the debates concerning the colonies specifically, see also Gauthier, *L'Aristocratie de l'épiderme*.
24 Malouet, quoted in Gauthier, *Triomphe et mort*, 209.
25 *Dictionnaire politique portative en cinq mots*, 1982, 112, quoted in Gauthier, *Triomphe et mort*, 236-237 n.14. Faye writes: 'Barnave, who in the autumn of '89 had been a man of the Left announces in July '91 the primacy of *real interests* over the enunciation of the rights. And in June '93 Robespierre – who has become the spokesperson of the Left – writes the second Declaration of the Rights and emphasizes in it "the necessity to enunciate these rights"' (Faye, *Dictionnaire politique portative en cinq mots*, 113).
26 Marx and Engels, *The German Ideology*, 31.
27 Gauthier, *Triomphe et mort*, 300.
28 Archives parlementaires, 2ᵉ série, 1802, t. 3: 'Rapport de Dupuy', 16 May, 692, quoted in Gauthier, *Triomphe et mort*, 352.
29 Gauthier, *Triomphe et mort*, 38.
30 Haynes and Wolfreys, 'Introduction', in *History and Revolution*, 2–3.
31 Robespierre, *Pour le bonheur et pour la liberté*, 84
32 Robespierre, *Œuvres complètes*, vol. 5, 62.
33 Linton, 'Robespierre's Political Principles', 53.
34 Cf. footnote 65 in Chapter 3 of this book.
35 See Perovic, *The Calendar in Revolutionary France*. Consider Perovic's suggestion that what most notably remains from the revolutionaries' failed attempt to establish the Republican Calendar may be 'an aggressive resistance to linear time. Thanks to this resistance, the Revolution was able to escape, as it were, its own epoch and become a myth applicable to all times and all places' (237).
36 Lasource, quoted in Gauthier, *Triomphe et mort*, 117.

37 Cf. how Hayden Whyte summarizes Rancière's attempt in *The Names of History*: 'What he has tried to do, as I see it, is place himself in the liminal zone between any given present and any possible past' (White, 'Foreword', in NH, xix).
38 Cf. Sellers, 'The Roman Republic and the French and American Revolutions', 348.
39 NH, 18–21; cf. Hobbes, *Leviathan*, 225–8 (170–2). This theme, too, is present in Marx's *The Eighteenth Brumaire of Louis Bonaparte* and its references to Oliver Cromwell and the English Revolution; see p. 16.
40 My reading is here diametrically opposed to that of Brian Whitener who argues in reference to *The Names of History* that Rancière is first and foremost 'a thinker of periods' ('Nonrelation and Untimeliness in Jacques Rancière's *The Names of History*', n.p.). According to my claim, Rancière is actually aiming to break with logics of periodization and is in favour of dissolution of a temporal consistency that allows such logics to sustain themselves. I do acknowledge that Rancière continues to utilize a certain kind of periodizing logic, such as that of the regimes of art. However (as I have pointed out earlier), he at the same time problematizes this periodizing approach.
41 Robespierre, *Pour le bonheur et pour la liberté*, 296; translation borrowed from Linton, 'Robespierre's Political Principles', 29.
42 *Le Moniteur universel*, vol. 20, 695, quoted in Wahnich, *In Defence of the Terror*, 67.
43 On the revolutionaries' obsession with conspiracies, both real and imagined, see Linton, 'The Tartuffes of Patriotism'.
44 Perovic, 'The French Republican Calendar', 5.
45 Robespierre, *Pour le bonheur et pour la liberté*, 41.
46 Linton, 'Robespierre's Political Principles', 42, 49.
47 Gauthier, *Triomphe et mort*, 30–1.
48 Karol, *The Second Chinese Revolution*, 12.
49 Robespierre, *Pour le bonheur et pour la liberté*, 287.
50 Ibid., 289.
51 Gauthier, *Triomphe et mort*, 168.
52 Robespierre, *Pour le bonheur et pour la liberté*, 289.
53 Cf. Jean-Paul Marat:

> When the constitution has been finally achieved and the fundamental laws have been recognized by the people alone, those in charge of different powers must be constantly under the surveillance of the citizens and controlled by the people. For this it is necessary that the constitution rests solely on people's exercise of their right to assemble as they will [*à volonté*]. It also requires establishing a way of communication between all the members of the empire, so that they can mutually enlighten each

other and to take unanimous decisions to repress their representatives, to force them to do what has to be done or to discharge them. (*L'Ami du peuple*, 269, 2 November 1790, 6)

54 Marat, *Écrits*, 151; cf. *L'Ami du peuple*, 26 September 1789, 16.
55 With the idea of rarity of politics Rancière joined Badiou and Sylvain Lazarus (see Badiou, *Logics of Worlds*, 26; cf. *Being and Event*, 17, 344).
56 The rarity of politics in Rancière is stressed, e.g., by Todd May in *The Political Thought of Jacques Rancière* (40). May has nevertheless argued that despite the rarity it is first of all a question of making it happen and tried to think ways around its ephemeral nature (*Contemporary Political Movements and the Thought of Jacques Rancière*, 22, 137). Finally, May has addressed his disagreement with Rancière on the principle of rarity ('Rancière and Anarchism', 127). Samuel Chambers who emphasizes the importance of the police order and tries to think 'The Politics of the Police' in Rancière has questioned the idea of rarity and claimed that it belongs to politics in its 'pure' form whereas for Chambers politics is never pure (21–2, 30). In a rather similar vein, Joseph Tanke interprets that politics is rare in its most radical forms (*Jacques Rancière*, 63). For me, 'rarity' is precisely the kind of temporal characterization which the logic of emancipation as such does not recognize. In this sense Andrew Gibson, who takes the principle of rarity in Rancière furthest, provides an interpretation which is useful by being philosophically almost diametrically opposite to mine. Thus, for Gibson rarity characterizes the temporal form of intermittency that in his analysis belongs to the historical reasoning in recent French philosophy shared by Rancière, Badiou, Proust, Lardreau and Jambet (*Intermittency*). Rarity and intermittency have served as a link to connect Rancière to Badiou (and Lazarus) also for Daniel Bensaïd based on which he has expressed his disagreement with them (*Éloge de la résistance à l'air du temps*, 44–5).
57 ME, 134; cf. Rancière, 'A Few Remarks on the Method of Jacques Rancière', 118.
58 Gauthier, *Triomphe et mort*, 170.
59 Rancière, *Hatred of Democracy*, 74; cf. DS, 68.
60 Rancière, 'L'Histoire aujourd'hui', 61.
61 In *On the Shores of Politics*, Rancière acknowledges that the effective invocation of the rights depends on their earlier 'force-entry' in the world of politics or on 'the violence of their inscription' (OP, 49). However, we cannot find in Rancière analyses of the violent processes which precede the internal logic of the rights. Rather, it is this logic itself which tends to be generalized beyond its historical point of emergence.

62 Here I disagree with Samuel Chambers who states that Rancière's appreciation of history means that for him 'you have to be located in *this* place' (Chambers, *The Lessons of Rancière*, 25). Obviously, I am arguing here for an opposite idea: as Rancière himself puts it, 'There is no reason why a speaking being should be "there" rather than "here", no special place for the sameness of any of us' (Rancière, 'Discovering New Worlds, 35). Chambers's reading should be seen in light of his attempt to link politics intimately to 'the police'. I will return to this question in conclusion.
63 Rancière, 'Les Énoncés de la fin et du rien', 71.
64 Two years before speaking about the paradox of politics (i.e. a division within a single notion), Rancière had already introduced in an article written in English a division between 'politics' and 'policy' along with a third term, 'the political', designating the medium where the two meet ('Politics, Identification and Subjectivization', 59). In *La Mésentente*, the division is famously translated into 'la politique' and 'la police', while 'le politique' ('the political') arguably loses any clear or distinctive role. In the English edition, these are rendered into 'politics' and 'the police'. There has been some debate on the importance of the third term for Rancière (which I will address briefly in conclusion). 'The political' and the debate over its importance can be related to Nancy and Lacoue-Labarthe's Heideggerian discourse on the ontologico-historical closure of the political which allows its retracing, or 're-treating' (Lacoue-Labarthe and Nancy, *Retreating the Political*). Although Rancière uses the term, his position is generally closer in this respect to Alain Badiou, who defends *politics* as a question arising from political practice rather than a primarily philosophical question of 'the political' (see Badiou, *Peut-on penser la politique ?*, 12). It can be questioned, however, whether Badiou's own supra-ontological account of the event really manages to turn the question away from the primacy of the 'philosopheme'. On Badiou and Rancière's relation to 'the political', see also Bensaïd's remarks in *Éloge de la résistance à l'air du temps*, 46–8.
65 Birnbaum, *Égalité radicale*, 93.

Conclusion

1 Rancière, 'A Few Remarks on the Method of Jacques Rancière', 122.
2 Deranty, 'Jacques Rancière's Contribution to the Ethics of Recognition', 145, cf. 150; see also Deranty, 'Rancière and Contemporary Political Ontology'.
3 Ibid., 136, 144, 140.

4 Chambers, *The Lessons of Rancière*, 53–7. Chambers shows, e.g., that Rancière introduces the notion of 'the political' in a specific context where he is asked to reflect on the term and its possible meanings in relation to his work.
5 Ibid., 49.
6 Ibid., 85.
7 Ibid., 87.
8 Ibid., 77.

Bibliography

Agamben, Giorgio. *Homo Sacer: Sovereign Power and Bare Life*. Trans. Daniel Heller-Roazen. Stanford, CA: Stanford University Press, 1998.

Agamben, Giorgio. *The Time That Remains: A Commentary on the Letter to the Romans*. Trans. Patricia Dailey. Stanford, CA: Stanford University Press, 2005.

Agamben, Giorgio . *The Use of Bodies*. Trans. Adam Kotsko. Stanford, CA: Stanford University Press, 2016.

Agamben, Giorgio. *What Is an Apparatus? And Other Essays*. Trans. David Kishik and Stefan Pedatella. Stanford, CA: Stanford University Press, 2009.

Althusser, Louis. *Essays in Self-Criticism*. Trans. Grahame Lock. London: NLB, 1976.

Althusser, Louis. *For Marx*. Trans. Ben Brewster. London: Verso, 2005. [Louis Althusser. *Pour Marx*. Paris: La Découverte, 2005.]

Althusser, Louis. *The Future Lasts Forever: A Memoir*. Trans. Richard Veasey. New York: New Press, 1993.

Althusser, Louis. *Lenin and Philosophy and Other Texts*. Trans. Ben Brewster. London: New Left Books, 1971.

Althusser, Louis. 'On the Cultural Revolution' [1967]. Trans. Jason E. Smith. *Décalages*, 1:1 (2014). Available at: http://scholar.oxy.edu/decalages/vol1/iss1/9.

Althusser, Louis. *Philosophy and the Spontaneous Philosophy of the Scientists*. Ed. Gregory Elliott. London: Verso, 1990.

Althusser, Louis. 'Student Problems' [1964]. Trans. Warren Montag. *Radical Philosophy* 170 (November–December 2011), pp. 11–15.

Althusser, Louis, Étienne Balibar, Roger Establet, Pierre Macherey and Jacques Rancière. *Reading Capital: The Complete Edition* [1965]. Trans. Ben Brewster and David Fernbach. London: Verso, 2015. [*Lire Le Capital*. Paris: PUF, 1996.]

Badiou, Alain. *Being and Event* [1988]. Trans. Oliver Feltham. London: Continuum, 2005.

Badiou, Alain. 'Beyond Formalization' (interview by Bruno Bosteels and Peter Hallward). In Bruno Bosteels. *Badiou and Politics*. Durham, NC: Duke University Press, 2011, pp. 318–50.

Badiou, Alain. *Circonstances, 2. Irak, foulard, Allemagne/France*. Paris: Éditions Lignes et manifestes, 2004.

Badiou, Alain. *The Communist Hypothesis*. Trans. David Macey and Steve Corcoran. London: Verso, 2010.

Badiou, Alain. 'The Lessons of Jacques Rancière'. In Gabriel Rockhill and Philip Watts. *Jacques Rancière: History, Politics, Aesthetics*. Durham, NC: Duke University Press, 2009.

Badiou, Alain. *Logics of Worlds: Being and Event, 2* [2006]. Trans. Alberto Toscano. London: Continuum, 2009.

Badiou, Alain. *Peut-on penser la politique?* Paris: Seuil, 1985.

Badiou, Alain. 'Roads to Renegacy: Interview by Eric Hazan'. Trans. David Fernbach. *New Left Review*, 53 (September–October 2008), pp. 125–33.

Badiou, Alain. *Theory of the Subject* [1982]. Trans. Bruno Bosteels. London: Continuum, 2009.

Balibar, Étienne. 'Althusser et Mao'. *Période*, 18 May 2015. Available at: http://revue periode.net/althusser-et-mao/.

Balibar, Étienne. 'Avant-propos pour la réédition de 1996'. In Louis Althusser. *Pour Marx*. Paris: La Découverte, 1996, pp. i–xiv.

Balibar, Étienne. 'Structural Causality, Overdetermination, and Antagonism'. In Antonio Callari and David F. Ruccio (eds), *Postmodern Materialism and the Future of Marxist Theory*. Middletown, CT: Wesleyan University Press, 1996, pp. 109–20.

Beistegui, Miguel de. 'The Subject of Truth: On Foucault's *Lectures on the Will to Know*'. *Quadranti*, 2:1 (2014), pp. 80–99.

Bell, David F. 'Writing, Movement/Space, Democracy'. *SubStance*, 33:1 (2004), pp. 126–40.

Benjamin, Walter. *The Arcades Project*. Trans. Howard Eiland and Kevin McLaughlin. Cambridge, MA: Harvard University Press, 2002.

Benjamin, Walter. *Illuminations*. Ed. Hannah Arendt and trans. Harry Zohn. New York: Schocken Books, 1969.

Bensaïd, Daniel. *Éloge de la résistance à l'air du temps. Entretien avec Philippe Petit*. Paris: Textuel, 1999.

Bensaïd, Daniel. *Marx for Our Times: Adventures and Misadventures for a Critique* [1995]. Trans. Gregory Elliott. London: Verso, 2002.

Birnbaum, Antonia. *Égalité radicale. Diviser Rancière*. Paris: Éditions Amsterdam, 2018.

Birnbaum, Jean. *Les Maoccidents. Un néoconservatisme à la française*. Paris: Stock, 2009.

Bosteels, Bruno. 'Archipolitics, Parapolitics, Metapolitics'. In Jean-Philippe Deranty (ed.), *Jacques Rancière: Key Concepts*. Durham, NC: Acumen, 2010, pp. 80–92.

Bosteels, Bruno. *Badiou and Politics*. Durham, NC: Duke University Press, 2011.

Bosteels, Bruno. 'Nonplaces: An Anecdoted Topography of Contemporary French Theory'. *Diacritics*, 33:3–4 (2003), pp. 117–39.

Bourg, Julian. 'The Red Guards of Paris: French Student Maoism of the 1960s'. *History of European Ideas*, 31:4 (2004), pp. 472–90.

Bourseiller, Christophe. *Les Maoïstes. La Folle histoire des gardes rouges français*. Paris: Plon, 1996.

Campailla, Giovanni. *L'intervento critico di Rancière. Democrazia, riconoscimento, emancipazione ottocentesca*. Rome: Meltemi, 2019.

Cartledge, Paul. *Democracy: A Life*. Oxford: Oxford University Press, 2016.

Cavazzini, Andrea. 'Le Maître impossible. Pour un bon usage du *Maître ignorant*'. *Le Télémaque*, 2:44 (2013), pp. 89–98.

Cavazzini, Andrea. *Le Sujet et l'étude. Idéologie et savoir dans le discours maoïste. Suivi de dialogue avec Yves Duroux*. Reims: Le Clou dans le fer, 2011.

Chambers, Samuel A. *The Lessons of Rancière*. Oxford: Oxford University Press, 2013.

Chambers, Samuel A. 'The Politics of Literarity'. *Theory and Event*, 8:5 (2005). Available at: http://muse.jhu.edu/journal/191.

Chambers, Samuel A. 'The Politics of the Police: From Neoliberalism to Anarchism, and Back to Democracy'. In Paul Bowman and Richard Stamp (eds), *Reading Rancière*. London: Continuum, 2011, pp. 18–43.

Chateigner, Frédéric. 'From Althusser to Mao: *Les Cahiers Marxistes-Léninistes*'. *Décalages*, 1:4 (2014). Available at: http://scholar.oxy.edu/decalages/vol1/iss4/6.

Cheek, Timothy. 'Introduction: The Making and Breaking of the Party-State in China'. In Timothy Cheek and Tony Saich (eds), *New Perspectives on State Socialism in China*. Armonk, NY: M.E. Sharpe, 1997.

Cheek, Timothy. *The Intellectual in Modern Chinese History*. Cambridge: Cambridge University Press, 2016.

Cook, Alexander C. 'Preface'. In Alexander C. Cook (ed.), *Mao's Little Red Book: A Global History*. Cambridge: Cambridge University Press, 2014, pp. xiii–xvi.

Cook, Alexander C. 'The Spiritual Atom Bomb and Its Global Fallout'. In Alexander C. Cook (ed.), *Mao's Little Red Book: A Global History*. Cambridge: Cambridge University Press, 2014, pp. 1–22.

Cornelisson, Goele. 'The Public Role of Teaching: To Keep the Door Closed'. In Maarten Simons and Jan Masschelein (eds), *Rancière, the Public Education and the Taming of Democracy*. Oxford: Wiley-Blackwell, 2011, pp. 15–30.

Davis, Oliver. 'Editor's Introduction'. In Oliver Davis (ed.), *Rancière Now: Current Perspectives on Jacques Rancière*. Cambridge: Polity Press, 2013, pp. 1–10.

Davis, Oliver. *Jacques Rancière*. Cambridge: Polity, 2010.
de Ste. Croix, G. E. M. *Athenian Democratic Origins: And Other Essays*. Ed. David Harvey and Robert Parker. Oxford: Oxford University Press, 2004.
Deleuze, Gilles. *Foucault*. Trans. and ed. Seán Hand. Minneapolis: Minnesota University Press, 1988.
Deranty, Jean-Philippe. 'Jacques Rancière's Contribution to the Ethics of Recognition'. *Political Theory*, 31:1 (February 2003), pp. 136–56.
Deranty, Jean-Philippe. 'A Journey in Equality'. In Jean-Philippe Deranty (ed.), *Jacques Rancière: Key Concepts*. Durham, NC: Acumen, 2010, pp. 1–14.
Deranty, Jean-Philippe. 'Rancière and Contemporary Political Ontology'. *Theory and Event*, 6:4 (2003), n.p. Available at: http://muse.jhu.edu/journal/191.
Deranty, Jean-Philippe, and Alison Ross. 'Jacques Rancière and the Contemporary Scene: The Evidence of Equality and the Practice of Writing'. In Jean-Philippe Deranty and Alison Ross (eds). *Jacques Rancière and the Contemporary Scene: The Philosophy of Radical Equality*. London: Continuum, 2012, pp. 1–13.
Derrida, Jacques. *Dissemination* [1972]. Trans. Barbara Johnson. London: Athlone Press, 1981.
Derrida, Jacques. *Margins of Philosophy* [1972]. Trans. Alan Bass. Brighton: Harvester Press, 1982.
Derrida, Jacques. *The Politics of Friendship* [1994]. Trans. George Collins. London: Verso, 1997.
Derrida, Jacques. *Rogues: Two Essays on Reason*. Trans. Pascale-Anne Braut and Michael Naas. Stanford, CA: Stanford University Press, 2005.
Didi-Huberman, Georges. *The Surviving Image: Phantoms of Time and Time of Phantoms—Aby Warburg's History of Art*. Trans. Harvey L. Mendelsohn. University Park: University of Pennsylvania Press, 2017.
Dikeç, Mustafa. 'Space as a Mode of Political Thinking'. *Geoforum*, 43:4 (2012), pp. 669–76.
Dikeç, Mustafa. *Space, Politics and Aesthetics*. Edinburgh: Edinburgh University Press, 2015.
Driver, Christopher. *The Exploding University*. London: Hodder and Stoughton, 1971.
During, Simon. *Exit Capitalism: Literary Culture, Theory, and Post-Secular Modernity*. London: Routledge, 2010.
Duroux, Yves, and Étienne Balibar. 'A Philosophical Conjuncture'. In Peter Hallward and Knox Peden (eds), *Concept and Form*, vol. 1. London: Verso, 2012, pp. 169–85.
Editorial, *Les Révoltes logiques*, 5 (Spring–Summer 1977), pp. 3–6.

Elden, Stuart. 'Another Sense of Demos: Kleisthenes and the Greek Division of the Polis'. *Democratization*, 10:1 (2003), pp. 135–56.
Elliott, Gregory. *Althusser: The Detour of Theory* [1987], 2nd edn. Brill: Haymarket Books, 2006.
Fajardo, Christian. 'Jacques Rancière: Aesthetics, Time, Politics'. *Journal of Aesthetics and Culture*, 14:1 (2022), pp. 1–12.
Faye, Jean-Pierre. *Dictionnaire politique portatif en cinq mots. Démagogie, terreur, tolérance, répression, violence*. Paris: Gallimard, 1982.
Feuerbach, Ludwig. *The Essence of Christianity* [1843], 2nd edn. Trans. George Eliot. New York: Dover, 2008.
Feuerbach, Ludwig. *The Fiery Brook: Selected Writings*. Trans. Zawar Hanfi. London: Verso, 2012. [*Gesammelte Werke*, vol. 9. Ed. Werner Schuffenhauer. Berlin: Akademie-Verlag, 1970.]
Foucault, Michel. *Dits et écrits*, vol. 2. Paris: Gallimard, 1994.
Foucault, Michel. *The Foucault Reader*. Ed. Paul Rabinow. New York: Pantheon Books, 1984.
Foucault, Michel. *The Hermeneutics of the Subject: Lectures at the Collège de France, 1981–1982*. Trans. Graham Burchell. New York: Palgrave Macmillan, 2005.
Foucault, Michel. 'Of Other Spaces'. *Diacritics*, 16:1 (1986), pp. 22–7.
Foucault, Michel. *The Order of Things: An Archaeology of Knowledge* [1966]. London: Tavistock, 1970.
Foucault, Michel. *Power/Knowledge: Selected Interviews and Other Writings, 1972–1977*. Ed. Colin Gordon. New York: Vintage Books, 1980.
Fraisse, Geneviève. 'Emancipation versus Domination'. In Oliver Davis (ed.), *Rancière Now*. Cambridge: Polity Press, 2013.
Fraisse, Geneviève. *La Sexuation du monde. Réflexions sur l'émancipation*. Paris: Presses de Sciences Po, 2016.
Freedman, Ralph. *Life of a Poet: Rainer Maria Rilke*. Evanston, IL: Northwestern University Press, 1996.
Friedman, Edward, Paul G. Pickowicz and Mark Selden. *Revolution, Resistance and Reform in Village China*. New Haven, CT: Yale University Press, 2005.
Furet, François. *The French Revolution 1770–1814*. Oxford: Blackwell, 1996.
Furet, François. *Marx and the French Revolution*. Trans. Deborah Kan Furet. Chicago: University of Chicago Press, 1988.
Furet, François. *Penser la Révolution française*. Paris: Gallimard, 1978.
Furet, François, Jacques Julliard and Pierre Rosanvallon. *La République du centre. La Fin de l'exception française*. Paris: Calmann-Lévy, 1988.

Gao Yuan. *Born Red: A Chronicle of the Cultural Revolution*. Stanford, CA: Stanford University Press, 1987.

Gauny, Louis-Gabriel. *Le Philosophe plébéien*. Ed. Jacques Rancière. Paris: Maspero, 1983.

Gauthier, Florence. *L'Aristocratie de l'épiderme. Le Combat de la Société des Citoyens de Couleur 1789–1791*. Paris: CNRS, 2007.

Gauthier, Florence. *Triomphe et mort de la révolution des droits de l'homme et du citoyen (1789–1795–1802)*, 2nd edn. Paris: Éditions Syllepse, 2014.

Gavi, Philippe, Jean-Paul Sartre and Pierre Victor. *On a raison de se révolter*. Paris: Gallimard, 1974.

Genette, Gérard. *Figures III*. Paris: Seuil, 1972.

Gibson, Andrew. *Intermittency: The Concept of Historical Reason in Recent French Philosophy*. Edinburgh: Edinburgh University Press, 2012.

Gibson, Andrew. '"A New Mode of the Existence of Truth": Rancière and the Beginnings of Modernity 1780–1830'. In Grace Hellyer and Julian Murphet (eds), *Rancière and Literature*. Edinburgh: Edinburgh University Press, 2016, pp. 99–121.

Gilles, A. 'La Cause du Peuple: marxisme ou anarchisme?'. *Communisme*, 9 (March–April 1974). Pagination from version available at: <http://ocml-vp.org/IMG/pdf/la_cause_du_peuple-marxisme_ou_anarchisme.pdf>.

Gramsci, Antonio. *Pre-Prison Writings*. Ed. Richard Bellamy and trans. Virginia Cox. Cambridge: Cambridge University Press, 2009.

Guobin Yaung. 'Mao Quotations in Factional Battles and Their Afterlives: Episodes from Chongqing'. In Alexander C. Cook (ed.), *Mao's Little Red Book: A Global History*. Cambridge: Cambridge University Press, 2014, pp. 61–75.

Guo Jian, Yongyi Song and Yuan Zhou. *Historical Dictionary of the Chinese Cultural Revolution*. Lanham: The Scarecrow Press, 2006.

Hallward, Peter. 'Reason and Revolt: Guy Lardreau's Early Voluntarism and Its Limits'. *Radical Philosophy*, 190 (2015), pp. 13–24.

Hallward, Peter. 'Staging Equality: On Rancière's Theatrocracy'. *New Left Review*, 37 (2006), pp. 109–29.

Hallward, Peter. 'Theoretical Training'. In Peter Hallward and Knox Peden (eds), *Concept and Form*, vol. 1. London: Verso, 2012, pp. 1–55.

Hamon, Hervé, and Patrick Rotman. *Génération*, vol. 2, *Les années de poudre*. Paris: Seuil, 1988.

Hanus, Gilles. 'Renverser l'ordre des choses. Méditations sur l'établissement'. *Les Temps Modernes*, 684–5 (July–October 2015), pp. 54–68.

Haynes, Mike, and Jim Wolfreys. 'Introduction'. In Mike Haynes and Jim Wolfreys (eds), *History and Revolution: Refuting Revisionism*. London: Verso, 2007, pp. 1–24.

Heath, Malcom. 'Introduction'. In Aristotle. *Poetics*. Trans. Malcolm Heath. London: Penguin Books, 1996.

Hegel, G. W. F. *The Phenomenology of Spirit*. Trans. A. V. Miller. Oxford: Clarendon Press, 1977.

Hobbes, Thomas. *Leviathan*. Ed. Richard Tuck. Cambridge: Cambridge University Press, 1996.

Hughes, Edward J. *Egalitarian Strangeness: On Class Disturbance and Levelling in Modern and Contemporary French Narrative*. Liverpool: Liverpool University Press, 2021.

Hyppolite, Jean. *Genèse et structure de la Phénoménologie de l'esprit de Hegel*, vol. 1. Paris: Aubier, 1946.

Important Documents on the Great Proletarian Cultural Revolution. Peking: Foreign Language Press, 1970.

Jones, Andrew F. 'Quotations Songs: Portable Media and the Maoist Pop Song'. In Alexander C. Cook (ed.), *Mao's Little Red Book: A Global History*. Cambridge: Cambridge University Press, 2014, pp. 43–60.

Jones, David M., and M. L. R Smith. *The Strategy of Maoism in the West: Rage and the Radical Left*. Cheltenham: Edward Elgar, 2022.

Kant, Immanuel. *Critique of the Power of Judgment* [1790]. Trans. Paul Guyer and Eric Matthews. Cambridge: Cambridge University Press, 2000.

Kant, Immanuel. *Critique of Practical Reason*. In *Practical Philosophy*. Trans. and ed. Mary J. Gregor. Cambridge: Cambridge University Press, 1996.

Kant, Immanuel. *Critique of Pure Reason* [1781/1787]. Trans. Paul Guyer and Allen W. Wood. Cambridge: Cambridge University Press, 1998.

Kant, Immanuel. *Groundwork of the Metaphysics of Morals*. In *Practical Philosophy*. Trans. and ed. Mary J. Gregor. Cambridge: Cambridge University Press, 1996.

Kant, Immanuel. *Lectures on Anthropology*. Trans. Robert R. Clewis et al. Cambridge: Cambridge University Press, 2012.

Kant, Immanuel. *The Metaphysics of Morals*. In *Practical Philosophy*. Trans. and ed. Mary J. Gregor. Cambridge: Cambridge University Press, 1996.

Kant, Immanuel. *Prolegomena to Any Future Metaphysics That Will Be Able to Come Forward as Science*. In *Theoretical Philosophy after 1781*. Ed. Henry Allison and Peter Heath. Cambridge: Cambridge University Press, 2002.

Karl, Rebecca. *Mao Zedong and China in the Twentieth-Century World: A Concise History*. Durham, NC: Duke University Press, 2010.

Karol, K. S. *The Second Chinese Revolution*. Trans. Mervyn Jones. London: Cape, 1975.

Kessel, Patrick (ed.). *Le Mouvement 'maoïste' en France*, vol. 1. Paris: Union Génerale d'Editions, 1972.

Lacan, Jacques. *Écrits*. Trans. Bruce Fink. New York: W. W. Norton, 2006.

Lacoue-Labarthe, Philippe, and Nancy Jean-Luc. *Retreating the Political*. Trans. Simon Sparks. London: Routledge, 1997.

Lardreau, Guy. *Dialogues avec Georges Duby* [1980]. Paris: Les Dialogues des petits Platons, 2013.

Lardreau, Guy. 'La Science est-elle policière?' (interview by Bernard Henry-Lévy). *Magazine littéraire*, 85 (February 1974), pp. 59–60.

Lardreau, Guy. *La Véracité. Essai d'une philosophie négative*. Lagrasse: Éditions Verdier, 1993.

Lardreau, Guy. *Le Singe d'or. Essai sur le concept d'étape du marxisme*. Paris: Mercure de France, 1973.

Lardreau, Guy, and Christian Jambet. 'Entretien avec Gilles Hertzog'. *Magazine littéraire*, 112–13 (May 1976), pp. 54–7.

Lardreau, Guy, and Christian Jambet. *L'Ange. Ontologie de la révolution, tome 1: pour une cynégétique du semblant*. Paris: Grasset, 1976.

Lardreau, Guy, and Christian Jambet. *Le Monde. Réponse à la question: qu'est-ce que les droits de l'homme?* Paris: Grasset, 1978.

Le Dantec, Jean-Pierre. *Les Dangers du soleil*. Paris: Les Presses d'Aujourd'hui, 1978.

Leese, Daniel. 'A Single Spark: Origins and Spread of the Little Red Book in China'. In Alexander C. Cook (ed.), *Mao's Little Red Book: A Global History*. Cambridge: Cambridge University Press, 2014, pp. 23–42.

Leese, Daniel. *Die Chinesische Kulturrevolution 1966–1976*. München: Verlag C.H.Beck, 2016.

Leese, Daniel. *Mao Cult: Rhetoric and Ritual in China's Cultural Revolution*. Cambridge: Cambridge University Press, 2011.

Leese, Daniel. 'The Mao Cult as Communicative Space'. *Totalitarian Movements and Political Religions*, 8: (2007), pp. 623–39.

Lei Han, Oliver. 'Sources and Early Printing History of *Chairman Mao's Quotations*'. Updated 10 January 2004. Available at: https://bibsocamer.org/BibSite/Han/.

Lenin. *Collected Works*, vol. 19. Moscow: Progress, 1977.

Lévy, Benny. 'Introduction aux Cercles Socratiques' [1978]. Available at: www.bennylevy.co.il/textes/IntroCS.asp.

Li Zhisui. *The Private Life of Chairman Mao*. Trans. Tai Hung-chao. London: Arrow Books, 1996.

Lin Biao. 'Foreword to the Second Edition of *Quotations from the Chairman Mao Tse-tung*'. In *Quotations from the Chairman Mao Tse-tung*. Peking: Foreign Language Press, 1966.

Linhart, Robert. *The Assembly Line*. Trans. Margaret Crosland. Amherst: University of Massachusetts Press, 1981. [*L'Établi*. Paris: Les Éditions de Minuit, 1978.]

Linhart, Robert. *Lénine, les paysans, Taylor. Essai d'analyse matérialiste historique de la naissance du système productif soviétique*. Paris: Seuil, 1976.

Linhart, Virginie. *Le Jour où mon père s'est tu*. Paris: Seuil, 2008.

Linhart, Virginie. *Volontaires pour l'usine. Vies d'établis (1967–1977)*, 2nd edn. Paris: Seuil, 2010.

Linton, Marisa. 'Robespierre's Political Principles'. In Colin Haydon and William Doyle (eds), *Robespierre*. Cambridge: Cambridge University Press, 1999, pp. 37–53.

Linton, Marisa. '"The Tartuffes of Patriotism": Fears of Conspiracy in the Political Language of Revolutionary Government, France 1793–94'. In Barry Coward and Julian Swann (eds), *Conspiracies and Conspiracy Theory in Early Modern Europe: From the Waldensians to the French Revolution*. Aldershot: Ashgate, 2004, pp. 235–54.

Lock, Grahame. 'Introduction'. In Althusser. *Essays in Self-Criticism*. London: NLB, 1976.

Loraux, Nicole. 'Éloge de l'anachronisme en histoire'. *Le Genre humain*, 27 (1993), pp. 23–39.

Löwy, Michael. '"The Poetry of the Past": Marx and the French Revolution'. *New Left Review*, 1:177 (September–October 1989), pp. 111–24.

Manceaux, Michèle. *Les Maos en France*. Paris: Gallimard, 1972.

Mao Zedong. *The Conclusive Scene: Mao Zedong's Last Meeting with the Red Guards*. Trans. Andrea Piazzaroli Longopardi. Helsinki: Rab-Rab Press, 2020.

Mao Zedong. *On Practice and Contradiction*. Ed. Slavoj Žižek. London: Verso, 2007.

Mao Zedong. *Quotations from Chairman Mao Tse-Tung*. Peking: Foreign Language Press, 1966.

Mao Zedong. *Selected Works*, vol. 5. Peking: Foreign Language Press, 1977.

Mao Zedong. *Works of Mao Zedong by Date*. Available at: www.marxists.org/reference/archive/mao/selected-works/date-index.htm.

Marat, Jean-Paul. *Écrits*. Ed. Michel Vovelle. Paris: Messidor/Éditions sociales, 1988.

Marat, Jean-Paul. *L'Ami du peuple*, 1789–92. Available at: https://artfl-project.uchicago.edu/content/lami-du-peuple.

Martin, Jean-Pierre. 'L'Épreuve du réel'. *Les Temps Modernes*, 684–5 (July–October, 2015), pp. 6–23.

Marx, Karl. *Capital*, vol. 1 [1867]. Trans. Ben Fowkes. London: Penguin, 1976.
Marx, Karl. *The Eighteenth Brumaire of Louis Bonaparte* [1852]. New York: International Publishers, 1963.
Marx, Karl. 'Preface to *A Critique of Political Economy*' [1859]. In David McLellan (ed.), *Karl Marx: Selected Writings*, 2nd edn. Oxford: Oxford University Press, 2000, pp. 424–7.
Marx, Karl. 'Theses on Feuerbach' [1845]. In *Collected Works of Marx and Engels*, vol. 5. Moscow: Progress, 1976.
Marx, Karl,, and Friedrich Engels. *The Communist Manifesto*. Trans. Samuel Moore. London: Penguin, 2015.
Marx, Karl, and Friedrich Engels. *The German Ideology*. In *Collected Works of Marx and Engels*, vol. 5. Moscow: Progress, 1976.
Marx, Karl, and Friedrich Engels. *The Holy Family*. In *Collected Works of Marx and Engels*, vol. 4. Moscow: Progress, 1975.
May, Todd. *Contemporary Political Movements and the Thought of Jacques Rancière: Equality in Action*. Edinburgh: Edinburgh University Press, 2010.
May, Todd. 'Kant via Rancière: From Ethics to Anarchism'. In Jimmy Casas Klausen and James Martel (eds), *How Not to Be Governed: Readings and Interpretations from a Critical Anarchist Left*. Plymouth: Lexington Book, 2011, pp. 65–81.
May, Todd. *The Political Thought of Jacques Rancière: Creating Equality*. Edinburgh: Edinburgh University Press, 2008.
May, Todd. 'Rancière and Anarchism'. In Jean-Philippe Deranty and Alison Ross (eds), *Jacques Rancière and the Contemporary Scene: The Philosophy of Radical Equality*. London: Continuum, 2012, pp. 117–28.
Mesner, Maurice. *Mao's China and After: A History of the People's Republic*, 3rd edn. New York: Free Press, 1999.
Michelet, Jules. *Introduction à l'histoire universelle*. Paris: L. Hachette, 1831.
Miller, Jacques-Alain. 'Action of the Structure' [1968]. In Peter Hallward and Knox Peden (eds), *Concept and Form*, vol. 1. London: Verso, 2012, pp. 69–83.
Myrdal, Jan, and Gun Kessle. *China: The Revolution Continued* [1970]. Trans. Paul Britten Austin. Middlesex: Penguin Books, 1973.
Nikulin, Dmitri. 'The Names in History: Rancière's New Historical Poetics'. In Jean-Philippe Deranty and Alison Ross (eds), *Jacques Rancière and the Contemporary Scene: The Philosophy of Radical Equality*. London: Continuum, 2012, pp. 67–86.
O'Neill, Onora. *Constructions of Reason: Explorations of Kant's Practical Philosophy*. Cambridge: Cambridge University Press, 1990.
Osborne, Peter. *Anywhere or Not at All. Philosophy of Contemporary Art*. London: Verso, 2013.

Osborne, Peter. *The Politics of Time: Modernity and Avant-Garde*. London: Verso, 1995.

Palmusaari, Jussi. 'Mao for Now' [review of Jacques Rancière, *The Method of Equality: Interviews with Laurent Jeanpierre and Dork Zabunyan*]. *Radical Philosophy*, 199 (September–October 2016), pp. 55–7.

Palmusaari, Jussi. 'Transgressing Temporal Hierarchies'. *Verso Blog* (4 July 2022). Available at: https://www.versobooks.com/blogs/5383-transgressing-temporal-hierarchies.

Perovic, Sanja. *The Calendar in Revolutionary France: Perceptions of Time in Literature, Culture, Politics*. Cambridge: Cambridge University Press, 2012.

Perovic, Sanja. 'The French Republican Calendar: Time, History, and the Revolutionary Event'. *Journal for Eighteenth-Century Studies*, 31:1 (2012), pp. 1–16.

Pestaña, José Luis Moreno. 'Castoriadis, Rancière: Quels apports pour une philosophie du tirage au sort en politique'. *Participations* (2009), Hors série, pp. 417–35.

Pippa, Stefano. 'Althusser and Contingency'. PhD thesis, Kingston University London, September 2015.

Plotinus, *Enneads*, IV. Trans. A. H. Armstrong. Cambridge, MA: Harvard University Press, 1984, pp. 1–9.

Poullain de la Barre, François. *On the Equality of the Two Sexes* [1673]. In *Three Cartesian Feminist Treatises*. Ed. Marcelle Maistre Welch and trans. Vivien Bosley. Chicago: University of Chicago Press, 2002.

Power, Nina. 'Which Equality? Badiou and Rancière in Light of Ludwig Feuerbach'. *Parallax*, 15:3 (2009), pp. 63–80.

Pozzana, Claudia. 'Althusser and Mao: A Political Test for Dialectics'. In Alex Taek-Gwang Lee and Slavoj Žižek (eds), *The Idea of Communism 3: The Seoul Conference*. London: Verso, 2016.

Proust, Françoise. *Kant. Le Ton de l'histoire*. Paris: Payot, 1991.

Quintana, Laura. 'Institución y acción política: una aproximación desde Jacques Rancière', *Pléyade*, 11 (January–June 2013), pp. 143–58.

Quintana, Laura. *The Politics of Bodies: Philosophical Emancipation with and Beyond Rancière*. London: Rowman and Littlefield, 2020.

Rae Yang, *Spider Eaters: A Memoir*. Berkeley: University of California Press, 1997.

Rancière, Jacques. 'The Aesthetic Dimension: Aesthetics, Politics, Knowledge'. *Critical Inquiry*, 36 (Autumn 2009), pp. 1–19.

Rancière, Jacques. 'The Aesthetic Heterotopia'. *Philosophy Today*, 54 (2010), pp. 15–25.

Rancière, Jacques. 'Aesthetic Separation, Aesthetic Community: Scenes from the Aesthetic Regime of Art'. *Art and Research: A Journal of Ideas, Contexts and Methods*, 2:1 (Summer 2008), pp. 1–15. Available at: http://www.artandresearch. org .uk/v2n1/pdfs/ranciere.pdf.

Rancière, Jacques . 'Aesthetics against Incarnation: An Interview by Anne Marie Oliver'. *Critical Inquiry*, 35 (Autumn 2008), pp. 172–90.

Rancière, Jacques. *Aesthetics and Its Discontents*. Trans. Steven Corcoran. Cambridge: Polity, 2009. [*Malaise dans l'esthétique*. Paris: Galilée, 2004.]

Rancière, Jacques. 'After What'. In Eduardo Cadava et al. (eds), *Who Comes after the Subject?* New York: Routledge, 1991, pp. 246–52. ['Après quoi?'. *Cahiers confrontation*, 20 (Winter 1989), pp. 191–6.]

Rancière, Jacques. *Aisthesis: Scenes from the Aesthetic Regime of Art*. Trans. Zakir Paul. London: Verso, 2013. [*Aisthesis: Scènes du régime esthétique de l'art*. Paris: Galilée, 2011.]

Rancière, Jacques. 'Althusser'. In Simon Critchley and William R. Schroeder (eds), *A Companion to Continental Philosophy*. Malden, MA: Blackwell, 1998, pp. 530–6.

Rancière, Jacques. *Althusser's Lesson*. Trans. Emiliano Battista. London: Continuum, 2011. [*La Leçons d'Althusser*. Paris: Gallimard, 1974.]

Rancière, Jacques. 'Anachronism and The Conflict of Times'. *Diacritics*, 48:2 (2020), pp. 110–12.

Rancière, Jacques. 'The Archaeomodern Turn'. In Michael P. Steinberg (ed.), *Walter Benjamin and the Demands of History*. Ithaca, NY: Cornell University Press, 1996.

Rancière, Jacques. 'Art is Going Elsewhere: And Politics Needs to Catch It' (interview by Sudeep Dasgupta). *Krisis: Journal for Contemporary Philosophy*, 1 (2008), pp. 70–6.

Rancière, Jacques. 'Autonomie et historicisme: la fausse alternative. Sur les régimes de l'historicité de l'art'. In Martin Kaltenecker and François Nicolas (eds), *Penser l'oeuvre musicale au xxe siècle: avec, sans ou contre l'Histoire?* Paris: CDMC, 2006, pp. 51–9.

Rancière, Jacques. *Béla Tarr: The Time After*. Trans. Erik Beranek. Minneapolis: Univocal, 2013. [*Béla Tarr. Le temps d'après*. Paris: Capricci, 2011.]

Rancière, Jacques. 'The Cause of the Other'. *Parallax*, 4:2 (1998), pp. 25–33.

Rancière, Jacques. *Chronicles of Consensual Times*. Trans. Steven Corcoran. London: Continuum, 2010.

Rancière, Jacques. 'Citoyenneté, culture et politique'. In Mikhaël Elbaz and Denise Helly (eds), *Mondialisation, citoyenneté et multiculturalisme*. Paris: L'Harmattan, 2000, pp. 55–68.

Rancière, Jacques. 'The Concept of Anachronism and the Historian's Truth'. *InPrint*, 3:1 (2015), pp. 21–48. ['Le concept d'anachronisme et la vérité de l'historien'. *L'Inactuel*, 6 (1996), pp. 53–68.]

Rancière, Jacques . 'The Concept of Critique and the Critique of Political Economy: From the *1844 Manuscripts* to *Capital*'. In Althusser et al. (eds), *Reading Capital: The Complete Edition* [1965]. Trans. Ben Brewster and David Fernbach. London: Verso, 2015 ['Le Concept de critique et la critique de l'économie politique des "Manuscrits de 1844" au "Capital"'. In Althusser et al. *Lire Le Capital*. Paris: PUF, 1996, pp. 81–199.]

Rancière, Jacques. 'Contemporary Art and Politics of Aesthetics'. In Beth Hinderliter et al. (eds), *Communities of Sense: Rethinking Aesthetics and Politics*. Durham, NC: Duke University Press, 2009, pp. 31–50.

Rancière, Jacques. 'De la vérité des récits au partage des âmes'. *Critique*, 769–70:6 (2011), pp. 474–84.

Rancière, Jacques. 'Democracy, Dissensus and the Aesthetics of Class Struggle: An Exchange with Jacques Rancière' (interview by Max Blechman et al.). *Historical Materialism*, 13:4 (2005), pp. 285–301.

Rancière, Jacques. *The Disagreement: Politics and Philosophy*. Trans. Julie Rose. Minneapolis: University of Minnesota Press, 1999. [*La Mésentente. Politique et philosophie*. Paris: Galilée, 1995.]

Rancière, Jacques. 'Discovering New Worlds: Politics of Travel and Metaphors of Space'. In George Robertson et al. (eds). *Travellers' Tales: Narratives of Home and Displacement*. London: Routledge, 1994, pp. 27–35.

Rancière, Jacques. *Dissensus: On Politics and Aesthetics*. Ed. Steven Corcoran. New York: Continuum, 2010.

Rancière, Jacques. 'Dissenting Words: A Conversation with Jacques Rancière' (interview by Davide Panagia). *Diacritics*, 30:2 (Summer 2000), pp. 113–26.

Rancière, Jacques. *Dissenting Words: Interviews with Jacques Rancière*. Trans. and ed. Emiliano Battista. London: Bloomsbury, 2017.

Rancière, Jacques. 'Divorcing the Hand from the Eye' (interview by Sezgin Boynik) (pagination by the author). (A published, slightly shortened version: 'The Divorce of the Eye and the Hand: Interview with Jacques Rancière by Sezgin Boynik'. *Rab-Rab: Journal for Political and Formal Inquiries in Art*, 4.1 (December 2017), pp. 90–102.)

Rancière, Jacques. *The Emancipated Spectator*. Trans. Gregory Elliott. London: Verso, 2009.

Rancière, Jacques. 'Les Énoncés de la fin et du rien'. In Georges Leyenberger and Jean-Jacques Forté (eds), *Traversée du nihilisme*. Paris: Osiris, 1994, pp. 67–91.

Rancière, Jacques. *En quel temps vivons-nous? Conversation avec Eric Hazan*. Paris: La Fabrique, 2017.

Rancière, Jacques. 'Entretien avec Julia Christ et Bertrand Ogilvie'. In *Cahiers critiques de philosophie*, 17 (February 2017), pp. 169–203.

Rancière, Jacques. 'Entretien avec Jacques Rancière' (interview by Nicolas Poirier). *Le Philosophoire*, 13:3 (2000), pp. 29–42.

Rancière, Jacques. 'Esthétique de la politique et poétique du savoir'. *Espaces Temps*, 55-6 (1994), pp. 80–7.

Rancière, Jacques. *Et tant pis pour les gens fatigués. Entretiens*. Paris: Editions Amsterdam, 2009.

Rancière, Jacques. 'A Few Remarks on the Method of Jacques Rancière'. *Parallax*, 15:3 (2009), pp. 114–23.

Rancière, Jacques. *Figures de l'histoire*. Paris: PUF, 2012.

Rancière, Jacques. *Film Fables*. Trans. Emiliano Battista. Oxford: Berg, 2006.

Rancière, Jacques. *The Flesh of Words: The Politics of Writing*. Trans. Charlotte Mandel. Stanford, CA: Stanford University Press, 2004. [*La Chair des mots. Politiques de l'écriture*. Paris: Galilée, 1998.]

Rancière, Jacques. *The Future of the Image* [2003]. Trans. Gregory Elliott. London: Verso, 2009.

Rancière, Jacques. *Hatred of Democracy* [2005]. Trans. Steve Corcoran. London: Verso, 2014.

Rancière, Jacques. 'How to Use *Lire le Capital*'. Trans. Tanya Asad. In Ali Rattansi (ed.), *Ideology, Method, and Marx: Essays from* Economy and Society. London: Routledge, 1989, pp. 181–9. ['Mode d'emploi pour une réédition de *Lire le Capital*'. *Les Temps modernes*, 328 (November 1973), pp. 788–807.]

Rancière, Jacques. 'I no longer have faith in Time'. In Nikolaus Hirsch and Shveta Sarda (eds), *Cybermohalla Hub*. Berlin: Sternberg Press, 2012, pp. 76–8.

Rancière, Jacques. *The Ignorant Schoolmaster: Five Lessons in Intellectual Emancipation*. Trans. Kristin Ross. Stanford, CA: Stanford University Press, 1991. [*Le Maître ignorant. Cinq leçons sur l'émancipation intellectuelle*. Paris: Fayard, 1987.]

Rancière, Jacques. 'In What Time Do We Live?'. In Marta Kuzma et al. (eds), *The State of Things*. London: Koenig Books, 2012, pp. 11–37.

Rancière, Jacques. *The Intellectual and His Double: Staging the People*, vol. 2. Trans. David Fernbach. London: Verso, 2012.

Rancière, Jacques. 'Interview with Jacques Rancière' (by Nina Power). *Ephemera: Theory & Politics in Organisation*, 10:1 (2010), pp. 77–81.

Rancière, Jacques. 'Introduction' [1976]. In Jacques Rancière and Alain Faure (eds), *La Parole ouvrière, 1830–1851* [1976]. Paris: La Fabrique: 2007, pp. 7–19.

Rancière, Jacques. *Ist Kunst widerständig?* Trans. Frank Ruda and Jan Völker. Berlin: Merve, 2008.

Rancière, Jacques. 'La Conception pseudo-marxiste de l'aliénation'. *Cahiers marxistes-léninistes*, 1 (December 1964), pp. 12–21. Available at: http://adlc.hypotheses.org/ archives-du-seminaire-marx/cahiers-marxistes-leninistes.

Rancière, Jacques. 'La Démocratie est-elle à venir? Éthique et politique chez Derrida'. *Les Temps Modernes*, 669–70:3 (2012), pp. 157–73.

Rancière, Jacques . 'La Méthode de l'égalité'. In Laurence Cornu and Patrice Vermeren (eds), *La Philosophie déplacée. Autour de Jacques Rancière*. Lyon: Horlieu, 2006.

Rancière, Jacques. 'La Nouvelle orthodoxie de Louis Althusser'. *Le Monde*, 12 September 1973.

Rancière, Jacques. 'La Paraphrase'. *Conséquence*, 1 (December 2015), pp. 35–9.

Rancière, Jacques. 'La Poétique du savoir'. *La Main de singe*, 11–12 (1994), pp. 68–72. Available at: http://www.multitudes.net/La-poetique-du-savoir/.

Rancière, Jacques. 'La Représentation de l'ouvrier ou la classe impossible'. In Philippe Lacoue-Labarthe and Jean-Luc Nancy (eds), *Le Retrait du politique*. Paris: Galilée, 1983, pp. 89–109.

Rancière, Jacques. 'La Scène révolutionnaire et l'ouvrier émancipé (1830–1848)' [1988]. *Tumultes*, 20:1 (2003), pp. 49–72.

Rancière, Jacques. 'Le Concept marxiste de rapport de production'. *Cahiers marxistes-léninistes*, 3 (publication date not available), pp. 1–12. Available at: http://adlc.hypotheses.org/archives-du-seminaire-marx/cahiers-marxistes-leninistes.

Rancière, Jacques. *Le Temps du paysage. Aux origines de la révolution esthétique.* Paris: La Fabrique, 2020.

Rancière, Jacques. *Les mots et les torts. Dialogue avec Javier Bassas.* Paris: La Fabrique, 2021.

Rancière, Jacques. *Les Scènes du peuple. Les Révoltes logiques 1975–1985.* Lyon: Horlieu, 2003.

Rancière, Jacques. 'L'Histoire aujourd'hui: des certitudes aux défis'. *Raison présente*, 108 (1993), pp. 57–69.

Rancière, Jacques. 'Literature, Politics, Aesthetics: Approaches to Democratic Disagreement' (interview by Solange Guénoun et al.). *SubStance*, 29:2 (2000), pp. 3–24.

Rancière, Jacques. *The Lost Thread: The Democracy of Modern Fiction*. Trans. Steven Corcoran. London: Bloomsbury, 2017. [*Le Fil perdu. Essais sur la fiction moderne.* Paris: La Fabrique, 2014.]

Rancière, Jacques. *Mallarmé: The Politics of the Siren* [1996]. Trans. Steven Corcoran. London: Continuum, 2011.

Rancière, Jacques. *Marx in the Woods*. Trans. Jussi Palmusaari. Helsinki: Rab-Rab Press, 2019.

Rancière, Jacques. 'Metamorphosis of the Muses'. In Mela Dávila (ed.), *Sonic Process: A New Geography of Sounds*. Barcelona: MACBA, 2002, pp. 17–30.

Rancière, Jacques. 'The Method of Equality: An Answer to Some Questions'. In Gabriel Rockhill and Philip Watts (eds), *Jacques Rancière: History, Politics, Aesthetics*. Durham, NC: Duke University Press, 2009, pp. 273–88.

Rancière, Jacques. *The Method of Equality: Interviews with Laurent Jeanpierre and Dork Zabunyam*. Trans. Julie Rose. Cambridge: Polity, 2016. [*La Méthode de l'égalité. Entretien avec Laurent Jeanpierre et Dork Zabunyam*. Montrouge: Bayard, 2012.]

Rancière, Jacques. *Modern Times*. London: Verso, 2022.

Rancière, Jacques. *Moments Politiques. Interventions 1977–2009*. Trans. Mary Foster. New York: Seven Stories Press, 2014.

Rancière, Jacques. *Mute Speech: Literature, Critical Theory, and Politics* [1998]. Trans. James Swenson. New York: Columbia University Press, 2011. [*La Parole muette. Essai sur les contradictions de la littérature*. Paris: Fayard/Pluriel, 2010.]

Rancière, Jacques. 'The Myth of the Artisan: Critical Reflections on a Category of Social History'. *International Labor and Working Class History*, 24 (Fall 1983), pp. 1–16.

Rancière, Jacques. *The Names of History: On the Poetics of Knowledge*. Trans. Hassan Melehy. Minneapolis: University of Minnesota Press, 1994. [*Les Noms de l'histoire. Essai de poétique du savoir*. Paris: Seuil, 1992.]

Rancière, Jacques. *The Nights of Labor: The Workers' Dream in Nineteenth-Century France* [1981]. Trans. John Drury. Philadelphia, PA: Temple University Press, 1989. [*La Nuit des prolétaires. Archives du rêve ouvrier*. Fayard/Pluriel: 2012.]

Rancière, Jacques. 'On *Aisthesis*' (interview by Oliver Davis). In Oliver Davis (ed.), *Rancière Now*. Cambridge: Polity Press, 2013, pp. 202–18.

Rancière, Jacques. 'On Ignorant Schoolmasters'. In Charles Bingham and Gert Biesta (eds), *Jacques Rancière: Education, Truth, Emancipation*. London: Continuum, 2010, pp. 1–16.

Rancière, Jacques. 'Only in the Form of Rupture' (interview by Peter Hallward). In Peter Hallward and Knox Peden (eds), *Concept and Form*, vol. 1. London: Verso, 2012, pp. 259–72.

Rancière, Jacques. *On the Shores of Politics* [1990]. Trans. Liz Heron. London: Verso, 1995. [2nd French edition: *Aux bords du politique*. Paris: Gallimard, 1998.]

Rancière, Jacques. *The Philosopher and His Poor* [1983]. Trans. John Drury et al. Durham, NC: Duke University Press, 2004. [*Le Philosopher et ses pauvres*. Paris: Flammarion, 2007.]

Rancière, Jacques. 'Politics and Aesthetics' (interview by Peter Hallward). *Angelaki: Journal of Theoretical Humanities*, 8:2 (August 2003), pp. 191–211.

Rancière, Jacques. 'Politics, Identification, Subjectivization'. *October*, 61 (Summer 1992), pp. 58–64.

Rancière, Jacques. *The Politics of Aesthetics: The Distribution of the Sensible*. Trans. Gabriel Rockhill. London: Continuum, 2004. [*Le Partage du sensible. Esthétique et politique*. Paris: La Fabrique, 2000.]

Rancière, Jacques. 'A Politics of Aesthetic Indetermination' (interview by Frank Ruda and Jan Voelker). In Jason E. Smith and Annette Weisser (eds), *Everything Is in Everything: Jacques Rancière between Intellectual Emancipation and Aesthetic Education*. Pasadena, CA: Art Center Graduate Press, 2011, pp. 10–33.

Rancière, Jacques. *The Politics of Literature* [2006]. Trans. Julie Rose. Cambridge: Polity, 2011.

Rancière, Jacques. *Politik und Ästhetik. Im Gespräch mit Peter Engelmann*. Wien: Passagen, 2016.

Rancière, Jacques. 'Postface pour la nouvelle édition' [2007]. In Jacques Rancière and Alain Faure (eds), *La Parole ouvrière, 1830–1851* [1976]. Paris: La Fabrique, 2007, pp. 332–42.

Rancière, Jacques. 'Préface'. In Pierre-Simon Ballanche (ed.), *Première Sécession de la plèbe*. Rennes: Pontcerq, 2017, pp. 9–23.

Rancière, Jacques. 'Sens et usages de l'utopie'. In Michèle Riot-Sarcey (ed.), *L'Utopie en questions*. Saint-Denis: Presses universitaires de Vincennes, 2001, pp. 65–78.

Rancière, Jacques. *Short Voyages to the Land of the People*. Trans. James Swenson. Stanford, CA: Stanford University Press, 2003. [*Court Voyages au pays du peuple*. Paris: Seuil, 1990.]

Rancière, Jacques. *Staging the People: The Proletarian and His Double*, vol. 1. Trans. David Fernbach. London: Verso, 2011.

Rancière, Jacques. 'Sur la théorie de l'idéologie. Politique d'Althusser'. *L'Homme et la Société*, 27 (1973), pp. 31–61.

Rancière, Jacques. 'Sur l'interruption' (interview by 'Groupe Interruption'), 14. June 2013. Available at: https://interruptionint.wordpress.com/2013/12/21/sur-linterruption-avec-jaques-ranciere/.

Rancière, Jacques. 'The Thinking of Dissensus'. In Paul Bowman and Richard Stamp (eds), *Reading Rancière*. London: Continuum, 2011, pp. 1–17.

Rancière, Jacques. [Untitled discussion of Badiou's *Being and Event*]. *Le Cahier (Collège international de philosophie)*, 8 (October 1989), pp. 211–25.

Rancière, Jacques . 'Un-What?' *Philosophy and Rhetoric*, 49:4 (2016), pp. 589–606.

Rancière, Jacques. 'Utopistes, bourgeois et prolétaires'. *L'Homme et la société*, 37–8 (1975), pp. 87–98.

Rancière, Jacques. 'What Does It Mean to Be *Un*?' *Continuum: Journal of Media & Cultural Studies*, 21:4 (2007), pp. 559–69.

Rancière, Jacques. 'Work, Identity, Subject'. In Jean-Philippe Deranty and Alison Ross (eds), *Jacques Rancière and the Contemporary Scene: The Philosophy of Radical Equality*. London: Continuum, 2012, pp. 205–16.

Rancière, Jacques, and Axel Honneth. *Recognition and Disagreement: A Critical Encounter on the Politics of Freedom, Equality, and Identity*. New York: Columbia University Press, 2016.

Rancière, Jacques, and Danièlle Rancière. 'The Philosophers' Tale: Intellectuals and the Trajectory of *Gauchisme*' [1978], in *The Intellectual and His Double: Staging the People*, vol. 2. Trans. David Fernbach. London: Verso, 2012. ['La Légende des philosophes (les intellectuels et la traverse du gauchisme)'. *Les Révoltes logiques*, special issue, *Les Lauriers de Mai ou les Chemins du Pouvoir, 1968–1978* (1978), pp. 7–25.]

Reid, Donald. 'Le Grand Récit des établis (et ses multiple entrées)'. *Les Temps Modernes*, 684–5 (July–October 2015), pp. 34–53.

Renault, Emmanuel. 'The Many Marx of Jacques Rancière'. In Jean-Philippe Deranty and Alison Ross (eds), *Jacques Rancière and the Contemporary Scene: The Philosophy of Radical Equality*. London: Continuum, 2012.

Rivenc, François. 'Quelques reflexions sur l'établissement en usine'. *Les Temps Modernes*, 684–5 (July–October 2015), pp. 24–33.

Robespierre, Maximilien. *Œuvres complètes*, vol. 5. Ed. Gustave Laurent. Gap: Louis Jean, 1961.

Robespierre, Maximilien. *Pour le bonheur et pour la liberté. Discours*. Ed. Yannick Bosc et al. Paris: La Fabrique, 2000.

Robson, Mark. 'Jacques Rancière and Time: *le temps d'après*'. *Paragraph*, 38.3 (2015), pp. 297–311.

Robson, Mark. '"A literary animal": Rancière, Derrida, and the Literature of Democracy'. *Parallax*, 15:3 (2009), pp. 88–101.

Rockhill, Gabriel. 'Glossary of Technical Terms'. In Jacques Rancière (ed.), *The Politics of Aesthetics: The Distribution of the Sensible*. Trans. Gabriel Rockhill. London: Continuum, 2004, pp. 80–93.

Rockhill, Gabriel. *Radical History and the Politics of Art*. New York: Columbia University Press, 2014.

Rolin, Olivier. *Paper Tiger*. Trans. Willian Cloonan. Lincoln: University of Nebraska Press, 2007.

Ross, Alison. 'Expressivity, Literarity, Mute Speech'. In Jean-Philippe Deranty (ed.), *Jacques Rancière: Key Concepts*. Durham, NC: Acumen, 2010, pp. 133–50.

Ross, Kristin. 'Historicizing Untimeliness'. In Gabriel Rockhill and Philip Watts (eds), *Jacques Rancière: History, Politics, Aesthetics*. Durham, NC: Duke University Press, 2009, pp. 15–29.

Ross, Kristin. 'Translator's Introduction'. In Jacques Rancière (ed.), *The Ignorant Schoolmaster: Five Lessons in Intellectual Emancipation*. Trans. Kristin Ross. Stanford, CA: Stanford University Press, 1991, pp. vii–xxiii.

Ruby, Christian. *L'Interruption. Jacques Rancière et la politique*. Paris: La Fabrique, 2009.

Russo, Alessandro. *Cultural Revolution and Revolutionary Culture*. Durham, NC: Duke University Press, 2020.

Russo, Alessandro. 'One Step, an Encounter'. In *The Conclusive Scene: Mao Zedong's Last Meeting with the Red Guards*. Trans. Andrea Piazzaroli Longopardi. Helsinki: Rab-Rab Press, 2020.

Saint-Just. *Œuvres complètes*. Ed. Anne Kupiec and Miguel Abensour. Paris: Gallimard, 2004.

Sartre, Jean-Paul. 'Avant-propos'. In Michèle Manceaux. *Les Maos en France*. Paris: Gallimard, 1972, pp. 7–15.

Sartre, Jean-Paul. 'Intentionality: A Fundamental Idea of Husserl's Phenomenology' [1939]. *Journal of the British Society for Phenomenology*, 1:2 (1970), pp. 4–5.

Schaap, Andrew. 'Hannah Arendt and the Philosophical Repression of Politics'. In Jean-Philippe Deranty and Alison Ross (eds), *Jacques Rancière and the Contemporary Scene: The Philosophy of Radical Equality*. London: Continuum, 2012, pp. 145–66.

Schiller, Friedrich. *On the Aesthetic Education of Man* [1795]. Trans. Reginald Snell. Mineola, NY: Diver, 2004.

Sellers, Mortimer. 'The Roman Republic and the French and American Revolutions'. In Harriet I. Flower (ed.), *The Cambridge Companion to the Roman Republic*. Cambridge: Cambridge University Press, 2004, pp. 347–64.

Shapiro, Michael. 'The Presence of War: "Here and Elsewhere"'. *International Political Sociology*, 5:2 (June 2011), pp. 109–25.

Shapiro, Michael. 'Radicalising Democratic Theory: Social Space in Connolly, Deleuze, and Rancière'. In David Campbell and Morton Schoolman (eds), *The*

New Pluralism: William Connolly and the Contemporary Global Condition.
Durham, NC: Duke University Press, 2008, pp. 197–220.

Shaw, Devin Zane. 'Cartesian Egalitarianism: from Poullain de la Barre to Rancière'. *PhaenEx*, 7:1 (2011), pp. 101–29.

Simons, Maarten, and Jan Masschelein. 'Hatred of Democracy and the Public Role of Education?' In Maarten Simons and Jan Masschelein (eds), *Rancière, the Public Education and the Taming of Democracy.* Oxford: Wiley-Blackwell, 2011, pp. 1–14.

Sini, Carlo. *Ethics of Writing.* Trans. Silvio Benso and Brian Schroeder.
New York: SUNY, 2009.

Smith, Jason E. 'From Établissement to Lip: On the Turns Taken by French Maoism'. *Viewpoint Magazine*, 3 (2013). Available at: https://www.viewpointmag.com/2013/09/30/issue-3-workers-inquiry/.

Stanguennec, André. *Hegel. Critique de Kant.* Paris: PUF, 1985.

Starr, John Bryan. *Continuing the Revolution: The Political Thought of Mao.* Princeton, NJ: Princeton University Press, 1979.

Tanke, Joseph J. *Jacques Rancière: An Introduction.* London: Continuum, 2011.

Toscano, Alberto. 'Mao and Manichaeism: An Episode in the Politics of Purity'. *Parallax*, 17:2 (2011), pp. 49–58.

Unger, Jonathan. *Education under Mao: Class and Competition in Canton Schools, 1960–1980.* New York: Columbia University Press, 1982.

Wahnich, Sophie. 'Archives, objet empirique et intuition du rapport passé/présent de l'historien'. In Myriam Bachir Curapp (ed.), *Les Méthodes au concret.* Paris: PUF, 2000, pp. 211–28.

Wahnich, Sophie. *In Defence of the Terror: Liberty or Death in the French Revolution.* Trans. David Fernbach. London: Verso, 2012.

Wahnich, Sophie. *La Longue patience du peuple, 1792. Naissance de la République.* Paris: Payot, 2008.

Wartofsky, Marx W. *Feuerbach.* Cambridge: Cambridge University Press, 1977.

Weil, Simone. *La Condition ouvrière.* Paris: Gallimard, 1951.

Whitener, Brian. 'Nonrelation and Untimeliness in Jacques Rancière's *The Names of History'*. *Política común*, 4 (2013). Available at: https://quod.lib.umich.edu/p/pc/?page=home.

Yan Jiaqi and Gao Gao, *Turbulent Decade: A History of the Cultural Revolution.* Trans. D. W. Y. Kwok. Honolulu: University of Hawai'i Press, 1996.

Index

achronie/non-time/timelessness 7, 9, 12, 18, 54, 83, 107, 177, 122, 133–5, 137–8, 145–9, 156, 161, 174 n.59, 201 n.35
activity and passivity 104–6, 110–13, 115, 118
aesthetics 8–10, 17, 98, 104, 108, 117, 119, 121
aesthetic regime of art 117
aesthetic judgment 110, 117, 119
Agamben, Giorgio 156, 200 n.32
Althusserianism 16–17, 19, 21–2, 29–30, 33, 35, 46–7, 64, 78, 81–3, 85, 142–3, 147–8, 170, 190 n.63, 202 n.70
Althusser's Lesson (Rancière) 10, 19, 21, 36, 46–58
anachronism/*anachronie*/untimeliness 4, 18, 120–4, 126–7, 129–38, 145, 149–50, 152, 158–60, 180 n.74, 185 n.19, 192 n.84, 198 nn.1–2, 198–9 n.6, 200 n.32
Annales School historians 71
antiquity 37, 149–51, 159
archē 15, 66
Arendt, Hannah 15, 156
Aristotle 100–1, 193–194 n.3
art 100, 108, 115, 187–8 n.39, 199 n.16
  contemporary 140
  regimes of 198 n.6, 205 n.40
axiom of equality 9–10, 15, 95

Badiou, Alain 130, 171 n.2, 177–8 n.43, 180 n.79, 186–7 n.33, 189 n.54, 192 n.95, 193–4 n.3, 206 n.55, 206 n.56, 207 n.64
  Being and Event 125
  The Communist Hypothesis 177 n.39
  and inaesthetics 196 n.34
  Metapolitics 193–4 n.3
  Theory of the Subject 75
Balibar, Étienne 29, 174 n.3, 175 n.13
beauty/the beautiful 106, 107, 110, 119

Beistegui, Miguel de 40, 179 n.64
Bell, David F. 85
Benjamin, Walter 171 n.6, 200 n.32, 201 n.49
Bensaïd, Daniel 206 n.56, 207 n.64
Bergson, Henri 22, 175 n.7
Birnbaum, Antonia 165, 192 n.95
Bosteels, Bruno 177–8 n.43, 180 n.79, 186–7 n.33, 192 n.95, 193–4 n.3
Braudel, Fernand 71
break
  between space and time 15, 76
  epistemological 20, 26–8, 38–9, 41, 52, 64, 175 n.14
  from science/theory 21, 24, 79
  historical 40, 42–3, 57, 67, 79–80, 83, 97
  Rancière's, with Althusser 19, 16, 83
  revolutionary/political 20, 22, 37, 52
  temporal 16, 44, 47, 57–8
  with time/temporality 58–9, 61, 63, 95, 159, 205 n.40
  see also rupture

Cahiers Marxistes-Léninistes 22, 29, 36, 176 n.24
Cahiers pour l'Analyse 29, 176 n.19
Campailla, Giovanni 201 n.40
capitalism 1, 23, 37, 41–2, 48–50, 58, 65, 199 n.20
cartography 69, 72, 81, 130, 185 n.16
categorical imperative 9, 173 n.38
causality 1, 5, 12, 23–4, 26, 31, 120, 175 n.13, 197 n.58
  expressive 23, 25
  mechanical 23, 31
  structural, 24–5, 29, 175 n.13
Cavazzini, Andrea 94, 190 n.67
Chambers, Samuel 168–9, 187–188 n.39, 206 n.56, 207 n.62, 208 n.4
Châtelet, François 56

China 30–33, 54, 80, 86, 161, 189 n.53
  Communist Party of 30–3, 88, 91
  see also Cultural Revolution (Chinese)
chronophobia 160
contradiction 24–5, 48, 55–6, 58–60, 68, 77, 89, 91, 94, 105, 156–7
cinema 116, 174 n.59, 196–7 n.55
citizen/citizenship 6, 153–4, 156–8, 160, 162, 153 n.53
Clarté 22
class struggle 13, 35, 44, 48, 50, 53–5, 142, 144–5, 147, 193–4 n.3
Cleisthenes of Athens 6, 172 n.25
coexistence 11, 111, 123
  egalitarian 3, 6, 14, 113, 120, 126–7, 130, 151, 158, 186–7 n.33
  spatial 4–5, 15, 67–8, 71–4, 115, 139, 141–2
  of times 1, 3–4, 5, 18, 30, 121, 138–42, 146, 150, 201–2 n.49
communism 13, 20, 28, 30–2, 60, 147, 176–7 n.30, 181 n.91, 183 n.3
community 11, 13, 59, 72, 95, 102, 108, 113, 120, 145, 163, 173 n.39, 195 n.28
  of science 53, 55
'The Concept of Anachronism and the Historian's Truth' (Rancière) 122–4, 126–9, 133
contiguity 6, 16, 41, 43–4, 158, 163, 165, 167, 170, 174 n.59
  see also discontiguity
Critique of Judgement (Kant) 8, 106, 110, 111, 118
Critique of Pure Reason (Kant) 3, 105, 118
Cultural Revolution (Chinese) 16–17, 19–20, 30–3, 37–8, 54, 63–4, 79, 84–7, 89, 91, 93–5, 97, 132, 147–8, 157, 161, 165, 170, 177 nn.32, 39, 41, 179 n.73, 189 n.53, 192 n.95, 193 n.103, 194 n.6

Davis, Oliver 100, 108, 124, 131
Declaration of the Rights of Man and the Citizen, *see* citizen/citizenship
Deleuze, Gilles 14, 174 n.59, 185 n.16
  and Felix Guattari 109
democracy 103, 125, 173 n.39, 203 n.12
  in antiquity 5–7
  to come 189 n.57

Jules Michelet on 70–1, 73
Mallarmé and 108
Maoism and 33
dēmos/demos 5–7, 66, 172 nn.24–25
Deranty, Jean-Philippe 167–8, 184 n.13
Derrida, Jacques 189–90 n.57, 190 n.61
detemporalization 15, 115, 141, 146
development 23, 24
  temporal/historical 1, 4, 8, 10, 13, 15, 20, 25–6, 34–5, 50–1, 57–9, 65, 84, 101, 124–6, 141–3, 152
  of theory 29, 175–6 n.15
  of the value-form 140
dialectic 12–14, 22, 34, 52, 75, 149, 168, 173 n.47, 175 n.14, 178 n.60, 182 n.108, 186 n.33
dialectical materialism 52, 175 n.14
Didi-Huberman, Georges 185 n.19, 200 n.32
Dikeç, Mustafa 15, 172 n.24, 186 n.30
disagreement (*mésentente*) 91–2
  see also dissensus
discontiguity 39–41, 43
discontinuity 20, 27, 30, 38–41, 52–3, 55, 63, 82, 126, 141, 179 n.63
disinterestedness 40, 112, 113
disorientation 66–7, 72, 74–7, 81, 84, 88–9, 91–2, 94–6
displacement 7, 20, 67, 107, 129, 135, 157, 174 n.59, 181 n.91
dissensus 92, 115
distribution of the sensible, see *partage du sensible*
division of labour 37–40, 47–8, 50, 54–5, 114, 180 n.89

education 5, 20, 30, 32, 50, 64, 85–8, 91, 93, 103, 107, 109, 115, 119, 124, 182 n.107, 190 n.69
Elliott, Gregory 54, 174
Engels, Friedrich 58–9, 149–50, 153
enquête 33–4, 178 n.47
epistemological break, *see* break
era/epoch (*époque*) 10, 14, 25, 40, 43–4, 54, 64–9, 72, 78–9, 84, 127, 129, 134, 174 n.59, 200 n.32, 204 n.35
établissement 17, 34, 63–9, 78, 80–1, 86, 97, 178 n.47, 179 n.72, 183 nn.2–3, 189 n.54, 196 n.39

see also *enquête*
étape, see stage
eternity 18, 54, 121–4, 127–33, 135, 149, 151–8, 160–3, 170

Fajardo, Christian 171 n.6, 172 n.29
Febvre, Lucien 123–4, 126–7, 130
Fénelon, François 86
Feuerbach, Ludwig 3–5, 13, 15, 23, 139, 153, 172 n.18, 200 n.29
  'Principles of the Philosophy of the Future' 4
  'Towards a Critique of Hegel's Philosophy' 3
For Marx (Althusser), 21, 53
Foucault, Michel
  archaeology in 198 n.6
  on the care of the self 103–4, 195 n.11
  and cartography 185 n.16
  on the concept of episteme 123, 179 n.63, 185 n.19
  difference between Althusser and 53
  on the Enlightenment 199 n.8
  on heterotopia 114
  Lardreau on 39–40
Fraisse, Geneviève 137, 196–7 n.55, 201 n.47
French Communist Party (PCF) 20, 29–30, 36, 51, 53–4, 147, 174 n.3, 176 n.23, 180–1 n.89
French Revolution 18, 124, 149–65, 170
Furet, François 74, 150, 152

Gao Yuan 177 n.41
Gauche Prolétarienne 16, 21, 35–6, 43, 46–7
  see also *gauchisme*
gauchisme 17, 65, 67–8, 83–4, 183 n.2
Gauny, Louis-Gabriel 13, 111, 113, 119, 196 nn.38–9, 199 n.20
Gauthier, Florence 153–4, 204 nn.19, 23
Gavi, Philippe, 190 n.64
Genette, Gérard 134–5
Gibson, Andrew 197 n.64, 200 n.32, 204 n.18, 206 n.56
Glucksmann, André 69, 185 n.16
Gramsci, Antonio 84

Hallward, Peter 44, 193 n.2, 198 n.2
Haynes, Mike 154
Hegel, G. W. F. 12–13, 20, 195 n.25, 197 n.64, 173–4 n.53
  Althusserian critique of 20, 22–3, 49, 82, 175 nn.6, 9
  Feuerbach's critique of 3–4
  and Lardreau 44
Heidegger, Martin 175 n.7
Heideggerianism 131, 200 n.29, 207 n.64
Hennebert, Marthe 73–4, 186 n.31
heterogeneity 25, 43
  see also homogeneity
heterotopia 113–14
historical materialism 52, 84, 141, 153, 181 n.91
historiography 70–2, 127, 149–50, 193 n.3
Hobbes, Thomas 159, 193–4 n.3
homogeneity 120, 127
horizontality 88, 117
Hughes, Edward J. 183 n.3, 194 n.9, 196 n.39
humanity/mankind 28, 46, 106, 109, 110, 115, 119, 137
  and inhumanity 11
humanism 22–3, 37, 51, 54
  anti- 28, 176 n.23
Husserl, Edmund 175 n.7
Hyppolite, Jean 173 n.53

The Ignorant Schoolmaster (Rancière) 86, 88, 190 n.65
imagination 117–19, 197 n.62
imitation 20, 87, 99, 128, 190 n.69
  see also repetition
impossibility 2, 20, 37, 41, 43, 52, 57, 73–4, 92, 103, 108, 111, 116, 123–6, 141, 144, 146, 156
  see also possibility
inner sense (form of intuition) 18, 104–6, 111, 113
intelligence 2–3, 11–12, 18, 86–7, 93–5, 114, 144
  class of 108, 112, 114
  equality of 2–3, 14, 94, 129–30, 136–7, 147, 191 n.76
  timelessness of 2, 11, 133, 135, 138

Jacotot, Joseph 5, 86–90, 92–5, 137, 144, 147–8, 151, 158, 190 n.69, 191 n.79

Jambet, Christian 78
　see also Lardreau
Jones, Andrew F. 90
judgement (Kantian) 8, 106, 110, 112, 130, 140

Kant, Immanuel 2–3, 8–13, 17–18, 49–50, 95–8, 107, 173 nn.39, 46, 47, 53, 195 n.25
　on aesthetics 104–21
　Lardreau on 44–5
　schematism in 118, 155, 197 n.64
Karol, K. S. 32
kingdom of ends (Kantian) 10–11, 173 n.39

Lacan, Jacques 75
Lacoue-Labarthe, Philippe 207 n.64
Lardreau, Guy 13, 16, 21, 28, 36–47, 83, 96–7, 170, 173 n.50, 179 n.73, 180 n.74, 180 n.76, 180 n.79. 183 n.2, 183 n.4, 184 n.7, 206 n.56
　L'Ange (with Jambet) 44–5
　La Véracité 45, 57
　Le Monde (with Jambet) 45
　Le Singe d'or 36–44, 51, 53, 55–6, 64–6
la nouvelle philosophie/les nouveaux philosophes 63, 69, 81, 83, 130
Le Dantec, Jean-Pierre 78
Leese, Daniel 89
Lefebvre, Henri 22
Lenin, Vladimir 24–5, 36, 38, 42, 52, 175 n.9, 178 n.60, 181 n.91
Les Révoltes logiques 69, 137, 142, 182 n.108
Lévy, Benny (alias Pierre Victor) 79, 81
Lin Biao 85, 87–8, 90, 92–3, 191 n.77
Linhart, Robert 66–7, 80–1, 189 n.54, 196 n.39
Linhart, Virginie 86
Linton, Marisa 205 n.43
literarity 17, 64, 76–9, 85, 157, 187–8 n.39, 188 n.40, 189 n.57
literature 85, 116, 188 n.40, 192 n.93
Little Red Book 64, 86–91, 93, 157, 191 n.70
Loraux, Nicole 134, 201 n.35

Mallarmé, Stéphane 108, 195 n.28
Mao Zedong 20, 22, 24, 28, 31–2, 35, 44, 52, 58, 68, 86, 91, 93–4, 148, 174–5 n.4, 175 n.6, 177–8 n.43, 184 nn.13–14, 193 n.103
Mao Zedong Thought 90, 91, 191 n.77
Marat, Jean-Paul 149, 162–3, 205 n.53
Marx, Karl 19, 21, 23–4, 38, 41–2, 50, 52, 58–60, 142, 148–50, 156, 174 n.54, 175 n.14, 175–6 n.15, 178 n.60, 180 n.89, 182 n.107, 193 n.3, 199 n.20
　and Friedrich Engels 58–9, 149–50, 153
　the young 10–12, 23, 29, 150, 173 n.47, 195 n.25
Marxism 12–13, 41–3, 51, 62, 64, 97, 153, 179 n.69, 181 n.102, 193 n.98
　Althusser's 19–20, 22–4, 28–9, 38
　orthodox 1
　post- 1, 12
Marxism-Leninism 87, 97, 179 n.67, 191 n.77
maxim (Kantian) 8
　of equality 95
　see also on a raison de se révolter/it is right to revolt
May 1968 4, 16, 19, 21, 30, 33–6, 55, 61, 69, 170
　post- 16, 35, 36
May, Todd 169, 173 n.39, 206 n.56
Michelet, Jules 70–4
morality 95, 112, 114, 152–3
multidirectionality 5, 25, 68, 71, 88, 94
　see also omnidirectionality
multiple times/temporalities 4–5, 7, 18, 20, 25, 30, 121, 127–8, 129, 131–4, 136–47, 149–50, 154, 158–9, 163, 165, 171 n.6, 185 n.19, 200 n.32, 201 n.49
　see also coexistence

The Names of History (Rancière) 70, 71, 74, 92, 122, 124, 132, 150, 186 n.30, 187–8 n.39, 205 n.37, 205 n.40
Nancy, Jean-Luc 207 n.64
narrative 6, 127, 135, 149
　discourse- 70, 186 n.23
　historical/temporal 59, 70–1, 73–4, 101, 134

neo-Platonism 45
The Nights of Labor (Rancière) 61, 111, 144, 147, 195 n.10, 199 n.20
Nikulin, Dmitri 185 n.22
nonplace 74–5, 186–7 n.33
novelty/the new 35–6, 45, 56–7, 78, 125, 187, 199 n.16

omnidirectionality 76, 88–91, 94–5
on a raison de se révolter/it is right to revolt 36, 41–2, 76, 148
opsis 100–1
orientation 13, 95, 112, 122, 127, 169
  historical/temporal 2, 11, 17, 44, 65–72, 75, 89, 96, 100, 101, 108–9, 143, 159, 184 n.7
  see also disorientation; *sens*
Osborne, Peter 18, 122, 139–41, 143, 171 n.2

Panagia, Davide, 192 n.94, 197 n.62
partage du sensible 7, 92, 105–6, 110
pedagogy, *see* education
People's Liberation Army 87, 91–2
periodization 125, 130, 133, 135, 159, 198 n.6, 205 n.40
Perovic, Sanja 204 n.35
Pippa, Stefano 175 n.13
place 4–8, 12–13, 47–8, 50–1, 54, 65, 70–1, 75, 77–8, 81, 90, 102, 111, 128, 146–7, 154, 157–8, 163–5, 167, 184 n.8, 186–7 n.33, 196–7 n.55, 202 n.70, 204 n.35, 207 n.62
  abstract 6
  any 85, 99, 114, 144, 163, 7
  see also nonplace; heterotopia; displacement
Plato 85–6, 105, 123–4, 127–31, 165, 190 n.61, 192 n.93, 193–4 n.3, 195 n.28
Plotinus 135
police, the 7, 13, 130, 165, 167–9, 172 n.29, 206 n.56, 207 n.62, 207 n.64
polis 128–9, 165
political, the 98–9, 167–8, 207 n.64, 208 n.4
possibility/the possible 7, 41, 60, 66, 71, 77, 79, 100, 103, 108, 123, 125–7, 130, 132, 192 n.93
  conditions of 4, 123–4, 126, 198–9 n.6

  see also impossibility/the impossible
Poullain de la Barre, François 137
post-Kantianism 12, 117, 119
Pozzana, Claudia 175 n.6, 176 n.29
practical reason (Kantian) 8–10, 12, 45
present, the 1–2, 5, 16, 21, 25, 35–7, 43–44, 46–7, 49, 51, 54–7, 59–60, 80, 83, 85, 90, 97, 99, 107–9, 115, 131, 136, 138, 141, 143, 150–1, 169
progress 1, 3–4, 20, 26, 28, 38–40, 42, 49, 52, 70, 73–4, 86, 93, 158, 167, 199 n.8
Proletarian Nights (Rancière), *see The Nights of Labor*
proletariat 10–11, 23, 29, 34–5, 42, 49, 55, 58–61, 64–8, 75, 77–8, 80–1, 83–4, 103, 111, 114, 127–8, 135–6, 142, 147, 150–1, 163, 184 n.8, 189 n.54, 189 n.56, 190 n.63, 192 n.95, 194 n.9, 195 n.10, 196 n.38
Proust, Françoise 13, 206 n.56
Proust, Marcel 134

Quintana, Laura 172 n.25

Rae Yang 91
Rancière, Danièlle 69
Reading Capital (Althusser, Balibar, Establet, Macherey, Rancière) 19, 21, 23, 25, 28–9, 40, 52, 53, 176 n.18, 202 n.70
Reid, Donald 183 n.3
Renault, Emmanuel 147
repetition 54, 87, 131, 190 n.69, 191 n.77, 190 n.69
Rilke, Rainer Maria 72–4, 186 n.31
Robespierre, Maximilien 149, 154–5, 160–3, 204 n.25
Robson, Mark 1, 189–90 n.57
Rockhill, Gabriel 187–8 n.39, 195 n.28, 196 n.38, 198 n.2, 198–9 n.6
Rolin, Olivier 199 n.20
Rome (antiquity) 149–51
Ross, Alison 187–8 n.39
Ross, Kristin 71–2, 123, 136, 186 nn.29–30, 190 n.65, 198 n.2, 201 n.44
Rossellini, Roberto 75
Ruby, Christian 186 n.29
rupture 15–16, 19–21, 27–8, 37, 39, 41, 44, 54, 61, 63, 65, 68, 80, 95, 97,

100–1, 109, 111, 113, 115, 124–5, 141, 147, 171
  see also break
Russian revolutions 25, 84
Russo, Alessandro, 177 n.30, 194 n.6

Saint-Just 149
Sartre, Jean-Paul 66, 116
'La Scène révolutionnaire et l'ouvrier émancipé (1830–1848)' (Rancière) 17, 98–103
Schiller, Friedrich 8, 17–18, 98, 106–9, 115, 119, 195 n.25
seismography, see seismology
seismology 68–9, 71, 83, 185 n.19
self 17–18, 98, 102–4, 106, 109–10, 112, 115–17, 119, 183 n.3, 194 n.8
sens 25, 65–6, 69–71, 74, 92, 119, 133, 186 n.24
sensus communis 8–9, 173 n.38
sex/sexuality 45, 137–8, 201 n.47
Shapiro, Michael 14
Shaw, Devin Zane 201 n.45
Short Voyages to the Land of the People (Rancière) 68–76, 183 n.3
simultaneity 3–4, 16, 47, 58–9, 68, 77, 88, 127, 141
socialism 23, 30–2, 50, 84, 184 n.8
society 11, 13, 24, 34, 42–3, 56–8, 84, 106, 108–9, 111, 182 n.107, 194 n.8, 195 n.22
  Althusser's theory of 37, 48–51
  capitalist 37, 199 n.20
  Chinese 30–1
  communist 60
  and the French Revolution 149, 154–7, 161
Soviet Communist Party 21, 31
Soviet Union, the 20
Sino-Soviet split, the 21
Smith, Jason E. 35
space-time 4, 7, 15, 60, 99, 100–1, 120–1, 142–3, 145–7, 150–1, 163–4, 186 n.30
space
  abstract 5–7, 9, 15, 77, 88, 121–2, 143–4, 146–7, 149, 163
  according to Kant 9, 12, 13, 18, 115–16
  between- 76, 78–9, 84, 158, 189 n.57
  common 11, 12, 157

cross-historical 121, 145, 158–9
disoriented, 67, 75–7, 81, 84, 88, 91–2, 186 n.33
empty 7, 77–8
Feuerbach's concept of 3–5, 15, 172 n.18
geographical 7, 69–71, 74, 89–90
social 4–5, 7, 14, 142
togetherness in 73–4, 146
virtual 4–5, 11, 12, 143
  see also contiguity; *dēmos*; disorientation; omnidirectionality; outer sense; space-time; spatiality; spatialization; spatial logic
spatial logic 1–3, 8–9, 13, 17, 41, 64, 67–8, 89–90, 158, 192 n.84
  see also space; spatiality; spatialization
spatiality 1–8, 12–15, 63, 67–68–72, 75–7, 98, 100, 102, 104, 109, 115, 117, 119, 121, 126, 131–2, 139, 141, 158, 167, 170, 171 n.6, 172 n.24, 185 n.22, 186 n.30, 186–187 n.33, 197 n.64
  see also space; spatial logic; spatialization
spatialization 81–2, 186 n.28
  of time 67–8, 70–6, 80
stage 3–5, 16, 23, 44, 67, 143, 158, 194 n.6
  and distinction between *étape* and *scène* 17, 43, 97–8, 101
  (*scène*) 98–104, 107, 119–21, 189 n.100, 193 n.3
  (*étape*) 44, 56–7, 59–60, 63–4, 78, 116, 126, 179 n.67
  see also *opsis*
Stalin, Joseph 37, 54, 174–5 n.4
Stalinism 22, 37, 54–5, 179 n.67
subject/subjectivation/subjectivity 27, 55–6, 75, 78, 94, 99, 101, 140, 157, 162–3, 173 n.39, 175 n.9, 189 n.57, 193–4 n.3, 198 n.6
  any 99, 198 n.6
  collective 195 n.10
  individual 113
  of history 56, 71, 73, 83
  political 66, 78, 98, 103, 194 n.8
  process without (Althusser) 55, 175 n.9
  of the Rights of Man and the Citizen 156
surface 71, 74, 90, 100, 115
  depth and 67, 88
  see also horizontality

substitutability 8, 103, 114
symptomal reading 51–3, 83, 178 n.60

Tacitus 74
Tanke, Joseph 48, 117–19, 206 n.56
Tarr, Béla 116
teleology 1, 17, 20–3, 28, 49–51, 63, 68, 72–3, 80, 168, 174 n.59, 193 n.98
temporalization 1, 13, 15, 46, 63, 65, 73, 83, 88–90, 106, 108, 110, 116, 118–19, 122, 124–5, 132, 135, 137, 140, 147, 155, 158, 161, 165, 171 n.2, 186–7 n.33, 189 nn.54, 57
Terror, the 160–1
theatre 17, 83, 99–101, 107, 193 n.2, 194 n.6
theoreticism 34, 37, 42, 54–5, 148, 174 n.3, 181 n.94
  anti- 47
time-determination 12, 118–19, 140, 165, 197 nn.58, 64

topography 2, 5, 7, 9, 20, 48, 88, 128, 130, 141–2, 146
Toscano, Alberto 180 n.76

Union des Étudiants Communistes 22
Union des Jeunesses Communistes – Marxistes- Léninistes (UJC-ml) 30, 33–5, 46, 53–6, 80–1, 176 n.24, 183 n.2

Wahnich, Sophie 160, 201 n.35
Wartofsky, Marx 3–4
Weil, Simone 183 n.3
Whitener, Brian 187–8 n.39, 198 n.2, 205 n.40
will 40, 86, 94–95, 140, 174 n.4, 179 n.64, 205 n.53
Wolfreys, Jim 154
Woolf, Virginia 4–5, 127
Wordsworth, William 68–9, 72, 184 n.15
working class, *see* proletariat

www.ingramcontent.com/pod-product-compliance
Lightning Source LLC
Chambersburg PA
CBHW070723020526
44116CB00031B/1477